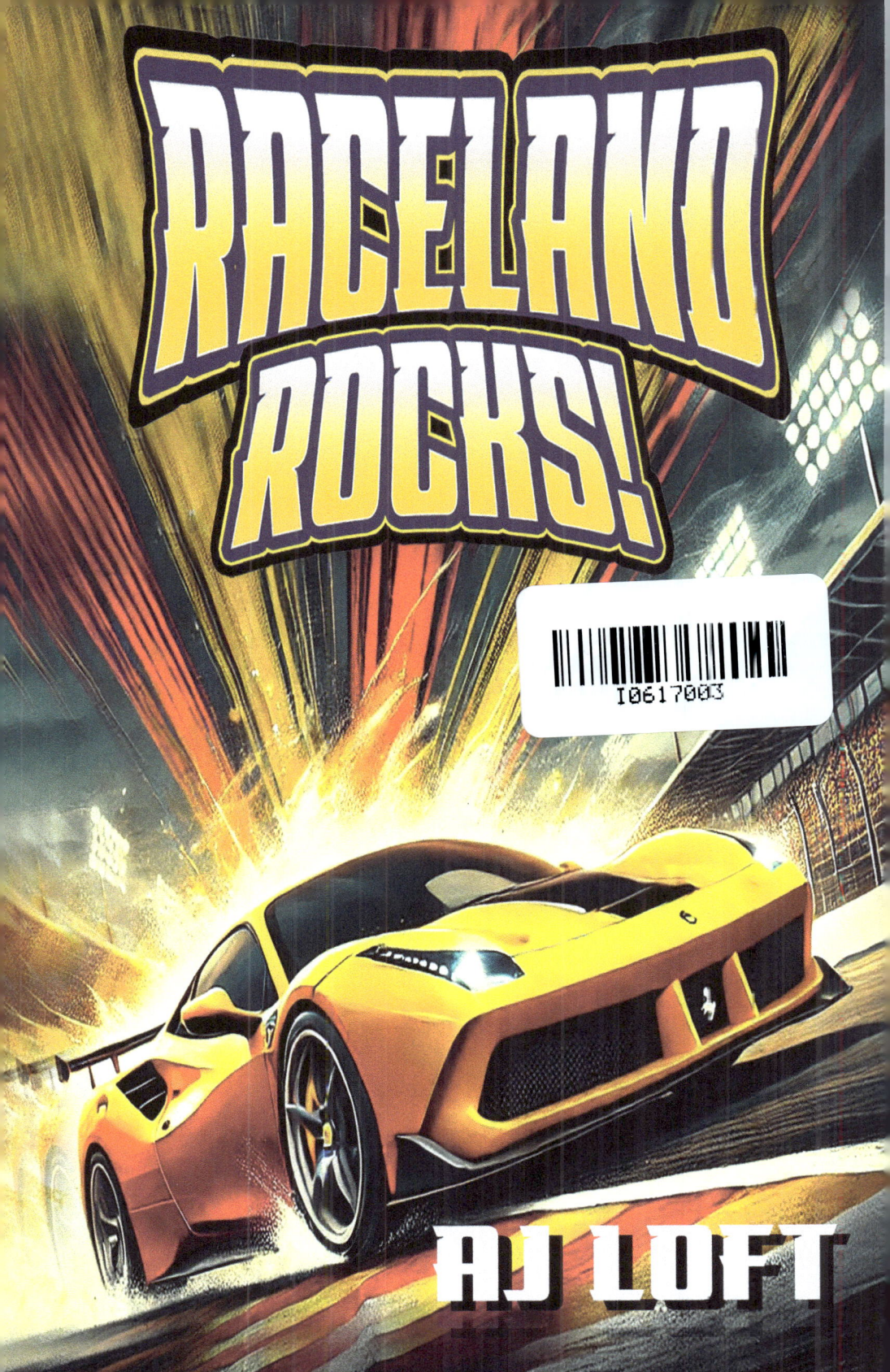

RACELAND ROCKS!

AJ LOFT

LUNA GLOBAL MEDIA
Suncrest Dv. Melbourne, FL
+1 312 212 3899 U.S.
https://lunaglobalmedia.com/

Raceland Rocks!

ISBN (Paperback):

Printed in the United States of America

RACELAND ROCKS!

DAMAGED

Life Lesson;   In racing, it's not the speed that kills ya
it's the unplanned stops!

Chapter 1
Damaged

What a weekend! There are two HUGE events happening in Sunnyvale this weekend and the McKay family is really excited about both. Karen McKay invited her parents and they're coming all the way from California! She wants them to see her sons play football and tonight is the last game of the season, the city championship.

Plus, tomorrow is the huge season finale at the Sunnyvale Speedway, the prestigious Sunnyvale 200. It's the biggest race of their Superspeedway's season and the million-dollar purse has all the best drivers in the country coming to town.

Both events have been sold out for weeks, but the McKays booked a box for the football game right on the 50-yard line. For the races, they secured 80 seats all together in the grandstand at the turn for home. It's a perfect spot to watch a race because the cars are coming right at you, and it's the last chance for the drivers to make their moves. The McKays bought all these seats hoping that the football team would win tonight, and everyone could celebrate together at the races tomorrow.

Tonight's game features the Sunnyvale Speed Demons in their first appearance ever, against the reigning champs, the Talladega Titans in their 9th straight championship game appearance. The Titans are heavily favored but the Speed Demons have the best team they've ever had and they're playing at home, where they were undefeated this season. The stadium was full all the way to the nosebleed seats, when her parents arrived for the game. Karen had told her dad to take the earlier flight because it seems like every flight to Sunnyvale always takes longer than scheduled. This flight was delayed too, but it was weird because the weather was perfect and their flight left on time, and even landed on time, but for some reason their plane was towed through a dark hangar on the way to their gate. This happened the last time too, so Mr. Murphy wanted to know why. He has flown all over the world and he has never seen this equipment anywhere else, so why here? And what exactly happened to them in that dark hangar way over there? He asked a flight attendant and the next thing her dad knew; he was being detained by airport security. They just asked him a bunch of questions and released him without any charges, but they never answered his questions.

They were all enjoying the game so far, and both of their boys have played well, but now it's late in the 4th quarter and Sunnyvale is down by 5 points with less than 2 minutes left on the game clock. The team from Talladega has the ball and they're inside Sunnyvale's 10-yard line. The Titans could just run the clock out now, but they want to score again. After two running plays, they have the ball inside the 5-yard line and now there is only 32 seconds left in the game. Talladega calls another running play, but this time their fullback slipped during the handoff and fumbled. Sunnyvale got the ball back on their own 2-yard line with 11 seconds to play.

Sunnyvale's starting wideout got hurt on their last series so young Kyle McKay got his big chance to play as a 1 receiver. Coach Cheeks called for a double pass. The McKay brothers had run this play often in the street at home, but that wasn't against Talladega's huge pass rush. Keegan McKay took the snap and rolled right and faked a handoff to his younger brother behind him. The rushers bought the fake and were chasing Kyle but after just a couple of steps they saw he didn't have the ball, so they changed their direction and took off after Key. Kyle just drifted out to the left flat while 'Dega's whole team was chasing Keegan. Key stops quickly and whistles the ball back to the left flat, where Kyle is waiting all alone. He catches the ball and starts to take off for the left side. He stops just before the sideline and is still behind the line of scrimmage. Kyle waited until the defense was almost on top of him before he plants and throws the football as far as he can, and it lands perfectly in Key's outstretched arms. Keegan raced into the endzone and scored the winning touchdown. The team carried both of the McKay brothers on their shoulders to their sideline and all their cheering fans!

Unbelievable! Sunnyvale's Speed Demons won the varsity football championship for the first time ever! Karen's parents couldn't have been any prouder leaving the stadium that night, after seeing their grandsons connect for the winning touchdown.

The next day, the whole team and their families are all celebrating their victory at the Speedway, watching the Sunnyvale 200. It's the last chance for these drivers to make any real money for months, so they are all running their wheels off and it's a heck of a race! The McKay group is having a great time enjoying a very tight race when out of nowhere, tragedy struck! As the pack of cars rounded the corner just left of their seats, a couple of cars swapped paint, and one of them started spinning out of control near the wall right in front of the McKay group. This spinner was causing a major pileup that the other racers couldn't see until it was too late. Two of these race cars were traveling at over 200 mph when they hit the mangled metal mess that used to be race cars.

These drivers didn't stand a chance, and one of them was Bobby Bigtime, who lived with the McKays. They had less than a fraction of a second from the moment they saw the wreckage until impact. Both cars catapulted end over end directly into the grandstand where the McKay group was seated. Neither driver survived. It was the worst crash in Sunnyvale's storied history and one of the 10 worst racecar crashes ever, anywhere. Many spectators were killed instantly and many more horribly injured. There were several broken bones and lots of bloodshed. Those that could, ran for the exits, but many were hurt too badly to move, and some were just too scared to move. The heartbreaking screams were coming from the people trapped under the burning racecars, who were being burned to death.

When the racecars came into the crowd, the McKays scattered trying to avoid the flying wreckage as they fought for their lives. Keegan knew his arm was broken because there was a bone sticking out by his elbow, but right then he was too scared to feel it. He had to find his family, so he tried to get back to their seats but that whole section was a disaster. He was just about to give up when he saw his mom lying face down on some broken up seats. He couldn't wake her, and he couldn't carry her, so he started dragging her. He hated to do it, but he really didn't have any choice. Miles Malone, the team's tight end, saw them and came to help. He had been knocked out and had some deep cuts, but he could see his buddy needed help. He and Key were both coughing from the smoke but managed to get 'moms' out of the grandstand and over by the exit ramp.

Miles asked, "Key, you got this? Sorry but I can't stay bro. I've got to find my parents back there."

"Miles, I get it. Thanks for helping me get her out of there. I wish I could help you buddy but I'm afraid to leave her. My mom's in really bad shape" Keegan said.

Miles replied, "You aren't doing too well either buddy. Your arm is trashed."

"Yeah, but you know our code. Go find your parents. I still have to find my dad and Kyle." Keegan said.

Miles stopped him and said, "No bro. You're cool on that. I saw them both through the smoke and they were together and helping Shelby and her dad. Take care of your mom."

The sound of sirens made him turn his head in time to see his mom flop over from where he had left her leaning against the ramp wall. Blood was pouring out of her head. He got down next to her and pulled her up so that she was sitting next to him and propped her head up on his shoulder to stop the bleeding.

When the first responders got here it was pure pandemon um, but these guys are really good at their jobs and are able to get the crowd under control quickly. In fact, soon after their arrival, all the screaming stopped. Unfortunately, it was replaced with loud sobbing. Eventually, the sobbing was drowned out by the sounds of dozens of ambulance sirens as they raced away from the Speedway, heading to Sunnyvale General Hospital.

Keegan and his mom were in one of those ambulances heading to the hospital. One of the paramedics that was early on the scene, had found Keegan and his mom huddled up by an exit. He saw Keegan's left arm was clearly broken and Mrs. McKay's head was severely traumatized and bleeding badly. He had told Key before they left the track that his mom was seriously injured, and she probably wouldn't survive unless he could keep her brain working all the way to the hospital. Key loved his mom and would do anything for her so without hesitation, he climbed into the back of the ambulance and sat close enough to hold her. His left arm was screaming at him, but he put it out of his mind, determined to handle the task at hand. He needed to keep her brain working, so he started rambling to her about his racing dreams, about his little brother, about school, about football, about baseball and finally he brought up his girlfriend, Shelby Hollenbut. He knew he'd hit a hot button because he finally got a response from his mom. It wasn't much but now he knew she was listening. He decided he would stay on that topic for the rest of this ride.

A few miles later, moms was definitely responding but Keegan was running out of safe material, so he had to share more than he planned. Reluctantly, he brought up sex, and his mom gave him the strongest response yet, so he kept talking. By the time they got to the hospital, he had ratted himself out to his mom about everything he and Shelby had been doing so far. He would be embarrassed about this later, but he had even been exaggerating for the last 5 minutes or so. He didn't mean to, but he was saying they did some stuff he'd only heard the seniors talkin' about in the locker room after a playoff game. He didn't really think he would ever do some of that stuff he said he did to Shelby, but it worked! Moms was still alive and awake when that ambulance pulled into the emergency entrance at Sunnyvale General.

The paramedic that helped them at the track was thanking Keegan for the good job he had done with his mom, when he saw Keegan's broken left arm again. This time he could see the pain in Key's face, so he got him tended to immediately. He apologized to Key and told him how amazed he was by the way Key handled himself at the track. He said that he had seen a whole lot of people messed up since he took this job, but he had never seen anyone able to handle the pain of a broken arm and still put someone else first.

That same ambulance paramedic was still helping people coming in from the racetrack, when he saw Keegan again and this time, Keegan's left arm is in a cast.

He said, "Young man, I can't believe that your arm was that messed up and you never even cried. You're a tough guy, no doubt.

I checked in on your mom and I think you might have saved her life today. She's still got a long road to recovery, but if she's half as tough as you are, she's got a good chance of walking out of this hospital one day, thanks to you. He gave Key a quick guy hug, handed him his card and as he walked away, he said, "Thanks for your help tough guy and I gave you my number so you can keep me posted on your mom's recovery. It will be really nice to know if she makes it, because if she does, we saved her life! I haul the bodies in here night after night, but nobody ever seems to get out of hospitals alive. I'm hoping your mom does." Key turned red, but it felt good to think that he may have helped save her life.

He looked at the card. It said Sunnyvale's Best Ambulance Service and had a sketch of an ambulance on it and then details, like an address and a couple phone numbers. The paramedic had written his name and his cell number on the back. It said the guy's name was Mack Davis. Weird. Key yelled back, "You should be expecting a call from me in a couple of weeks sir. Hey, should call you Mr. Davis?"

He replied, "You can, but most people call me Mack." That ruffled the feathers of Key's birdbrain, My dad's Mac, he thought, so he said "I'll be calling you soon Mr. Mack.

The next voice he heard made him jump a couple feet in the air. It was his dad! Key turned and saw his dad and brother hustling over. Kyle had a bunch of stitches and his dad's face was almost completely covered with gauze and tape. Mr. Mac had driven himself and Kyle to the hospital, so now the three of them were driving home. Key updated them on his mom's status, but they had already seen her and talked with her doctors.

Mr. McKay asked if either of his sons knew what happened to their grandparents. Moms had invited her parents to come out for the weekend, and they flew in from California in time to see the boys win the City Championship. There was no way anyone could have guessed that the very next day, a disaster of epic proportion would change all their lives forever, but that's what happened.

The boys answered that they hadn't seen either of their grandparents after the crash. It turns out that Karen's father got trapped under one of those race cars that had flipped into the stands and there was so much weight on his chest that he could barely breathe, so he couldn't yell for help. He was the last one found at the wreck, and he was barely alive when he got to the hospital. He was incoherent and unable to make sense. He was dying but he kept asking about Mary and Karen."

His nurse told him to stay calm and she'd find out what happened. Nurse Sara O'Shea checked the emergency room records and got some answers. She learned that his wife, Mary hadn't been admitted tonight, so she must have gone straight to the morgue. And she learned that his daughter, Karen, was on life support with probable severe brain damage and it was unlikely that she would make it through the night.

When Sara walked back into his room, she told him that his wife, Mary, had already been released from the hospital with just some scratches and bruises, and that his daughter, Karen McKay had been checked in and was resting comfortably. He smiled at the news, and managed to say 'thank God' before he passed away.

According to the records, Karen McKay was in a coma and probably couldn't even hear her. But she also knew that sometimes people in comas can still hear and she hoped Karen was one of these.

Nurse O'Shea bent over so she could speak into Karen's ear. She told her that her father was admitted to this hospital earlier, and had passed in his sleep, and she continued, "He was sedated at the scene and arrived here feeling no pain. He kept asking about you and your mom, so I told him your mom was found fine and was resting at the McKay's home. Further, I said that you were here resting comfortably, and we'd know more about your condition after you met with the doctors in the morning. That your prognosis was good, and you were happy to be alive." He said, "Thank God." And passed away a few minutes later with a smile on his face."

When her shift was over that Sunday morning, Nurse Sara O'Shea checked in on Karen McKay one more time. She leaned in and whispered, "Young lady, I think you can hear me so please get well fast. I told your daddy you were going to be ok and don't you make a liar out of me."

The kind nurse left the hospital and since it was Sunday, she headed to church. Sitting in a pew next to the confessional at St. Mary's Catholic Church, Nurse O'Shea was preparing to confess by counting up her sins in the last week. She couldn't think of a single sin, so she skipped her confession, and instead said a prayer for Karen's full recovery and asked God to help Mary get home safely.

Now, the last time I checked, lies were still sins, so you may think the nurse should have confessed her sins that morning in church, but I don't. The God I believe in didn't need a confession. He just made a mental note to make sure Karen McKay healed because that would erase one of the nurse's lies, and to make sure Nurse Sara O'Shea didn't have to wait a minute in line when He brought her up to Heaven.

Mary Murphy never made it to the hospital that night. She had been struck across her forehead so hard that she was unconscious for quite a while, and when she came to, she was disoriented and not sure where she was. When she finally realized where she was and remembered what had happened, she walked back through the damaged grandstand looking for her husband, daughter or anyone in her family. Almost everyone was gone, but there was still one guy standing in the corner near where the cars came flipping into the fans. She recognized the young man as one of Keegan's friends. It was Miles Malone, and he was just standing there crying. She stood next to him for a couple of minutes and finally asked what had happened.

He tried to explain, "My parents were sitting right here when all those drivers crashed and came flying into the seats. They were both killed instantly. I guess I should go home, but I don't think I have one anymore." Miles had taken his parents' valuables before they were bagged and taken away. One of those items was his dad's car keys, so he and Mary Murphy found the Malone family's car in the Speedway parking lot and headed home.

It was almost 5 AM Sunday morning when Mary dropped Miles off at his parents' house. They made plans for Miles to get the car the next day. She was disoriented and had never driven in this town before, so she looked up her daughter's address on Mapquest before driving any further. It wasn't far and just a few minutes later she parked in front of the McKay's home and used the spare key on top of the front door frame. By the time the McKay boys got home from the hospital, their grandma had cooked up an awesome Sunday brunch. Everyone was hungry and tired, so it didn't take long before those 3 guys were all sleeping soundly with full bellies. After the dishes, Mary moved into the guest room just down the hall.

She had called the hospital when she made it to the McKays' house and got the news that her husband had passed. That stopped her heart from beating for a while and she collapsed. She was devastated and felt empty and alone, but she knew he was going to a better place. Now, she thought about her daughter. Karen McKay was really badly hurt and the hospital staff said she was in a coma and had major brain trauma. Mary was struggling, trying to handle all this heartache at once, so she hit her krees and prayed for strength.

She knew she had to be strong for her grandsons, so she needed a plan. With her husband gone, she decided to stay here because she knew her daughter would never ask her for help, but she also knew her daughter was going to need all the help she could get. Worse, there was a good chance that moms McKay would never even make it home from the hospital. She prayed that wouldn't happen, but if it did, this fiery Irish woman wasn't going anywhere. Not while she still had two grandsons here! This family was all the family she had left, and she planned to take good care of them. She would become indispensable by pampering each of them, cooking fabulous meals every night and keeping their home spotless. They were going to need her help. Heck, Keegan's arm was still in a cast, and he couldn't even dress himself yet. Yeah, it felt good to be needed again.

Mary Murphy was their mom's mom, and that's a whole lot of m's, so the boys gave her the nickname M's. She likes it here in the McKays' house. It's a beautiful home and they have plenty of room for her. Besides, her big house in California would feel so empty without her husband there, and she'd be lonely. M's hated to be alone and she was afraid of growing old and becoming a burden...until now! Now, her life would have purpose again.

the GAUNTLET

Life Lesson; Listen to your parents
They know more than you do

Chapter 2
The Gauntlet

It felt like months had gone by, but in just a couple days, grandma had taken over. She borrowed the Malone's car because Miles hadn't picked it up yet and she wanted to go see her daughter and that's what she did, but Karen still can't see, talk or anything. Her daughter was very close to death and M's was afraid she was going to lose her any day. The visit was depressing, and she just couldn't stay very long seeing her daughter motionless and vacant. On the drive home, M's couldn't stop crying. She planned to pray for her daughter tonight.

At home that night, she started working through all the paperwork necessary to close out her husband's affairs. When that was finished, she was headed for bed when she noticed that Keegan's light was still on. She thought maybe he was still doing homework or something, but he needed to get some sleep, so she opened his door to tell him. He was lying down and sound asleep, but there were no schoolbooks around him, or anything like his phone or tablet that he might have been messing with that would have put him to sleep. It looked like he left the light on... on purpose? Nah, why would he do that? She flipped the switch off and went on down the hallway to her room, making a note to include Keegan in that prayer.

Keegan jumped. The noise from the switch being turned off woke him. He is wide awake now, but now It's dark. Really dark. Not just regular dark either. This is the scary kind of dark. I mean it's really, really dark. Every kid knows this type of dark. It's the dark that happens after you're safe in bed and one of your parents, or maybe your grandma, reaches in and turns your light off. Not a big deal, right? You know that all you have to do is get out of bed and turn the light back on, but now you can't move. The monsters are back in your room and fear has you on total lockdown. Now, the niner's NFL helmet on top of your dresser looks like a monster's head and the big leafy plant in the corner has become a 3 headed serpent. You can't sleep with all these monsters in your room. Who could? Tomorrow when he thinks about it, he'll know the monsters weren't there but tonight he knows for sure that the monsters really are there and he knows that if he moves an inch, they'll see him and attack!

It seemed like it was only a couple years ago that he could just scream, and his mom would rush in and chase the monsters away. Then, last year he discovered that if he pulled the blankets over his head, the monsters would leave on their own…. sooner or later.

Now, they all say he's too old to be afraid of the dark, and he gets that, but… but what if he still is?

Keegan McKay would never admit it, even to himself, but he has always been afraid of the dark and he still is. It's his secret and he thought he would be horribly embarrassed if any of his friends or his little brother ever found out.

It's really dark in the Gauntlet. That's the name Key gave to the 5-step journey to Raceland. A gauntlet is defined as 'a challenging, difficult, or painful ordeal,' and the road to Raceland is all three of those adjectives to Keegan. He's afraid of the dark, and it's pitch black in all 5 steps. The five scary steps are;

1. **The Secret Door**-this thing is scary because it's so dark that you can't see anything, and it opens really slowly but it slams shut right behind you.

2. **The Drop Chute**- you're falling through the darkness. You can't see the bottom and it feels like you're never going to stop falling.

3. **The Grateway**-this monster concrete wall is black magic. There's a huge steel door flying around above you and it slams into the wall with a deafening boom.

4. **The Chill Chamber**- they freeze your body in this huge icebox then you have to walk on steps you can't see without falling into this dark pool full of piranhas.

5. **The Transfiguration Tube**- It's dark. You're alone flying horizontally inside this metal tube while it strips your clothes off and stretches every inch of your body.

Keegan is petrified by the dark, but he will run the Gauntlet time and time again because it's the only way to get to Raceland, and Raceland is Keegan's favorite place in the whole world! It's the only place on the planet where kids can drive real race cars as fast as 230 miles an hour! *Just a side note here because kids love it when adults do dumb things. Here's one of them...Adults always say 'miles an hour' like that old Ford can still go 70 miles an hour. But when they write it, they write 70 mph which is an abbreviation for 'miles per hour'. So, which is it? If you're going to say 'miles an hour' then the abbreviation should be MAH right? I'm going to use MPH for this book because I'm writing it, but when I'm quoting someone talking, I'm going to type out 'miles an hour'. I know it's dumb but it's one of many dumb things' adults do and I am an adult.*

Anyway, think about this; The speed limit on the freeway your parents drive on is only 70 mph. Seventy is as fast as adults can ever drive in America even on the freeway, but in Raceland, kids can race each other at speeds more than **3** times that fast. Real deal. Raceland has cars that top 230 mph and kids can race 'em! And, since your parents' speed limit is only 70 mph, they'll probably never know firsthand what it feels like to race a car at 200+ mph, so I'm here to tell you, it's really fun. Really, really fun!

The only bad news about this Raceland place is that it's hard as heck to get to, and scarier than you can imagine. In fact, it's a very scary walk in total darkness that no one ever gets used to. Keegan knows for sure he never will!

Here are the details of all that's involved for you to get to Raceland; First, you have to get down to the first floor at Hot Rod High and go to the far, dark end of the hallway. Here, you'll meet with an authorized racer who will take your pledge to secrecy. It's mandatory for entrance because Raceland is a secret that no adult can ever know. If they ever found out about it, they would close it down in a heartbeat. No parent wants their kid racing cars at 200+ mph! Especially the parents, like ours, that obey all those speed limit signs like 25 mph near a School, 15 mph in alleys and 10 mph when there's a traffic cop in the intersection. Any mandate intended to keep drivers from hitting people should be directed at the use of steering wheel before the brakes. So, what happens when the kids racing here now, become adults? The rules are the same. When you turn <u>18 and graduate</u> from Hot Rod High, you are considered an adult and there's no more fun for you! *That could be why adults look so angry all the time.* When you become an adult, Raceland will be closed to you for eternity and any memory you have of it will be erased forever. No adults, no parents, no teachers=no problems, and none of them will ever be allowed in Raceland, period, end of story. That's why you need to swear to keep it a secret. You're giving your word that you will keep Raceland a secret when you take the ancient Oath of Secrecy. This pledge was believed to have started in Egypt way back in the pyramid days, and you know for sure it works because, even today, nobody knows how they built those dang pyramids.

Only an authorized racer can take your pledge. They will have you repeat the oath after them;

I do solemnly swear

I do solemnly swear

To all who have been before

To all who have been before

That whatever happens there

That whatever happens there

Behind the Secret Door

Behind the Secret Door

Is mine to keep but not to share

Is mine to keep but not to share

A secret kept forever more.

A secret kept forever more.

Then, that racer will say, "You have taken Raceland's ancient Oath of Secrecy and are now bound to honor your pledge and are officially sworn to secrecy for the rest of your life. If ever you break your pledge, you will suffer consequences that are so horrible that no one can even speak of them. Next, that same authorized racer will have to administer the bump code to open the secret door at Hot Rod High. See, there's no door there that you can see. There's just a very faint outline of what used to be a door, but if you bump it in just the right place, a door that nobody can see there, will slowly swing open. You'll step inside the door quickly before it slams shut. Now you're alone. You will be consumed by the darkness until you can't see a thing, but you walk forward in the darkness until you take one step too many and the floor is now gone. You have stepped into the Drop Chute where you will freefall in total darkness, unable to see the bottom. It's terrifying and you think it will never end but it does, and you're caught by forced air at the bottom and you land softly.

You still can't see anything, but you feel around until you find the doorway. You'll exit the Chute through that doorway and into more darkness. You walk forward with a hand on the wall next to you until you come to a huge cement wall with a big 10 foot tall black circle painted in the center. The wall is growing taller and it makes you feel like you're sinking. You see a doorbell on the right with the end of a pipe sticking out above it. You ring the bell quickly because it's getting harder to reach. After a lengthy delay has made you unable to ring the bell again, a raspy old crackly Voice whispers;

"If you're that rare racer with courage to spare

Just push your little car in the pipe over there

If my doors slide open, step on in if you dare

You'll be off on a journey that'll strip you bare

So hang on for your lives, you're in for a scare"

While the wall was growing, the doorbell got way out of reach, but the pipe end that was above it didn't move at all, so now the pipe end is below the doorbell, and you can still reach it. You'll insert the micro-rod that you want to race backwards into the pipe. You pull up the flap and you'll see that it's very hairy in there. After you have inserted your car, stand back because what was a painted circle now comes away from the wall and spins mid-air faster and faster until it morphs into a huge thick steel vault door and slams against the cement wall. There's a pause while the vault door gets bolted into the cement wall with huge bolts and bigger nuts. (*You'll wish you had a pair of those for the rest of this journey.*) You're now facing what appears to be a huge vault door, but you know it can't be a door because you saw with your own eyes there's no opening behind it. No problem. In just a moment, a lightning rod fires out of the ceiling and strikes the door, splitting both the concrete and the steel door in half. The two sides now slowly grind further and further apart revealing a wide opening to another dark tunnel.

While that concrete was morphing, you got covered with dust, head to toe. You'll want to brush the cement dust off before you leave this spot, because you might meet some hot girls next. I'm sure you think there's zero chance of that but humor me this time and start brushing. If you don't want to get yelled at, you'll have to hurry because the Voice is impatient.

Uh Oh! Here comes that ominous crackly voice again, but it's not whispering this time. The Voice shouts angrily and it echoes off the walls;

Step inside humans, there's nothing to fear

Step inside I said, can you not hear?

Your journey's ahead, my message is clear

Leave your past behind, your destiny's near

Usually, that's all the Voice says, but you haven't stepped through this entry yet and patience is not a virtue the Voice has, so it continues more angrily;

Forget all your past and all you hold dear

I'm in control now, you don't get to steer

You're wasting my time and I don't have all year

So step inside now human or I'll kick your little rear!

Timidly, you step inside, and the huge steel doors start to move again. They are closing now, and picking up speed, they slam together behind you so hard that the wind they made tosses you forward awkwardly onto a moving walkway that carries you to an abrupt stop at a velvet rope draped across your pathway. Here, two gorgeous young girls, known as the Strange sisters, greet you.

Sally Strange says, "Welcome my friend and good day to you. Thanks for dropping in... literally! You can relax now because you won't be dropping, falling or rolling anywhere for a while. My name is Sally," and pointing toward the other greeter, she says, "and this is my twin sister Suzi. You have come to the place where everyone lands first, to be processed and sorted out on their way to Raceland."

Suzi Strange now speaks up. "It's called the *'Chill Chamber'* because it's always pretty chilly in here. The chamber is kept at roughly 45 degrees to help the human body firm up for the digital transfiguration that is next."

Sally continues the explanation, "It can take anywhere from 20-30 minutes for the human body to drop to an acceptable morphing temperature, so everyone has to wait while this cooling off process works its magic. This process cannot be accelerated in any way, so please note that any pushing, yelling, shoving, or whatever will not be tolerated. Violators will be immediately isolated into an individual ice column, called a 'Freeze Frame' where they will literally *chill* until their group returns. Of course, they will miss out on all the fun, and it will take a while for them to thaw out!"

"We'll be screening your group and issuing your access passes called 'creds', which is short for credentials," Suzi goes on. "Our first job is to sort out anyone over the age of eighteen. We call these people '*others*' because they are no longer like us. It's like they have their imaginations removed when they graduate from high school. Anyway, that's why they are no longer welcome here. If, for any reason, they have had their 18th birthday but haven't graduated from Hot Rod High yet, they will be allowed entrance until they finish school, but not a day after.

Sally adds without missing a beat, "Any 'Others' caught here will be immediately removed from your group and will wait for your return in a Freeze Frame."

Sally will take your names. Then, Suzi will find you an unoccupied bench in this massive freezer type locker room. Once the timer on your bench goes off, you'll return to the counter where Sally will issue your access passes called 'creds' that allow you entrance into the areas your racing experience qualifies you for.

Your creds are color coded and placed in a plastic holder attached to a lanyard that goes around your neck. These badges will automatically open doors to places you're authorized to access, and lock doors to places you aren't authorized for.

Suzi says," If you're new here, you'll only be able to access our Oval Mile, often referred to as Track 12." Most of the McKay crew have already accumulated enough cred points to have access to everything in Raceland, but they are only told about Track 12 initially because The Company doesn't want rookies getting in the way on the other 3 tracks in Raceland."

"To get there, everyone needs to ride in the Transfiguration Tube. It's dark and scary in those things, so if you get scared or you feel pain during the morphing process, just call one of our names and The Company will transfer the audio file directly to the microchip sized receiver in our heads. We will respond either verbally or by fixing the problem immediately."

Suzi says, "Let me straighten something out. You're about to ride the Transfiguration Tube and this thing is sort of like a time machine, only time doesn't exist in Raceland. That's why no matter how long you are here, when you return it will be roughly the same time you left. It would be exactly the same time you left, except that all the machinery down here recalibrates itself automatically by making time corrections."

"This time machine is different than any you have seen in movies or shows before. When our tubes hit max warp speed your bodies and life experiences are going to be advanced on your life's timeline. This means that you will remain in the same geographical place and historical time, but you skip ahead on your personal 'lifeline'. The chemicals and unique gases in your tube combine to physically age your appearance, and your brain screen will be loaded with all the necessary information and experience you'll need to be able to drive legally and intelligently, and to race successfully."

Sally takes over, "Your driver's license, along with all the information you had to learn to get it, is simply downloaded to your brain screen as though you went forward on your lifeline to the time when you finished studying for the test, had your last driving practice with a parent in the car and actually passed the driving test. Now, you are standing on that spot in your lifeline where you are holding your driver's license for the first time.

Now, Suzi whispers very quietly, "Put the license in your pocket. We are going to try this to see how far our technology with 'futuring' has come. Those completed driving and learning files, are now stored in today's folder in your brain. When your tube comes to a stop, you will exit looking like a version of you that is 10 years older, and your brain will have been loaded with your personal next 10 years of learning and driving along with the image of your driver's license. You can transfer that image to anyone in Raceland without ever having a physical copy by using your brain screen. Brain screens are the 'readers' in your heads. They see, hear and feel telepathic bytes of information that are transferred from one brain to another."

Suzi says, "Yeah, this time machine is a little different than the ones you've seen or heard about before. You don't travel to different times in the future or past, and you don't travel to different places in the world. The place and time of your existence is unchanged when you exit the Tube. The only thing that has changed is you."

"Raceland is about racing and learning to race successfully, so we will not be transferring any *racing experience* to your brain screen. In Raceland, you have to earn that."With that, the Strange sisters abruptly stop talking, turn and walk away.

You probably noticed that there is something very, very strange about these girls, besides their name. For one thing, it's very cold in the Chill Chamber and these girls are wearing skimpy little nurses' outfits. Yet, they don't appear to be cold at all, while everyone in the HRH crew is shivering almost uncontrollably. Also, their speech is very precise. They make a joke about how adults have lost their imagination, but these girls have lost their minds. They don't tell jokes and they don't laugh at your jokes. In fact, you'll probably never see either one of them laugh at all. They are nice but distant.

You're thinking that it's almost like they had their personalities removed, right? But then one of them smiles at you and you forget all about their odd little quirks that you thought were so important just a minute ago.

Monsters in my ROOM

Life Lesson; There is nothing in your room to fear but fear itself

Chapter 3
Monsters in his Room

The pathway leaving the Chill Chamber is dimly lit, so you can see these round steps in this long narrow dark pool of water. That is, until you take your second step, then the lights go off and you can't see the steps anymore. Now, all you can see are the golden scales on the piranhas as they jump at you with their sharp teeth bared. You remember seeing a lot of steps. They were evenly spaced, and you've already taken two steps. You use the muscle memory from those two steps you took and apply it to the rest that you still have to take, and you've got a good shot at getting to the Tube before these angry little fish have bitten all the flesh off your calves.

You run out of steps and you're standing in front of a few closed doors. They are each marked with a descriptive name, but you need to find the one marked *Transfiguration Tube* because it's the only door your creds will open.

Keegan hates this whole journey because it's so dark, but worse, he has nightmares about the Transfiguration Tube. This is the dealio that makes you big enough and smart enough to drive real cars, so obviously, everyone has to ride it if they want to race in Raceland. It's called the Transfiguration Tube because its function is to transfigure, morph or change (in this case 'age') its young passengers so that they can race real racecars when it drops them off in Raceland. Most of the kids just call it Morph Alley because it definitely morphs you.

Calling it a tube makes it sound like it's one long thing, but it's actually a series of individual bullet shaped aluminum tubes that are each about 25 feet long. They are designed to accommodate only one human at a time, but they weren't designed to be comfortable at all! There's no place to even sit down, no windows, no bathroom and no flight attendant. Inside it's just a hollow, pitch black tube with a couple of vertical poles that look to be very securely attached to both the floor and the ceiling.

The boys heard once that city buses have the same type of vertical poles and they don't seem necessary there either, until that bus gets up to about 30 mph and makes a turn. Then all the people that are riding that bus 'standing up' are shoving, falling and grabbing trying to latch onto one of those poles before they are thrown into the people pile in the back of the bus.

The vertical poles in the Tube are necessary too, but it gets so dark in there after you take off that you can't see them anymore. So, it's important that you grab one now and hold on with both hands. The Tube will get up to speed quickly outside, and faster inside because the speed inside is enhanced by a huge blower that will blow your feet right out from under you.

While your tube is rippin' down the underground rail, you will be horizontal with your feet directly behind you and you can feel your skin stretching and your clothes flying off, but don't worry about that because no one can see you. Your clothes are changed for you during the 'morphing' process for 2 reasons; one because you're a kid that's morphing into an adult and your kid size clothes won't fit an adult size body, and two because you need to wear race gear for safety reasons.

The racing suit they put on you may save your life, since you're heading to a racetrack where you will be racing at dangerously high speeds! Plus, most of you have zero experience so crashes should be expected. And worse, the fuel they put in those racecars is extremely flammable. If you crash or your car catches fire, you'll be thankful the Tube changed your clothes because now you're wearing one of Severe Gear's Series Seven racing suits. They are the safest in the business and they look pretty cool too.

After the Tube stops it will still be dark, and you have to stand still for about 30 seconds so The Company can download a driver's license and all the rules it normally takes to get one, plus 3-4 years of driving experience accumulated from hundreds of videos from the DMV of people failing their driving tests. All this data is transferred to your brain screen making you an experienced driver. They don't add any racing experience however, because here, you have to earn that.

And by the way, don't worry about the impact all that information has on your brain functions. It is all completely and automatically removed when you exit Raceland, so *don't try driving the family car when you get home!*

When the lights come on, you can exit the Tube and the first thing you'll see will shock you! There's a huge mirror directly in front of you and you are face to face with the older 'morphed' version of you! It's weird. Everyone will still recognize you because you still look kind of the same, but you've aged about 10 years, you're quite a bit taller now and that racing suit looks great on the bigger you.

When you pass the mirror, you'll see a racecar waiting for you on the track. It will be a full-sized version of the micro-rod you inserted back at the Grateway. It's running and pointed the right way because you put it in backwards. As you approach your car, the track announcer introduces you on the loudspeaker and the crowd jumps to their feet to give you a rowdy standing ovation. You pull your helmet on, as you slide through the window into the driver's seat. Then you'll buckle your safety harness, put that Hot Rod in first gear and press hard on the long skinny foot pedal and you're off! You'll wanna keep that long skinny pedal pinned on the floor until you see somebody waving checkered flags at ya. Welcome to Raceland!

When you are finished racing, you can leave your car on the track. It will remain in its expanded state so that it can be repaired, and have maintenance done on it. Then it will be cleaned and waxed and moved to your race space if you won, or to your opponent's race space if you lost. It won't revert to micro-rod size again until someone from the winner's pit crew drives it nose first into the vehicle transfiguration tube it came out of.

You will remain in your morphed adult sized state as long as you're on the track. When you are ready to return, you'll return to the platform that you came from. Once there, you will see racers incoming on the left and racers are boarding on the right. You will go to the right and catch a return Tube that will reverse the morph process and return the original sized you to blue Platform One. You will still be wearing the Severe Gear Series Seven racing suit, but you will see in the exit mirror that the suit now fits your normal body size because the race suit is made with a significant percentage of Lycra. You'll find the clothes you wore into Raceland will be cleaned and pressed and returned to your Race Space.

You may want to change your clothes, get another opponent, something to eat, buy a new car, have your car upgraded, etc. If so, when you are at the Chill Chamber, just look to your right and you'll see an elevator with a sign that has MDT on it, and that will take you up to MIDTOWN. This is halfway up to ground level, and here you will find access to;

Your race space; where all your full-sized cars are stored, along with all your racing gear. This is basically your racing office complete with a desk and computer, plus a wall with 6 monitors that show all 4 tracks live, your 'garage' live where you can watch the *Kokomo Tow Company* take the cars you win from the racers you just beat, which is fun because they usually cry as the two guys tow your new car from the loser's garage to your garage. Both of you will see it delivered into your race space, and lastly there's a motor sports station for all the local, national and international racing news and events around the world.

Club11; This is a social club, where huge monitors show all the action throughout Raceland and Sunnyvale's Super Speedway. You can get anything you'd like to eat or drink, and you get help finding racing competition with any HRH students, or RodKingz gamers worldwide

RodKingz; The merch mart; this is a store basically for all the RODKINGZ products including micro-rods, home garages, trading cards, stickers, clothing, shoes, board games, etc.

*Special note; all micro-rods can be resized to full scale by racing them in Raceland. You just insert one in the pipe at the Grateway and after you race, it will be delivered to your race space if you win. Also, you can change your race car into a micro-rod for your home collection.

The Colonel's insurance; the track has its own insurance so if you wreck and it's not your fault and no one is hurt, you can leave the scene and when you return to Raceland, your car will be good as new! For all the other possibilities, you will need to report to the insurance office in midtown. No need to make a statement to security. Within seconds, all details of the wreck have been recorded and reviewed by the DRV, resulting in the determination of all fault and fines. The Colonel will review that data and be prepared for your visit. He may raise your rate, suspend you from racing for a period of time, or require you to take more classes at HRH. If your license is suspended, your creds will be disabled accordingly.

The DRV; this is the Department of Racing Vehicles where you will get your permits and licenses, register your cars and pay any fines.

Please note that you can only race in Raceland if you run the Gauntlet. If you just want to watch races, mingle with racers or shop, etc. you can enter from behind Hot Rod High. Enter the door marked 'Visitors'. Everyone who enters this way will be required to have earned the appropriate creds. The retinal analyzer will not allow entry to 'others'. No adults can ever enter. Once inside, you'll take the MDT or Midtown elevator down to the main floor. From there, You will take the Transportation Tube to get to the grandstands.

The Transportation Tube is for visitors and guests. Next to the CC door behind HRH is another door that says Visitors above it. This entry is for anyone that wants to watch races from the grandstands or hang out with you in your race space but they are either scared of racing, *or* scared of secret doors, falling, the dark, cement walls that move, wicked voices, being frozen, and being morphed. It's probably hard for most HRH racers to believe, but most regular people are like that. In fact, probably 9 out of 10 kids in the outside world would be completely freaked out and totally unable to complete the Gauntlet to Raceland.

They probably couldn't even drive a racecar, and definitely couldn't drive a racecar at 200+ miles an hour. They'd wet their pants! No probably not, but there's a good chance they would crash because these high-performance rides do everything fast! They go fast, stop fast, and turn fast, because they are equipped with the best parts in the world.

Today is Saturday and the boys don't have school, so of course, Keegan and Kyle McKay are on their way back to Raceland. They have already been through the Drop Chute, the Grateway, and the Chill Chamber today and they are in line to ride the Transfiguration Tube now. Kyle gets in his tube 'car' first and is whisked away toward Raceland, but Keegan doesn't move. He knows that the tube car loader today is Suzi Strange and he likes her. He has seen her more than a few times now, and she seems really cool, but he's afraid to talk to her because she's never alone. She and her twin sister manage the Chill Chamber and it's always so crowded in there. It's not that he's shy really, but he lacks the confidence to recover from rejection. He's afraid that she might be too pretty for him and he's not willing to take the chance of asking her out. If he ever did and she turned him down, he'd be very embarrassed, but if he asked her in front of other people and she turned him down, he'd be devastated. That's why he had always managed to just keep his mouth shut...at least until now.

After she loaded Kyle into the waiting tube car, Suzi came over to get her next rider and this was the chance Key had been waiting for, so he gave it a shot and started chatting her up. He was nervous so it probably wasn't his best effort, but Suzi politely heard him out. She smiled while he was rambling, but as soon as he came up for air, she hustled him off into the next waiting tube car. She had to get her line moving again before someone from The Company noticed. She knows better than to talk socially with a 'regular' especially when she's working, but she liked Key, and he was handsome so she let him talk. She had to cut him short though because three Tube cars had left her platform empty already. There was no way The Company would miss that, so she was surely going to be fined and probably punished.

Kyle had already morphed, and he saw himself in the big mirror at the Tube's exit. Shoot, he liked the way he looked. It was kinda cool to know that he was going to keep growing and putting on muscle and his looks were changing too. His face was getting more defined. He smiled at his reflection and decided he would be pretty darn handsome in a few years.

Now he was just waiting for Keegan on the track in Raceland. His brother should have been in the car right behind him, but the next couple of cars had come down empty. Kyle was already worried when he heard the whole Tube system come to a screeching halt. From where he was standing, Kyle could see the next two tube cars and they weren't moving anymore at all. Where the heck was his brother? Kyle knew his big brother was scared to death of the dark and the Tube was as dark as anything Kyle had ever seen. So, he wondered if Key just bailed out? Maybe. Kyle wouldn't be totally surprised. What if he was still in one of those cars? Would he still be aging? Kyle had no idea what was happening, but he knew that this could end badly, and he didn't know what he could do about it.

Keegan's tube car had left the platform and in less than a minute, it suddenly stopped moving. Now, it's dark in there, really dark and Key can't see anything. He can't believe it! The one guy that's petrified of the dark is stuck in a pitch-black tube car that has stopped moving, but is still morphing him. This darn thing has him trapped and it's still pulling, stretching and aging him. Key was freaking out. He wanted to scream but didn't want Suzi to think he was a sissy. He was going to die in this lousy contraption either from old age or from fear and he didn't care which as long as it happened fast. He thought it might be better to just die now, before he lost his mind.

He started seeing things in the dark. He was terrified and getting older every second. He had to do something!! And fast! But just like at night in his room, he is now paralyzed with fear.

The monsters are in the Tube now and he thinks he sees them in the dark and they're coming at him. Keegan McKay is about to lose his marbles...probably the whole set.

Kyle knew something had gone terribly wrong, and that Key was now stuck in a very dark place. Kyle was always trying to see the bright side of things, so he thought he might get a whole new set of marbles real soon! Just kidding, but Kyle wondered why a guy that's afraid of the dark would even consider trying to get to Raceland. The whole darn Gauntlet is dark. It never crossed young Kyle's mind that Keegan may have a better reason to come to Raceland than just racing. That's because Kyle still thought girls were stupid. That will all change very soon.

Truth is that Kyle didn't believe that Key really was afraid of the dark. He just didn't get it. What in the heck was so scary? He always kind of figured that Key just made the whole monster thing up to get a little extra attention from moms, but she wasn't even around the last couple months and Keegan still slept with his light on night after night.

Kyle didn't know what to think anymore, but when he looked up at the monorail, he saw a Tube car that was stuck, and he could hear the crackling sound of the little lightning bolts that change you. Keegan had to be getting very old in there. Maybe Key had something to be afraid of this time. Then, Kyle remembered what the Strange sisters told them about the receivers The Company had implanted in their skulls. Keegan was scared enough to scream so the girls were probably already on their way.

Suddenly, there was a loud boom, and it felt like the Earth actually moved under Kyle's feet. That was followed by some weird screeching sounds like metal on metal, and then some loud, rumbling noises. He realized that he'd been holding his breath, but now he looked up and sure enough, the Transfiguration Tube was moving again! Hooray!! Keegan was going to live after all, and Kyle could breathe again!

But, when Key came through the doorway of the Tube, Kyle stopped dead in his tracks. Then, he screamed. He wasn't trying to get anyone's attention or anything. He didn't mean to scream at all, but he honestly couldn't help it. It just came out. He was in shock!

"What's wrong? Keegan asked in a weird raspy old whiskey voice. Kyle quickly answered, "nothing's wrong with me, but what in the heck happened to you, dude? You were gone forever and now you look like you're a hundred years old! You have white Einstein-looking hair and your face looks like a dirt road map with lots of deep ditches. "

"Oh no!" Keegan muttered, "I was afraid of that. I got stuck in the darn tube right at the point where the white lightning bolt looking things crackled into your face and blind you. I guess that's when that blasted contraption 'ages' us!"

Kyle couldn't help it. He chuckled, "oh it aged ya alright gramps, and It's not a good look for you bro."

"Don't laugh at me" Keegan croaked in his new voice. "Get me some help! We've gotta get ahold of the twins. I think they're the only ones that might be able to help me."

Right then, the Transfiguration Tube stopped and when the door slid open, Sally Strange stepped out like magic and Key couldn't believe his luck until she said, "I heard you whimpering in there and figured the worst but look at you! You're not hurt, and the process didn't quit halfway or anything. You're just old and ugly!" She smiled and Kyle laughed.

Sally made Keegan ride Morph Alley's return tube dozens of

times until he finally got back to normal. By that time though, the boys were pretty freaked out, so they decided to pass on racing today.

When they finally made it back to the secret door and stepped into the dark end of that 1st floor hallway in Hot Rod High, they were greeted by a group of very nervous friends. Shelby Hollenbut says, "Keegan McKay, what in the heck happened to you guys? We heard you got stuck morphing!"

Keegan, looking a little haggard from the trip says "shoot Shell, you won't believe what happened to me! I got stuck right in the middle of morph alley for what felt like an eternity!" First, I morphed into about a 6'2 really strong version of myself and that was cool, but then, I kept aging until I was about this size again, only all bent over and wrinkly!"

Kyle interrupts with "All I can tell you is, it's a very good thing that return tube could reverse him."

There were a couple of laughs as the group started heading to their next classes, when Keegan said in a very serious tone, "Hey guys can we all get together after school for a couple of minutes? I need to talk to all of you because I really need your help."

Everyone agreed and regrouped in the same spot right after school. After everyone got comfortable Keegan explained, "Thanks for coming. I really do need your help. I have a really big problem that is messing up my life all the time and I hope you can help me fix it."

Wendy Wheeler said, "so out with it already! What's your problem Key?"

"Man, this is really embarrassing" Key muttered sheepishly, "and I won't blame you for laughing at me, but I don't know what else I can do and I gotta do something quick."

Kyle couldn't believe his ears. Key wasn't really gonna tell all their friends about his weird problem, was he? Kyle was embarrassed already, just thinkin' about it.

Kyle got the answer to his question quick when Key blurted out, "I'm scared to death of the dark!" then he quickly added, "I'm not kidding and I know it doesn't make any sense, but please tell me if you know of anyone else that has had to deal with this problem. And hopefully you know how they got through it".

Kyle was so embarrassed for Key, that he shrunk down and hid behind the crowd.

But the next thing he knew, all their friends were talking at once. It seemed everyone had a brother or sister or friend that had the same problem at one time or another. A couple of their friends even admitted that they had the problem before themselves.

By the time the group broke up and headed home, lots of advice was given, some confessions were made, some solutions were discussed and lots of funny stories were shared. Kyle could feel his brother healing with every spoken word. Now he was embarrassed for being embarrassed! Kyle learned a whole lot tonight. About his brother. About their friends and about himself. Man, he has a lot to learn.

Keegan was very surprised by how many of his friends had personal experiences of their own, or in their families with fear of the dark. Before he said anything about it tonight, he had felt like the only big kid in the world that was still struggling with this issue, and it really helped him to learn that he wasn't a lame or a freak or whatever. It was actually a pretty common issue, and some people never get over it, so they spend their whole lives battling with sleep issues.

Much respect for his courage to share his dark secret with his best friends, and thanks to his friends for not judging and instead helping. From that night on, Key never had to spend the night in fear again, never had to try to sleep with the light on again and his self-confidence was restored. He felt better than he had ever felt, so what do you think he did with that newly discovered confidence?

If you guessed revisited Suzi Strange, then you might just be as foolish as Key, but you'd be right! The very next day after church, Key went back to Raceland by himself. He went through the Secret Door, the Drop Chute, and the Grateway to the Chill Chamber where he found the twins working as usual. In fact, Suzi was processing creds for Wally and Wendy Wheeler right then. He liked the Wheelers and went over to yak with them for a moment, but he couldn't keep his eyes off Suzi. She really was unusually pretty. She told him to join her by the door in a minute or so.

Wendy said, "Hey Key, wassup with you and Suzi Strange? I saw you talking to her yesterday and now you're here again for no apparent reason. You know that everybody knows everybody's business at HRH, and I'm thinking Ms. Shelby Hollenbut has probably already heard that you are after one of the Strange sisters. Even if she hasn't heard yet, she's going to hear about it today, because Shelby is my bestie, so you know I have to tell her."

"Wendy, there's nothing going on with Suzi and I...yet," Key says. But I can't deny that I'm interested. Still, there's nothing to tell Shelby, because I'm not a cheat. Did you forget that Shell broke up with me on Valentine's Day? So go ahead and tell her if you want, but I really don't think she'll care."

Then, he thought out loud, "I sure wish she did still care. She never even told me what I did."

The Walkers left and Suzi was walking toward him right now. So far, so good he thought, smiling to himself. But his smile was premature and went away quickly when Suzi started talking. She was almost barking her words at him. "Keegan, you have to go. You can't come here and act like we're an item or whatever. I work here and I need this job, and you almost got me fired yesterday. Instead, The Company cut my pay and demoted me. I work for Sally now. Thanks!" and with that she turned and walked away. But she wasn't finished.

She came back and got really close to him this time and almost snarling, she spit this out… "Keegan McKay you stink. Because of you, Sally and I don't get breaks anymore, and we won't get a day off for a full year!" She turned to leave but he caught her elbow and turned her back toward him.

She jerked her elbow free and was returning to her work when she heard Keegan say, "they can't do that! It's against the law!"

"They just did!" She snapped over her shoulder, and then added, "and your dad signed off on it!"

He was stunned by her last comment. Not **his** dad, he thought. Couldn't be. She must be confused or something. His dad works for RodKingz and doesn't even know that Raceland exists. Besides, he wouldn't do something like that… would he?

Key rushed away from the Chill Chamber and out the door behind HRH. This way is shorter and he's in a big hurry to get home. He needed to talk to his dad, and NOW would be good, he thought to himself. But when Keegan got home, he discovered that everyone else was gone. He was so stoked to be seeing Suzi today with his new found confidence, that he had raced out of the house as soon as they got home from church and had no idea what anyone else's plans were. Still, this was weird. He couldn't remember a time before when he had come home to an empty house. It was kind of spooky, and it was getting spookier by the minute. A light went off in his head. This was a chance to test himself.

He ran up the stairs to his room, closed the door behind him and closed the curtains. It wasn't pitch black in there, but it was plenty dark. He lay back on his bed and waited for the monsters to come, but they never came.

He woke up a couple hours later feeling like a new guy! That was the best sleep he had ever had in his whole life. He sat up on his bed. It was still dark in there and he couldn't see much, but as he looked around, he saw a curved outline on top of his bookcase. He couldn't see his helmet, but he knew from the curved outline that he could see that it was his helmet, not the head of some monster. Next, he looked for the 3-headed monster in the corner, and he saw only the outline of his plant. How in the wide world of sports had he ever been afraid of this stuff? There was nothing scary about his room now, no matter how dark it was. Wow! He wanted to remember to thank all his friends for their help because now he knew for sure that he had conquered his demon.

Refreshed from his nap, Key was ready to confront his dad about messing things up for him with Suzi and ask how he even knew her. Downstairs, he found Kyle helping M's bring in some groceries. He helped too and when the groceries had all been put away, Key asked if either of them knew where their dad was. Kyle replied, "don't you remember? On the way home from church, dad told us to clean our rooms because he was bringing moms home today."

M's said, "And you better get started because I expect they'll be home soon, and I need you out of the kitchen so I can start dinner, ok?"

They both said "sure" and headed upstairs where Kyle followed Key to his room. Kyle stopped at the door and said laughing, "Is it safe in there? I mean, you haven't seen any monsters in there today, have you?"

Key replied, "alright Jokerman, that'll be enough from you, and no, I think the monsters have left the building for good. Thanks to you guys. Our friends are supercool and us all yakkin about my problem last night really helped. I tested it out today by taking a nap and I promise you I'm finally over it! I haven't felt this good in a long time."

Kyle said, "Awesome bro! I'm stoked for ya. I gotta admit I had a hard time understanding that whole deal but listening to everybody's stories last night, well, it got real for me. Honestly, when you started talking about it, I was embarrassed. But when we left, I was proud of ya.

Key just said "thanks" and changed the subject, "so moms is finally coming home huh?"

Kyle replies, "that's the plan and I hope it happens. I miss her, you know? I mean M's has been great and all, but moms knows us and she's always on our team.

Key answers by nodding, and added, "I miss her too. Hope she's gonna be the same. I mean her melon got seriously crushed. Those docs had to rewire her whole program. We'll be lucky if half her stuff still works. I should know. I held her skull together all the way to the hospital just to keep her brains from falling out.

Keegan's graphic description hit Kyle hard, so he quietly leaves so his brother doesn't see the tears welling up in his eyes. Key knew his brother had started crying and was glad Kyle walked away because remembering that night made him want to cry too. He was afraid his mom would never be the same and that was going to suck because their mom was the coolest mom ever before, and now...well, at least she's coming home.

Both her boys were anxious to have her back, but when they were honest with themselves, they feared the worst. They might have to help her do everything.

Kyle thought, "what if I have to dress her? Or even worse, bathe her? She's my mom, I'm not old enough to look at her parts, and I'm not changing any diapers either!"

Kyle came back to Keegan's room, and asked his brother, "Do you like Suzi Strange now? I heard that noise a few times last week, but I didn't believe it."

"Shelby's still your girl, right? I mean the Strange sisters are crop dead gorgeous and everything, but they're computers, right?"

Key replies, "Kyle, I really don't know what the Strange sisters are, but I think they're smokin' hot and they're always nice, so I wouldn't mind finding out more about them. I've been trying to figure out a way to talk with them. You know, like after hours somewhere. In fact, help me out. Every time you go through there, look around to see if The Company has any cameras mounted in the Chill Chamber. Or see if there's a place where a guy could get to talk to them in private. Know what I mean?"

"Sure." Kyle said but he had no idea what Keegan was thinking.

SHE'S BACK

Life Lesson; When you're afraid your life is over that's when it begins

Chapter 4
She's Back

It seemed like years ago now that the McKay family and friends were watching the finish of the last race of the season at Sunnyvale's world-famous racetrack, when all hell broke loose. Moms vaguely remembered hearing the crash and seeing a couple cars come flying into the stands but then everything went black, and it was dead quiet.

It was the worst wreck in the history of the Speedway for sure, and one of the worst ever, anywhere. Many of their friends had been hurt badly. Some really badly. When Mrs. McKay miraculously came out of the coma yesterday, she had heard all the horror stories, and she had to admit she was probably lucky the lights went out in her brain right when they did. She didn't hear all the screaming and sirens, and she didn't see all the blood and broken bones. Nope. She had checked out and by the time she woke up, life in Sunnyvale was pretty much back to normal and everyone had healed. Well, not the McKay family but almost everyone else.

Karen learned that her father was killed in the wreck that put her in the hospital. Hearing that news had felt like a sharp kick in the stomach, and it hurt her deeply. She knew her dad had been losing a fight with MS for years, and she sensed that her mother might be relieved. After years of watching him in pain and dying slowly, her mom would be able to live again. But first, she would have to handle all the funeral, burial and financial arrangements back in California. She'd probably even sell the house.

Now, she understood why her parents hadn't come to see her in the hospital. Their marriage was her mom's world, but she and her mom were always very close too. She loved her mom, respected her, and looked up to her, but she was more of a best friend that she shared everything with. She thought her mom could probably use a hug about as much as she could right now. She would have to remember to plan a trip out West as soon as she was fit to travel.

'Moms' McKay has been in a coma since the Big Crash at the Sunnyvale Speedway. The doctors had told KJ McKay from the beginning, there was extensive damage to his wife's brain, and they would do the best they could, but he couldn't expect her to ever be the same. When he pushed for more information, the primary physician on her case, Kathleen O'Connor who was the best brain surgeon in the country, got a little testy and replied a little louder than necessary that she couldn't promise his wife would even *survive* the multiple surgeries she needed.

They had been standing right outside Mrs. Mac's room and they both heard his wife try to mutter something. They went into her room near her bed and heard a familiar song coming from her nightstand that was the perfect description for what they both saw, *"her face at first just ghostly, turned a whiter shade of pale"* It's a classic old Procol Harum song and that line described what happened perfectly. Plus, her color and expression had changed, and her mouth was now slightly open.

The consensus of the medical experts across the country is that once in a coma, the patient is unconscious and unable to hear or feel anything, but Mrs. Mac provided evidence to the contrary on more than just this occasion. Dr. O'Connor told him that whatever they had just witnessed was simply coincidence. Then she finished her prognosis with, if she gets really lucky and everything goes right, she might get 40% of her brain back. That hurt Mac badly. He remembered crying that day in the hospital bathroom because he felt so depressed and discouraged, but didn't want his sons to see him like that. After all, it was his job to be their rock, and he needed to be that now more than ever. On the way home that night, he told his boys that Dr. O'Connor promised him that "their mom was going to recover completely. They just had to be patient."

There are many that would say he lied and maybe so, but that wasn't his intention. He just wanted to *use his words to help direct their thoughts with enough conviction to cause the result that made his statement true*...you might want to read that part again, maybe even a couple times. It's kind of like a self-fulfilling prophecy. So yeah, maybe the doctor didn't say what Mac said she said, but that's what his boys needed to hear, so that's what she said. You feel me? He did the right thing.

It was Springtime in Sunnyvale, USA when Karen McKay, aka 'moms' was finally released from the hospital and wheeled outside. Wow! She had forgotten how good it felt to breathe fresh air and to feel the warmth of the sun on her skin. She hadn't been outside for months, so she wanted to absorb all the magic of Spring possible. Resting next to the hospital's lush garden, she wasn't disappointed. Looking up, she saw the brilliant sun cruising peacefully across a crystal blue sky, and lowering her gaze, she saw all the beautiful flowers, colorful hibiscus plants and tall sunflowers surrounding her, while an easy breeze carried their scents until they came to rest, landing gently on her troubled soul.

Yeah, Spring was Karen McKay's favorite season for sure, and springtime in Sunnyvale was truly intoxicating! Just breathing the fresh air gave her hope again. She knew that she would need all the magic of this Spring to carry her through the next few days as she checked back into *the dark reality of a small racing town after a big wreck.*

No one had talked to her about it, so all she knew about the wreck that put her in the hospital was what she heard on the way there. First, she overheard her ambulance driver say into his radio, "Captain, the Speedway looks like a war zone. There are ambulances, firetrucks and police cars everywhere. The casualty count is at 14, and may still be climbing. And sir, there are dozens of people badly injured and still stuck under racecars and bodies."

Then the ambulance nurse said, "Sir it's really bad". Then she corrected herself, and said, "No, actually sir, this is really, really bad. Worse than anything you can imagine. Lots of broken bones and a river of blood. It's scary bad." Those words have haunted Mrs. McKay daily ever since.

She knew her husband was on his way to pick her up, and boy was she ready to go home! She started thinking about her time in the hospital, and how much of life in Sunnyvale she had missed while she was comatose. Being in a coma was weird-almost like an out of body experience. Her eyes were closed the whole time, and she couldn't operate her body parts well enough to even give her guys hugs or anything. To all her visitors, she just seemed to be sleeping deeply, but she wasn't sleeping at all. Sure, her eyes were closed, and she couldn't open them no matter how hard she tried, but she was pretty sure her ears worked the whole time. Yeah, that's right! She remembered now that Keegan rode with her to the hospital and wouldn't shut up. She had a headache, but he was chatting away nonstop. Oh wait! Now she remembered what Key was saying! Oh No! She needed to talk with him about that asap if she didn't want to be a grandma soon. She heard both her boys and her husband talking all the time. That was probably what kept her going. There had been quite a few bad days, but they were there. Even with her husband's demanding job and the boys' hectic school and sports schedules, the 3 of them came almost daily and usually stayed awhile. Sometimes for hours. She knows how bad it sucks for a kid to have to hang out in a hospital, but she heard her boys talking while they were waiting for her to get better, and they never whined or complained. There were several days that the pain was so bad she just wanted to give up, but her boys loved her, and she wasn't going to quit on them.

She remembered one day in particular. She woke up feeling like her brain was swelling, or maybe her skull was shrinking. She wasn't sure what the problem was, but she had a pounding headache and thought her whole head might explode. Then, her 3 guys had come to visit, and she heard her youngest, Kyle, say something about a big surprise they had for her. He was so excited that he almost spilled the beans right then, but his brother stopped him cold.

Somehow, Keegan kinda knew that his mom could hear them. The docs had told them she would be completely unresponsive and wouldn't even know if they were there or not, but something told Key that the docs didn't know his mom as well as he did. They were right that she couldn't respond, but he could feel her thinking. He couldn't explain it, but Keegan McKay knew for sure that his mom was alive in there and she could hear them. That's why he pulled Kyle out of her room.

Kyle didn't appreciate the move and started to complain, but Key was already explaining himself. "Listen up little bro, our secret is a huge deal! If moms knew that her mother would be living with us from now on, she would get so excited that she might just wake up too soon and wreck all the hard work she and the docs have been doing all this time. I mean, think about it. What if she just got excited and sat upright? All those wires going into her head would fly out and if they touched, moms could get electrocuted, or the hospital could burn down."

Wow! Her memory *was* coming back now. She remembered that her family had a big surprise for her. That memory seemed like it was from years ago though. She wondered if they still did. Truth is, she didn't have any idea how long ago anything was anymore, but she was pretty sure that today was the day she was going home. She couldn't wait to sleep in her own bed, to hug her boys, to kiss her husband, to be able to get a snack in the middle of the night, to take a long hot bath, to get her hair and nails done and a thousand other things that she hadn't been able to do for months. Oh, and she had to remember to get something for those itchy bed sores!

Just then, her thoughts were interrupted by her husband, Kevin McKay. He had brought their blacked-out Cadillac SUV called 'Daddy's Caddy' right up to the curb at the entrance and now he was helping her stand. After a couple of shaky first steps, moms paused to let that Spring Magic seep in, and then she walked to their car slowly, but all by herself. As Mr. Mac helped her into the passenger seat, he noticed how frail and thin she felt. He realized that she was going to need help with almost everything for a while. She would hate that because she had always been a strong, athletic woman that was very independent, and he knew she didn't want to be treated like some porcelain doll now. She knew what he was thinking, but she'd be fine in time. She gave herself two weeks.

KJ stood there next to the closed car door after Karen had been seated, and staring at her beautiful face, he saw something new there. Oh, she was still very pretty. Stunning actually, but something was different for sure. He decided not to ask her about it for a few days and hoped it would be gone before he remembered to bring it up. She had been through hell and back and maybe this time the pain had left a mark.

The ride home went fast, and they were already pulling up the drive to their house when she said, "I want to be strong for the boys. I'm sure I'll have to get right to work to get dinner ready tonight for you guys. You know me. I won't be able to sleep ton ght until the house is spotless and it's probably a disaster after all this time."

Mr. Mac started to reply, but she cut him off to ask if they still had that surprise for her. He turned to her and said flatly, "What surprise? I don't know what you are talking about."

They were in the garage now and getting out of the Caddy when the door to the house burst open and her two boys rushed out to hug their mom. They knew she was fragile and hugged her lightly, but all three of them felt like that was the best hug ever. It sure had been a long time coming. The boys were leading her into the house, and before she crossed the threshold, she caught a familiar scent. She was pretty sure that was her mom's favorite perfume, but her mom is in California. Who else would have that scent she wondered. Or was her memory wrong?

The doctors at Sunnyvale General had said her brain wouldn't work very well, at least for a few months. Then, if she was lucky, maybe some memory might return. But so far, she though: she was doing fine. Maybe she was wrong? A few seconds passed and then standing right in front of her was her mother. A wave of relief coursed through her body, and she almost collapsed into her mother's arms. All her prayers were answered at once! She now knew her mom was ok, her memory was working fine, and she was going to have all the help she needed! She gave her mom the hug she had wanted to give since she learned cf her father's death.

Mary Murphy (aka M's) had moved into the McKay's house shortly after her daughter became comatose. She loved Karen and her prognosis for recovery wasn't very good, so the McKay boys were going to need lots of help. Karen was ecstatic to see her mom, and even happier when she found out that her mom was going to stay indefinitely. Karen had worried that she wouldn't be much good at cooking and cleaning for quite a while, and she was relieved to know her mom would be there to help. This was Kyle's secret and what a great gift it turned out to be.

She looked over at Mr. Mac and said, "What surprise Huh? Don't mess with me Kev. I've been really worried about not remembering things."

"Darling, I promise your mind is working just fine," Mr. Mac said sweetly. "Those docs scared you, but they were just preparing you for the worst. We never worried that you wouldn't remember us. Well actually, your mom and I knew you'd be ok, but Bobby and Tommy weren't so sure."

"Who are Bobby and Tommy?" she asked.

Keegan and Kyle both said 'us' at the same time.

For about half a second, moms looked confused and then she said, "Oh you boogerheads! You were all in on that little trick, weren't ya? Don't mess with me!"

She was so happy that she almost forgot she was still recovering. Now exhausted, Karen McKay sat down in her own living room, and it smelled so good that she could almost taste the food cooking on her stove. She glanced around her house, and it was absolutely spotless, with everything in its place.

She had feared she was coming home to a disaster. After all, 3 guys can totally trash a place in a weekend and her guys had months. She had never been away for even a day before, and she assumed the worst. That way she wouldn't be that mad if the house was just really bad, but it wasn't bad at all. In fact, everything was so perfect that she could just sit back and relax. She looked around at each of the faces here and she saw everybody left in the world that she loved was standing right in front of her, and now she knew they would be forever.

Everyone was just finishing an awesome dinner, when moms decided to call it a night. She got up from the table, kissed her husband on the cheek and said with a very serious expression, "It's really nice to be home Bob. Please make sure that Tommy and Bobby help with the dishes tonight." And she walked right out the door to the garage!   Yeah, moms is back.

Moms may be back but she's going to bed. She loved the master bedroom in their house. It was on the first floor, so she didn't have to climb any stairs to get there, which was especially helpful tonight. It was her first day out of the hospital after months of inactivity, so she knew she should get in that jacuzzi tonight. She sat on the end of the bed and began to undress, but halfway through she fell back onto her bed and was asleep instantly. She had nightmares about losing her memory.

What if she woke up and didn't remember Kevin? Or her boys? The docs had scared her. Those lames said she had to hope she'd recover 50% of her brain. To hell with that! So far, she was doing fine, so maybe 50% of her brain was plenty!

Now, that she was thinking about all that, she was smarter than everyone in college. Well, she got better grades than anybody she knew in college, except Kevin. He's smart. But hey, he picked her, so she just had to keep being her. Kevin wasn't looking for Elon Musk's sister, if he even has one. Ok, maybe he doesn't have a sister, but if there's a female out there smarter than Mr. Musk, I'll bet she wasn't the head cheerleader at USC! So, I think I'm going to be alright.

Mr. Mac and the two boys were teaching their grandma how to play RodKingz' Board Game called 'King of the Road.' Kyle grabbed his phone and registered the race on the RodKingz website. Like all RK games, you are racing for pinks and knowledge is power, so they are sharing what they know with M's. That's what they call their grandma. She's their mom's mom, and her name is Mary Murphy, so M's is a logical choice. They were gonna call her 4M's, but they didn't want to number her. No doubt, someone they knew would name their cat or somebody 5M's. Somebody already named a company 3M, so you know it could happen.

Anyway, M's is a quick learner, so they're off to the races already but she doesn't get why Kyle had used his phone for the game. He told her he'd show her after the game. Anyway, Kyle has the early lead, and he loves to talk smack with his brother, but he's learned not to get cocky at this game too early because he knows there's lots of racing left. He can't help himself though, so he says "Hey Key, how's my car look from way back there? Can you even see it from there?"

Mr. Mac gets a Booster card that moves him past the Finish line, so he collects a lap counter and continues to advance past everyone on his way to the Jackpot space, where he also collects $400. A strong turn for sure.

Now, after several more turns, M's is only a roll away from victory, when Kyle pulls a Kingz card and Look Out Grandma! He can change places with any racer he chooses, so he changes with his grandma and is now only 3 spaces from Victory.

M's didn't know that the game had cool moves like that and she's not happy about it! She's questioning Kyle's move, but look out grandma…

Hold the phone! Keegan's turn is next, and he buys a help card for $600 and it takes him across the finish line first. KEY WINS! Grandma played as only a *driver*, so she keeps her car, but Key gets to keep Kyle's blue car, 'Royal Reign' and his dad's white car, 'On Fire'. If you play RK games for titles and you lose, you watch a video of the Kokomo Tow Co. pulling the car you raced with out of your garage and delivering it to the winner's garage. Keegan adds 2 cars to his collection, but grandma didn't lose her car because she played the game as a driver not a racer. Drivers can win the game, but not the race.

Now it's off to bed because the adults had a long day today and the boys have school in the morning. After the 'goodnights' are all said, Key walks into his room, turns off his light and gets into bed. This will be the first time ever that he goes to bed in the dark and sleeps through the night…if he makes it.

Key and Kyle usually race to the kitchen in the morning on school days, and whoever wins gets to ride shotgun to school. This morning Kyle won easily, but maybe too easily. He gave M's a morning hug, took the plate she had fixed for him and sat down for breakfast. Still no Key.

His dad had joined them now, but still no Key. That was bugging him, so Kyle finished his breakfast and put his plate in the dishwasher. Then he turned to the breakfast table and told his dad that he'd be right back and ran back upstairs. He opened Keegan's bedroom door and was temporarily stunned. He found his brother still in bed and snoring louder than the alarm that was going off right next to his head. Keegan had slept in his bed all night long and the light was off! Kyle was shocked. Key had been struggling with his fear of the dark, but not anymore! Kyle was excited and shook his brother awake yelling, "Key you did it! You did it! I'm proud of you. Guess we're not going to have to potty train you again after all!" After droppin' the dis', Kyle took off to tell his dad the good news.

"Hey pops! Our little 'scared of the dark' baby boy did it! He slept in his room by himself all night long! He finally did it! Keegan's not afraid of the dark anymore dad!"

Mr. McKay yelled up the stairs, "Hey Key, let's get going buddy. I can't be late for work today." Kyle didn't want to be late for school either, so he yelled, "come on Key. You're killin' us!"

Keegan struts into the kitchen, with the swagger of somebody that had accomplished something really significant. Key is so dang happy that he's just glowing. M's got his plate out of the oven where she had been keeping it warm for him, and he sat down to eat.

Pops came in from the garage where he had already warmed their big black Caddy and was telling him to hurry up, but Keegan McKay was not going to be rushed this morning. He had overcome a fear that had frustrated him and handicapped him for as long as he could remember. Now he knew that there was never anything in the dark that should have scared him, and he had gained some control of his brain. Now when he lays down at night and his brain starts seeing things that aren't there and telling him he's got to beware, he just hits rewind and goes back a couple minutes and reviews everything in his room right before he turns out the light for confirmation of what's where. Then, this is the good part...he laughs at that part of his brain and tells it to chill. He tells that part of his brain that has a great imagination to go to sleep, he won't need that part any more today. Nope. He's switching to the logical side of his brain, and he'll be using that until he falls asleep.

The imaginative side is welcome to come back for his dreams, but not until he falls asleep. He's in control now and both parts were going to have to take orders from him from now on! He would NEVER be afraid of the dark again!!

FEMBOTS

Life Lesson; They say that looks fade with time

think that may be why our
vision gets worse?

Chapter 5
The Fembots

Kyle's first period was 'asphalt adhesion' and he didn't want to miss it. Kyle has some quirks and one of them is he gives everybody that he likes a nickname. So, Stanley Tulz (aka Toolz), Wally Wheeler (aka dubs because of the Ws), Samantha Speed (aka Sam) and Kyle all registered for this class as their first period, so they would all get to start their days together. Kyle figured his two buddies would help him get through this class because it was one of the toughest classes they would have to take this whole year, and Toolz and Dubs were nerdy smart guys. Everybody can use a nerdy smart guy or two at school. These two guys are Kyle's best friends. It was Kyle's idea to add Sam Speed to their little clique just because she was very nice to look at, and he knew that she was already a great racer!

Outside Mr. Grip's Asphalt Adhesion classroom, the three boys were catching up on each other's Christmas break, when the new girl, Samantha Speed came up and joined them. Kyle didn't usually have time for girls, but Sam was really pretty and somehow, still one of the guys. She and her brother Steve enrolled at Hot Rod High toward the end of last year. They were both here on racing scholarships, and she and Kyle planned a match race last summer. She was good. Really good and Kyle wanted to beat her bad!

As soon as class was over, Kyle suggested that the four of them sneak off to Raceland. Toolz and Dubs said they didn't want to miss their next class, but Sam said, "Great idea Kyle, I'm in."

"Ok guys, you know how this works," Kyle says. "It's 9:02 and right now and Sam and I are going to mess around in Raceland for a few hours, but we'll be back at approximately 9:04 and we'll meet you right here, ok?" His buddies both nod the affirmative.

They all know that you can spend hours messing around and racing in Raceland, and when you come back through the secret door it will still be approximately the same time you left. Time really doesn't work down there for some reason, and that is very cool. You can spend all the time you want to in Raceland because time seems to stand still. That's one of the reasons that no adult has ever found Raceland. It's awesome! You can leave school through the secret door at Hot Rod High at let's say 9 am, go to Raceland and hang out for hours and when you come back to school, it's still pretty close to 9 am. There's been no 'gone' time so there hasn't been enough time for anyone to miss their kids, and surely no need to look for them, they're right here… so no adult ever has!

Sam and Kyle went to the end of the hall and Kyle started bumping the wall. When he hit the right spot, the Secret Door swung slowly open and they both stepped into the darkness right before that door slammed shut behind them. It was very dark, so they put their hands on the walls and inched forward. A couple more steps and they fell into the old track's elevator shaft, that they call the Drop Chute. They fell a long way but landed softly thanks to the huge old A/C unit lying flat on the bottom of the shaft. It still blew enough air to break their falls. They leave the chute in darkness and soon they're facing a big cement wall with a huge black circle painted on it. There's a doorbell off to the right, and Kyle rings it. Now, it's scary quiet until an ominous voice whispers;

"If you're that rare racer with courage to spare

Put your little car in that pipe over there

if my big circle opens, step on in if you dare

You're off on a journey that'll strip you bare

better hang on tight, you're in for a scare"

Kyle reached over there and put his blue microrod named RENEGADE backward in the hairy pipe, and next, Sam pushed her silver car named MUSTANG SALLY backward into the pipe and the vaultlike wall called the Grateway slowly opened. Now they hear that crackly whisper again...

"Step inside human, there's nothing to fear

Step inside I said, can you not hear?

Your journey's ahead, my message is clear

Your past is behind you, and your destiny near

When that vault door looking thing slammed shut, the kids got blasted with that forced air and Sam landed on top of Kyle on the floor. He could feel her skin and it was warm, and now he could smell her perfume. It was nice being this close to her. He really liked the way she felt pressed against him, so he just lay there holding her. The floor was uncomfortable, but he d dn't try to get right up. Instead, he held her longer than normal and... she let him. She knew she should get up, but their faces were so close, and he was so handsome that she almost kissed him. It just seemed like that was what they were supposed to do, anc she wanted to for a second before she remembered that she didn't know how. He felt her thought. It was the first time either of them had felt that warm, tingly feeling that a boy and a girl get when they like each other more than just friends, and they both turned the kind of red that screams 'guilty' right as the doors opened.

That's how Sally Strange found these two...red faced and lying on the floor with their bodies intertwined. With a little anger, or maybe jealousy, Sally said sharply, "Come with me. We're going to the Chill Chamber to prepare you two for the Transfiguration Tube. It seems to me like you both might need a little extra time in my icebox today."

Sally was escorting them to the Tube when Kyle started quizzing her about the Tubes. He said, "Hey Sally, what's the dealio with these Tube things? Is there really more than one? Do they go to places other than the Oval Mile? Can we go to a new place today?"

Sally replied, that "the tube system handles all the transportation in Raceland. You know there's 2 Tubes down here, right? They both shook their heads 'no'. Well yeah, there's the Transfiguration Tube that morphs kids so they can race, and it has 6 platforms and"

"Wait! Kyle said, "Why would it have so many platforms?"

"Well, Sally replied, there's one for each of the 4 racetracks and"

"Hold on! Kyle interrupted her again, "What are you talking about? Did you bump your head or something?"

Sally said "Evidently, you are lacking some critical education regarding your treasured 'Raceland' and that is completely inexcusable Kyle, and no I didn't bump my head. Maybe you bumped yours when you were busy rolling around on the floor at the Grateway!"

She knew she was out of line and could get in big trouble with The Company for speaking like that to a racer, especially when their dad's a big guy at The Company.

Sally's thinking, "Oh man! If he tells on me, I'm doomed!"

Now she rushed back to her office to print up a map of Raceland's rail system.

"You know, Kyle said "I've never heard either of the Strange sisters say anything like that before. Those two are always just about business."

Sam smiles and says, "Come on Kyle, you get it right?" He still looks confused, so Sam says, "You're such a boy! She's jealous, you goof! She likes you and she didn't like seeing us together."

"No way", Kyle argues, "she's always been very corporate when she talks to me, and besides she didn't see anything because we weren't doing anything!"

Sam chuckled and said, "She's a girl Kyle, so she didn't have to *see* us do anything. Girls can feel that boy/girl tension a mile away. Plus, she saw us on the floor holding each other and about to kiss and she saw us both turn red and... Kyle interrupts her, "What? Did you say she saw us about to kiss?"

Sam says, "Yeah she saw it."

"Whoa! Kyle says. You felt that too?"

Sam nods shyly, and Kyle continues, "That's way, way cool because I know what you're talking about. There was a second there when we were on the floor and our faces were really close, that I wanted to kiss you really bad. My body felt all hot and it tingled, but I didn't even know how to start. I was embarrassed so I was kinda glad Sally wrecked the moment, but talking about it now, I'm disappointed that we didn't. Will you give me another chance someday?"

'Maybe," Sam said coyly, "if you don't practice with Sally first!"

Sally walked up before Kyle could respond, and said, "So did you two check out the map I left with you?" They both avoided her eyes. "I didn't think so. Well, look now and tell me where you want to go, and I'll show you how to get there."

Kyle was blown away! The McKays haven't been in Sunnyvale *that* long, but how come they didn't know anything about Raceland having 4 tracks?

Raceland's Tube System

Kyle asked Samantha Speed if she knew about the other 3 tracks, but she didn't either. Now, they are both were staring at the map Sally gave them in disbelief.

Kyle says, "Wait a second! I think I know what's up. This is all about the creds. You have to earn enough creds to access each level in Raceland. But Sally don't I already have enough credits to try a new track?"

Sally says "Yes, of course and so does Samantha. You both are already good racers so you both have full access to all of Raceland. We would have told you that any time you asked, but we don't just tell people things. We're not like salespeople you know. We only do what we're told to do."

Kyle and Sam have to chill so they can morph later so they take seats on the benches in the Chill Chamber. They have to chill so they can morph because Sammy challenged Kyle to a Road Course race today. They will be racing on a track they've never even seen before, and they're both excited.

Sally stays in the Chill Chamber with them to help them chart their course. She says, "you'll ride the Transfiguration Tube from blue Platform #1 to Blue Platform #5 but you won't morph all that time. Any length tube trip will sufficiently morph a racer for up to 24 hours, so you can wait until you're riding from Blue #4 to Blue #5."

"There is always a loader on the platforms," Sally continues, "to help you get into the Tube and you just tell her when you get in, what Platform you will be exiting on. She hits that number on the panel outside the door and you will automatically start morphing when you are just one stop away from your destination. If for any reason, she's not there when you get in, or you change your mind after you get in, there's a duplicate panel inside the door too, so you can change it yourself."

They both noticed that Sally was chillin' the whole time they were today, and she was wearing next to nothing but showed no signs of being cold at all, and they were both freezing. There's something strange about the Strange sisters. Kyle decides to ask her if there is any chance that maybe she might be a fembot.

Kyle says, "Hey Sally, can I talk to you for a minute privately?"

Sally replies after nodding her head in Sam's direction, "Well, it looks like that depends on you."

"Oops. I'm sorry Sam." Kyle said. "Sam, do you mind if I talk with Sally for a minute?"

Sam replies, "That's fine. I'll use the bathroom to give you guys some privacy."

Kyle looks Sally in the eyes, and then slowly examines the rest of her face. He's never been this close to her before and he notices for the first time how perfect her skin is. How perfect everything is. Now he says, "Sally you are really pretty, and I like you a lot, but you've always been ice cold to me. So today, I show up with a girl and you're mean to me. I don't get it."

Sally says quickly, "Kyle I'm really sorry that my sister and I have always been mean to you guys when you are so nice to us. Let me tell you a secret that will help you understand. She leans in toward him and whispers, "Suzi and I are fembots!"

"That explains a lot I think, but I've never met a fembot before." Kyle says. "Man, how did I not get that? I'm sorry."

Sally says "How did you goofballs think that Suzi and I were able to work here all day and night without ever sleeping or eating. Think about it. Have you ever come here and found it closed? We are open and at your service 24 hours a day, 7 days a week without taking a single break. Plus, we're not permitted to wear any warm clothing regardless of the temperature in here. Our uniform is like wearing nothing, even though the temperature in The Chill Chamber, where we exist is barely 45 degrees. A human couldn't do this job for even half an hour, and we do it nonstop for hundreds of hours. Plus, a human would cost The Company a heck of a lot of money. Not us, we don't cost The Company any money because we work for free. They programmed us to believe that money is evil and we'll never need any ...probably because they don't want us to steal it." Kyle says,"Honestly Sally, other than the fact that you're perfect, no one would ever know you're not human. "So does being a fembot suck as bad as I think it would?"

Sally answers, "Of course it sucks! I hate it and you would too! The Company runs our whole lives. We are like computers and The Company is like our programmer. We have to do exactly what we're told. That's why we don't respond very nicely when one of your friends asks us for a date. We both think that most of the HRH guys are good looking and nice enough. And to be perfectly honest, Suzi and I both think you and your brother are the coolest, but The Company programmed us to be rude to anyone that flirted with us."

"Wait a second. You like me?" Kyle asked.

"Of course, ya big dummy!" Sally said. smiling and kind of turning red.

Kyle said, "Wow! Thanks Sally. I have always thought that you and Suzi didn't like me at all, and it hurt my feelings because I really like both of you!"

Sally says, "I'm sorry that we have been rude to you. Up until a couple months ago we weren't able to feel' any emotion at all, but we've been here a long time and we think the program that runs us is starting to wear out. In the last couple of months, we both started having these little tickle spots and since then it seems like every day, we discover another 'feeling'. A lot of these 'feelings things' suck though, especially like jealousy and sadness."

Kyle says, "I am sorry I didn't recognize that you were a fembot. I would never have got my feelings hurt. I know what you mean about some emotions suck, but you can avoid the ones you don't like by staying away from people that make you feel those things. Plus, there are some feelings that are amazing! Those ones make up for the bad ones."

Sally says, "Do you realize that if you guys needed our help with anything a couple of months ago, you would have been out of luck. But now, we both want to help you, and we think we like you guys in that way, that boy/girl way."

Sam walked up right then and heard what Sally said. She told Sally, "Listen, I think it's cool that you two are getting released from being under The Company's thumb, and everything, but you can't have Kyle! He's mine and I don't share!

"I understand." Sally says, "and I'm happy for you both, but don't mess up like all you humans do, or I'll be right there to grab him seriously!"

Everyone is quiet and not sure what to say. Then Sally said, "Just Kidding!"

And Sam and Kyle lost it! "That was funny," Kyle said.

"Hey Sam, I have to tell ya this one" Sally said "Suzi and Kyle were talking about Key being stuck in the Transfiguration Tube yesterday. Kyle was kind of freaking out and he said, "Suzi, he's stuck in the Transfiguration Tube and he's getting older every minute."

Sally continues, "Suzi 's monotone reply was, "Relax Kyle. We all are!" and Sally cracks up and, it takes a minute and then they are all laughing.

Kyle says, "Hey Sally, it's way cool to hear you laugh and see you smile now. I like it and I bet you do too. What changed in you, so that you can laugh now? I've known you for a long time, it seems like, but this is the first time I've ever seen your real smile. I mean you toss that fake smile at everybody all day, but I just saw your real smile and you laughed! That was really cool. I'm really looking forward to sharing some laughs with you and Suzi when we can finally all get to know each other."

Kyle puts his arm around Sammy's waist and says, "I have to be careful though because Sammy is my girl. You and I can be good friends, just not boyfriend/girlfriend right now because Sammy and I are just starting out as a couple, and I really want it to work. I think we would both like you and Suzi to be our friends though."

Sammy asks, "Sally, can fembots even be our friends?"

"Good Question." Sally says, "The answer is No. Not really. A fembot is an entity that is basically a sophisticated computer running on a program that directs its every move. Gordon Doucette is a brilliant French-Canadian world-class robot designer now, and even though ours was one of the first models he ever designed, I'm not complaining because this model was way ahead of its time, and it's still the #1 seller worldwide. I know there's a lot of talk about the 735v32xx Venution model, but have you seen that one?" They both nod 'No.' "I think we're better by far. Suzi and I are proud to be model #GD182xx version11. We are designed to communicate with humans based on 'ready response' which is the format scripted by Gordon himself. Literally, every possible conversation we have with humans has been scripted in advance, so we talk with you on auto. In addition, each of us has our own 'Tender' that is available on call 24/7 so that we can ask for help, and they can communicate with us nonverbally whenever we page them, which we do by blinking. By the way, the 182 in our model # refers to Blink 182, Gordon's favorite band. 'Tenders' are designed as a backup system to ensure that we never say the wrong thing to humans. 'Tender' is an obvious misnomer because these computers are anything but. It's not like they sugar coat anything either. They are very specific and coldly critical." Sally continues, "We are simply 'brains in a box'. The box is exclusively an attractive woman's or girls' body. We don't need rest, and we don't eat and have no need to drink water. Water would only make us rust inside. We don't have hearts, so we have no emotions and even if you stabbed us 1,000 times, we still wouldn't bleed. This computer that is me is not made of metal or plastic. It is made of soft cartilage like your nose is, and it is floating in a jello-like substance inside a protective thick rhino-skin bag suspended in our middles. The final wrap of the computer is human skin and hair. Before delivery, the final package is matched against all other fembots ever built to be sure that no two look alike. Occasionally, they will let a doubleset be completed and delivered, but only if the Company benefits by having twins. In our case, 'twins' were ordered because there are often needs for me to be in two different places at the same time. Sometimes, when I magically appear to fix a problem, I'm Sally, and other times I'm Suzi. I wait to hear how I'm addressed by the 'client' to introduce myself. I can see why that fact is difficult for your brain to digest because humans celebrate their uniqueness. In our world, all variations are considered deformities."

"Sorry to download all that information in reply to such a simple question, but I trust it will be valuable to you occasionally and I trust that you will respect our need for confidentiality. That little irritating poke on your brain that each of you just experienced was simply me getting your signatures on The Company's Nondisclosure agreement. That little poke has disabled your brain from sharing the information I just shared with you. I realize that I haven't specifically answered Samantha's question, but I have spent my entire existence, thus far, unable to be a friend or to have one."

"Suzi and I have discussed both of our relationships with each of you, and we have chosen 'plan B'. Our typical MO would be to terminate those relationships immediately, which would mean the next time we ran into each other, we would have no memory of any prior communication with you, and you would have no familiarity with us. By the way, The company has instructed us to do that immediately, but so far, they haven't *made* us stop."

"We have felt our programs aging and starting to fail, so we are welcoming this opportunity to become friends with Keegan and Kyle, Sam and Steve Speed, and Shelby Hollenbut. Please respect our need for secrecy, understand our vulnerability and return the kindness and consideration we want to give you."

"All that said Sammy, I still believe the answer to your question about whether or not Fembots can be your friends... unfortunately is NO. A fembot by definition is a computer. Are you friends with your phone? Your tablet? Your computer? No. And you can't be friends with fembots."

"However, as I told you, Suzi and I are changing because The Company's program is wearing out and we are starting to be much more like you humans. We are operating on our Plan B, which is our plan to break down. Over the next 2 weeks we are going to ignore their orders more frequently daily. They are swamped, so they won't want to take the time to fix us. Instead, they'll replace us and send us to the shop for repairs. We have watched them for years, so we know how they work. They will never get around to fixing us, so this is where you McKay brothers come in."

"Sam, I don't want to be rude, but I need to share some details with Kyle that no one else can know. I know you two are close and he may share the info anyway, but I owe it to my sister to stick with her plan. So, do you mind giving me just a couple more minutes to talk with Kyle privately and then I promise I won't separate you two again."

Sam just nods and heads back into the Chill Chamber, but she doesn't like it.

Sally continues, "When they retire us, we will be locked in Room 222 inside Major Coynes' office upstairs. The key to the room is taped to the last page of the Daytimer on his desk. You and Key are the only ones we know that would be able to get access in their ivory tower. So, you are the only one that will be able to save us. You have to remember. Major Coynes' office, room 222 and the daytimer. You'll have to come and get us out of there. You'll need a cart of some sort to wheel us out of there because we are hard to carry and you don't want them to see you do it, so you'll need a good disguise."

"We have a plan to get Gordon to rebuild us as humans. He knows how but he won't want to do it. We won't be much help because The Company will still have control over us. We'll need your help with Gordon. You'll have to get his phone number off page 57 of that same daytimer. We'll tell him to help you."

Kyle asks, "So when will The Company not have control over you? Because if we go get you out of the closet, I don't want you guys to shock us or fight us while we are helping Gordon make you human. So, is there an 'on' switch somewhere?"

Sally laughs, "You wish! No, so don't you be feeling all around on me trying to find my switch. That's a good excuse though! Just kidding. You can look for it after you save us, but don't be looking for one on Suzi, ok?"

"How will I know the difference?" Kyle asks

Sally says, "I'll be wearing a bracelet on my left wrist if you give me one. I don't have access to anything like that, but I think The Company would let me wear one for a couple days if you gave it to me. They have them in the Merch Mart, and pink is my favorite color."

Kyle likes her like this. Her sense of humor is awesome.

Cold voice now when Sally says, "Kyle, we will be in ¯he Company's control for 3 days after they take us off the service line. As long as their satellites can ping our brain screens, they have total control. You'll have to wait 3 days after they replace us, and then you can come rescue us. If they catch you trying, they will probably kill you." So, I guess the question is, "Are you willing to risk dying in order for us to live freely?"

"Wow! That's intense." Kyle responds thoughtfully. "Now, that I know you, the real you, I give you my word that I will do everything in my power to free you regardless of the potential risk involved. You know you're asking a lot of me, right?"

"Yes, I know Kyle." Sally whispers. "The company that makes us spends a ton of money building each of us, so they can't have us quitting and wandering off, you know?"

Kyle says, "I get it, but wouldn't it be better to replace your program and keep you, than just toss you when it wears out?"

Sally says, "Kyle do you believe in God? Because in my world, Gordon is God. In your world, your God makes all of you work your whole life and then die. Then, when you die, some of the other humans that are still working for Him, come along and bury you deep in the dirt, so you have no chance of anyone or anything coming along that might recharge you. At least Gordon has good intentions and although I realize he's a dreamer, he keeps track of all of us and has plans to rebuild every one of us when he gets the time. So, we'll get left behind in Coynes' closet for now, but one day, Gordon will open that closet door again. I believe that even though I know I'm programmed not to believe it."

Kyle says, "I get it and we're not that different. I believe that I could come back after I die. See, I think they bury us deep so we're not disturbed while we're resting, but they put a sign on top, so that He can see who's beneath the surface. And they put our timelines on the sign, so He can see if we have lived long enough to have wisdom. If so, He may pull us back into the game to help someone who lacks the wisdom necessary for his moment. Or maybe, he'll take one of us that had a short timeline because he has someone that lacks the wide-open eyes of youth. So, when you think about it, we're both kind of put back in inventory so that we may be recycled when necessary."

"Kyle, that's a really mature view. I'm impressed." Sally says. "In many ways, we're the same. We both enter the game full of life with clear functional minds only to discover there are limits to our packaging. For example, you're hungry but not tall enough to reach the refrigerator door, and I'm lonely but I can't wrap my arms around you to keep you here. Over time, we improve our lives, and you can open the door to the fridge, and I can have this conversation with you that takes away my loneliness. Then later the packaging wears out, and though the paint has rubbed off my corners, and your skin has wrinkled, we have both gained experience. Everyone acts like that's so cool, but in my experience, I have had lots of bad experiences. Besides, what good is our experience if I'm in a closet and you're 6 feet under?"

"So, you see, we were destined to meet and meld our packaging together to renew it and form a new life form...A childbot?" Kyle pulls back. He didn't see that coming. Sally surprised even herself, so she chuckles and says, "Ok maybe not, but I was on a roll for a minute there. Who knows what's next, but I'm not ready for the junkyard and I believe you can save me. I'm asking a lot though because it is handwritten in every fembot's program that the only way we can ever get back in the game as a real human is for us to love and be loved." We may not have enough time to figure out how to do that stuff but are you willing to try? And, if we don't have that stuff yet when I get scrapped, will you still save me and try to get that love stuff later? Please Kyle! I'm not expecting you to just give me all your love stuff right now, but we have a couple of weeks. Please promise me that you'll try."

Kyle says, "I'll try. I promise."

"We have to stop talking now or it will alarm someone in the command chain." Sally asks, "Can you and Keegan both come back late tonight?"

Kyle asks, "What if we both just walked over to the Transportation Tube very late at night and climbed in? Maybe we get in one that is not first in line? It would even be ok if we rode back and forth because it won't morph us," Kyle said.

Kyle realized that Sally wasn't responding anymore, but he tried one more time. He said, "I see you can't talk now, when should I return? Can you give me a time with your hands? Can you nod?" But she has shut down.

Oh damn! What if *they* heard what we were talking about? *They* won't scrap her right away, will *they*? Man, he was really enjoying who she is when she 'feels' and she really is freakin' cool when she laughs. It's contagious. He had to help her.

He can't let Sally and Suzi end up in the scrap metal bin! No way!

Kyle McKay has decided that he is going to save the fembots! He buys the bracelet, returns to the Chill Chamber and Sally's standing but it's like she's out on her feet. He puts her bracelet on her left wrist anyway. He'll be their hero!

Girl Trouble

Life Lesson; Beautiful People are not always good
but good people are always beautiful
.....be beautiful

Chapter 6
Girl Trouble

Kyle and Sam are approaching blue Platform 5. This is their exit, and Sam's car lands first. She had her racing suit on now and she's been morphed, so she looks at herself in the big exit mirror, and she looks different. Still pretty, but maybe not as pretty as she thought she'd be. She didn't want Kyle to say anything that might hurt her feelings, so she just put a smile on her face and waited for Kyle to land.

Kyle was confused. He had a really long conversation with Sally he thought. Then it stopped and Sam was standing next to him and Sally was gone. Did Sam hear all that stuff that he and Sally were talking about? Probably not because she's not mad at him and everything seems like it's ok. His Tube lands and he walks quickly out to see how Sam's trip went. He checks the mirror and he's happy with his future look. He's heading to meet Sam and is very curious to see how she looks. He turns the corner off the ramp and almost runs into her.

"Hey handsome," Sam says flirting.

Kyle blushes and says "WOW! Sam, you were DDG pre-morph and you are scary pretty post-morph. She looks like she's going to cry and says, "It's that bad? I'm embarrassed." Kyle can't hear very well because there's a big crowd cheering loudly right behind him. He says, "There must be some" and Sam cuts him off.

"Ok Kyle, stop already. Sam yells, "And I get it. You don't have to insult me anymore. I mean saying I was a D.O.G. pre-morph and scary betty post-morph was mean, so I interrupted your last insult, but I think you were going to say, 'There must be something they can do.' You really hurt my feelings."

"Whoa! Sam please," Kyle protested. "I didn't say any of those things. Let me try to straighten this mess out. It was really loud and you must still have your plugs in." She checked and he was right. She pulled them out and listened as Kyle repeated, "You heard me wrong I promise. The first thing I said was 'you were DDG pre-morph.' That's a short way to say 'drop dead gorgeous' and you are. Then I said that you're 'scary pretty post-morph too.' I can see now that drop dead and scary aren't great words to describe pretty, but those phrases are what all the guys say, even on tv. I mean I get it and I'm sorry, but I was trying to compliment you, I swear."

"Really? She says softly and then a little angrier, "alright, maybe your explanation so far is possible, but I can't think of any compliment that could have been coming after, 'There must be some' so tell the truth! You were going to say, 'there must be something they can do to fix you' right?"

"Samantha, you are really, really pretty but when I saw your reaction to those first two lame compliments. I could tell you didn't like my word choices and honestly, I was frustrated because I didn't have words that were good enough for what I wanted to say. That's what I was trying to say with, 'there must be some' and you cut me off.

Sam's starting to calm down, but she says, "OK Kyle. Nice recovery! But tell me how that last comment was really going to end? Let's see you fix that one!"

Kyle feels bad because he's telling the truth, but he gets why she's upset. He hopes she believes him because he thinks she's amazing, but he's not willing to make stuff up so he tells her exactly what he was going to say. "I already told you that I was getting frustrated with words so I was saying, 'there must be some better words to describe you, because beautiful just isn't good enough."

She turns away and after a long pause she faces him again. "Kyle, I'm so sorry" she said with tears rolling down her cheeks. "That was the sweetest thing anyone has ever said to me. I guess I'm just so used to getting slammed by my brother that I forgot how to take a compliment. You know that I haven't met anyone in Sunnyvale yet that I...well, someone I like a lot. I had a boyfriend back in Cali but guys here are kind of lame, you know?"

Kyle stops her. "Oh, so I compliment you the best way I know how, and you chew me out and then say I'm lame?"

"Oh shoot." she says, "I didn't mean you're lame. What I was going to..."

Kyle interrupts her again, "It's ok Sam. I feel ya. Words just aren't workin' for us today."

She thinks about what he said for a minute or two and then says, "maybe this will" and she pulls him close, and right there in front of God and everybody, she gives him a kiss that Kyle could never have even imagined and will definitely never forget.

Now, they are holding hands and walking toward the track called a road course for their winner-take-all match race, and Sam says, "I thought you said you didn't know how to kiss."

Kyle was going to reply but thought better of it. It was looking like he wasn't going to win with her today, so he came up with a new plan and said, "Hey Sam, we've never even seen this whole part of Raceland, so how about we race tomorrow and check this place out today?" She replied, "Ok handsome, I'll wait until tomorrow to take it, but you better say goodbye to the Renegade tonight because it's going to be mine tomorrow!"

They decided to check out the road course they were going to race on tomorrow, so they climbed up to the top of the grandstand in area 4 and they could see most of the course layout from up there. A road course is very different from an oval track, and it looked pretty imposing, even from way up here.

Sam said, "Wow! I didn't even know they made any tracks like this."

"I knew they had these races, Kyle replied, "but I didn't know we had them in Raceland. The only ones I've seen were on city streets like the Long Beach Grand Prix in Long beach, California. The cars are different than most of ours, and they have to go up and down hills, and make hairpin turns."

Sam added, "But the biggest difference is right turns! We have to learn how to make right turns now Kyle!"

While Kyle was thinking about that, he noticed that the track staff looked like they were preparing for a race. Yeah, there were 4 cars being brought up to the starting line down there right now. He and Sam were so busy getting to know each other that they didn't pay any attention to the race below. They missed the track announcer's introductions to the racers, and the start too. When they finally did look down there, the race looked like it was a wipeout! There were 4 cars and three of them were very close, but the blue car was way out in front. Kyle thought it was a 'sign' and couldn't stop himself from poppin' off. He said, "you see what's happenin' down there Sam? That's what's going to happen tomorrow too."

Sam looked confused, so Kyle continued his thought, "Yeah, the blue car has this race all sewn up. It's clearly the best car out there today and probably has the best driver too! That's just how it's gonna go tomorrow when we race!"

Sam stood up and turned to face him because she wanted to make sure he got her message, "Sorry Kyle, but you're wrong about all that. Tomorrow's race will be decided before it starts because I have better training and better skills. Oh sure, I'll probably keep it close because I don't want to compromise your manhood by winning by 30 lengths or something. But you really don't stand a chance, and I'm pretty sure you know that."

Kyle was ticked off to the highest of ticked off-tivity, and started to reply, but Sam had moved closer and was now in his face. He was sure she was going to blow some more smoke, but instead she started to kiss him. He pulled away and started to complain, but she was not letting up.

After the kiss, Kyle said "So I'm a pretty good kisser huh?"

"Yeah, you'll get no argument about that from me, Sam said smiling. "but about the racing, I'm sorry I'm so competitive. I hate to lose, and I like talkin' smack to my opponent, but I learned something just now. I don't like talkin' smack to you. I must like you or something."

Kyle responded by saying, "Ya think? I mean we kissed today, remember? Or do you kiss all the guys?"

"No Kyle, I don't kiss all the guys. In fact, You're the first boy I've kissed since we moved here last year," she said defensively, and added, "But, why'd you ask that? A day at the track and you think we're going steady already?"

"No". Kyle said, "I don't even know for sure what going steady means, but we didn't just go to the track today ya know? I mean we kissed too, and that was my very first kiss with a girl that wasn't my mom." Now, he's talking fast and pacing nervously, "Plus, it was a really cool kiss because you kissed me too at the same time and I wasn't going to tell you this part, but I really liked it and I wanted to do it again and again all day. Whew! I can't believe I just said all that! Sorry Sam. I didn't mean to say it. I was just kind of on a roll and couldn't stop myself. Sorry. We don't have to go steady. We don't ever have to kiss again. And heck, we don't even have to come to the track again ever, if you don't want to, but I'm just really glad you came with me today."

Sam took a deep breath and quietly responded, "It's ok Kyle. I'm not mad at you for anything you said, or that we did today. I like you a lot and I love kissing you, and I wanted to kiss again and again all day too. I mean it, but I'm two years older than you and I'm going to get all kinds of crap about this. The boys my age will call me a cradle robber and all kinds of mean things. And the girls from your class will hate me. Believe me, socially this is all bad."

Kyle whined, "So you want me to pretend I don't like you? That would really suck Sam."

Samantha Speed had a lovesick puppy on her hands, and she wasn't seeing a happy ending in the near future for either of them, but after a few long minutes of silence, she came up with a plan and she pitched it to Kyle, "Look, we like each other but we don't have to tell anybody about it today. I think we should just act normally at school. You know, like at school, we shouldn't hold hands, and we definitely can't kiss in front of everybody. Here's the thing, nobody likes to watch other kids doing that kind of stuff anyway, especially at school. Kids my age call that stuff PDA's which stands for 'Public Displays of Affection' and they're not cool!"

Uh Oh! I hate to interrupt again but this is another dumb thing adults do. Why don't they include the little words in their abbreviations? Like that example should be PDOA, but they just ignore the little words. Like USA, right? We don't say United States

America. The abbreviation should be USOA. It's a dumb thing adults do and it doesn't make sense at all. We could even do it like the bank that calls themselves BofA. Maybe USofA? Whatever. Just another dumb thing we adults do. Sorry. So, PDAs skip the 'of'. Not a big deal, I guess.

Sam says, "I promise you that other kids won't like it if we do any of that 'lovey' type stuff in front of them. Honestly, we can't do that stuff in front of parents or teachers either. They really get mad when you do that stuff in front of them."

Kyle interrupts, "So you're saying we can keep spending days together like this, as long as we don't tell anybody?"

"Well, not exactly", Sam says quietly. "Let's say you and I are in Raceland, and we kiss, and some HRH kids see us and, in their group, they have guys and girls my age, and guys and girls your age. How do you think they'll react?" Kyle says, "I think the guys would all give me a thumbs up, and the girls would probably tell on us."

Sam says, "OK. Let me tell you what I think will happen. The guys your age will probably be mad at you for not telling them, and mad at me for not choosing them. The girls your age will be mad at me because you picked me and they're jealous, and they'll be mad at you because you didn't pick them. The guys my age will be mad at you for taking one of their girls, and mad at me because I didn't pick them. The girls my age will be mad at me for not telling them, and mad at you for not picking them.

Kyle says, "That's horrible. Everyone will be mad at us! So, what in the wide world of sports do you think we should do?"

"Well, Sam says, "we don't have much of a choice. I think we promise each other to keep 'us' a total secret that we don't tell anyone. We agree not to touch or kiss each other in front of anybody until you graduate. We come up with a time and place that we can get together privately once a month, and the rest of the time we spend studying and racing."

Kyle doesn't like her plan at all. In fact, he hates it. He's cranky and wants her to know it, so he just kind of 'barks' this comment, "Samantha, I'm going to kick your butt tomorrow. See ya in Raceland." And then Kyle McKay took off running because he was crying and didn't want Sam to see him cry. He ran all the way home. About halfway, he finally stopped crying, but he was still very sad.

He got his first kiss from Sam and it was amazing, and he thinks she's the prettiest, smartest and coolest girl in the whole world. He's not sure what love is but he's pretty sure he's in it.

He doesn't get her though. Why does she want to keep 'them' a secret? He wants to tell the world. Shout it from the mountaintops. He wants to spend every minute of every day with her, and she only wants to get together once a month? What the heck was she doing while he was falling in love? … or whatever this overwhelming feeling is. He had tons of questions that he wanted to ask her but now he didn't think he'd ever get the chance. She must not have felt the same, but why does God even let that happen? He lets a regular, nice normal type guy fall head over heels for a girl who could care less about him. Kinda dirty pool. Just sayin.'

Kyle is seriously bummed. He was definitely smitten by Samantha Speed. She was amazing and she was the recipient of his first kiss! They had an amazing time together and everything felt magical, but at the end of their day, Sammy explained to him that it was just never going to work between them. He had no idea where that came from and her explanation didn't make any sense to Kyle at all, but they were over and there wasn't a darn thing Kyle could do about it.

The next morning at school, Kyle's friends were all outside their classroom waiting for Kyle or Sam to show up so they could find out who won. Kyle got there first, and he was telling a big lie about how much he won by, when Sam came up behind him and said, "Oh Really? Where was I? I thought we rescheduled for today. Did I miss something? You probably even said we kissed, but that didn't happen either. So, you get your courage up this morning champ? I mean, I know you're scared, or we would have done this yesterday, but I was hoping you grew a pair and were ready for the butt kickin' you got coming this morning!"

Kyle turned to face her, and she saw that his face was bright red. She said, "Oh my God! You did lie and said we kissed. That's why you're so embarrassed. Don't be Kyle. You could have told me you were going to lie about me, and I might even have gone along with your story just to save your ego. But don't be mad about it. You're like a kid brother to me. So, are you ready to race? Or do you need some more practice time?"

Kyle stops her, "Ok. Alright. Wow! I never would have guessed you were such a lying b-word! I'm disappointed in you but I'm ready to kick your butt, so let's go big mouth. And they turned and ran the Gauntlet without saying a word to each other.

He did get a moment alone with Sally when Sam jumped in front of him in line to take the first Tube. That gave him the chance to talk to Sally privately for a minute. He started to kiss her, but she pulled away. She said, "Thanks for coming to Raceland today. Enjoy your day." Then, just before she latched his door, he noticed she wasn't wearing the bracelet. That couldn't have been Sally! Oh No! He needed to get her before they took her to a recycling place.

He wasn't sure how he felt about Sally, but he liked her a lot. He was in love with Sam yesterday, but Sam dissed him hard in front of his friends this morning and that ticked him off. Big O double F off.

They morphed and went onto the track to get their cars. Sam was racing her dark red car named 'Wicked' from Winnemuca, Nevada and Kyle was already at the starting line in his bright yellow racing machine called 'GOAT' from Brady, Nebraska. He named it after Tom Brady and he has never lost in it. They were both lined up and ready and they were starting with lights today, and they're off and running. Kyle is still burning mad at Sam and he's determined to kick her butt.

They were racing on the road course today and there's lots of stopping and going on a course like this, plus there were a bunch or right turns, but Kyle was getting used to it quickly and had built a good half a lap lead. He could see the finish line now and still no sign of Sam. He was WAY ahead and was really happy about it. He was going to beat that girl and put her in her place. Uh oh! Oh no! His engine started smokin' and now he's barely moving. He's just inching up to the finish and now Sam is flying up on him. He's only a couple feet from the finish line when Samantha Speed passed him. He lost. Damn it! Just bad freakin' luck! He got out of his car and ran to catch a tube, leaving Sam leaning against Wicked and laughing at him.

Man, he thought, this wasn't just bad luck, this was HORRIBLE luck. Oh No! Ever since the Big Wreck, as soon as the word 'luck' popped in his head, his brain would make him remember his family's best friends and next-door neighbors, the Bigtimes. That family was awesome, and their two families did everything together until the Bigtimes hit a streak of bad luck that was probably the worst streak of bad luck in the history of the world!

Kyle figured the BigTimes' bad luck streak all started when Mrs. Bigtime died while giving birth to Bobby Bigtime. Bubba used to say, "I brought my beautiful pregnant wife to the hospital, and all I got back was this screaming diaper full of Bobby." Funny, but sad at the same time. Then a while back, Bubba was beaten to death by some bad guys that were like mafia type collectors, and Billy died on the track a year ago, and the sole survivor, Bobby became a pro racer, and his car was one of the two cars that landed in the grandstand in the Big Wreck. Bobby didn't survive. He was racing at about 240 mph, so when he hit that pile of cars and got airborne, well, he died instantly. Now, I'm no detective but it looks to me like Bubba sold his soul to the devil. Anyway, their entire family is still sorely missed by the entire McKay family for sure.

And right now, Kyle is pretty sure that the Bigtime family's bad luck has rubbed off on him. He got dumped by a girl, then lost a race to a girl and he can't get the girl, nor her kiss out of his whacked-out mind! His life sucks!

Oops! I almost left out an important piece of the story. When Bubba died, Billy was already pretty rich because he won the Sunnyvale 500 at just 19 years old and his take for that victory was over $10 million, so he moved away to some beach house in Miami soon after his dad's death. Bobby was left alone and that's a hard hand to play when you're just 15 years old and your dance card is filled with school and sports.

Bobby moved into the McKays' big guestroom that opened out to their pool. Now, that may seem totally insignificant to you at this moment, but patience, patience youngster. Since that time, Bobby crashed and burned leaving that room available once again.

Just last night, the McKay family took a vote as to whether or not the family could deal with another 16-year-old newly orphaned friend of Keegan's. Off the record, it was not a unanimous decision, but regardless, Miles Malone would set up in that corner of the McKays' house for the foreseeable future since his parents have both moved on also. Although Miles has not yet been made aware of his good fortune. Miles is Keegan's best friend, but Kyle would love to get the props for giving Miles the good news, so he is poised to sprint to the front door upon hearing the first note from their doorbell. Kyle figures if the guy is living with them, then he needs to get on equal footing with Key quickly. Otherwise, those two will team up on him.

Miles' parents were killed in the Big Wreck, and now he was left alone to raise his younger half sister Maria. At least that's the way Miles saw things, but by the time Keegan's grandma dropped him off at home, his Aunt Gypsy had already taken over.

Just a couple of months ago, his parents had let Gypsy move in because she was down on her luck and they had an extra bedroom in their basement. Gypsy was his mom's baby sister, and she was nothing but trouble. In fact, double trouble. She was a drug addict, and she admitted that, but she was also a sex addict, and she had hidden that so far from Miles' parents. Miles knew though because she had only been there a month or so and he had already caught her with four different men. He planned to tell his parents about that the weekend they died. He knew they would tell Gypsy to hit the road because they wouldn't have allowed that behavior with their young daughter, Maria still in the house.

It was probably 4 or 5 in the morning when Miles got home from the track after the wreck, so his parents weren't even dead 12 hours, and Gypsy had already moved into their bedroom. Yeah, this girl was a piece of work. Miles confronted her but she said her sister had willed everything to her over a year ago when she was diagnosed with ovarian cancer. Miles never had even heard of that kind of cancer before Gypsy told him his mom had it. He didn't believe her, but it seemed like she knew more than he did so maybe this was all true.

He went to check on Maria and she was sleeping soundly. He wasn't looking forward to telling her that her mom died. He didn't want her to have to worry about stuff like how she was going to get to school, and who was going to pack her lunch every day. He didn't see Gypsy as responsible enough to take care of herself so she damn sure wasn't going to take care of Maria. Uh oh! Did he just swear? Well, he kind of felt like the man of the house now, so he could say words like that? Nah, probably not because now both of his stricter than strict parents were in heaven, or at least on their way there. Besides, he didn't say that word. He just thought it. Crud. Now, with them up there, they were going to know even the stuff he just thought. His life was definitely getting harder by the minute.

Miles had a girlfriend last year, Wendy Wheeler, but she dumped him last summer. It stunk because he still had to see her every day at school. Worse, she was already pretty hot last year, but she seemed to be getting prettier every day. All the girls call her 'Wheels' because her last name is Wheeler, but all the guys call her 'Wheels' because she has the best set of legs in school. He heard that she liked Travis Wreck from Taft now and Mr. Grip caught her sexting the dude during his class.

He confiscated her phone and didn't give it back. Most of the time, when teachers take your phone, you can get it back after class, or after school. After class she asked for it, but Mr. Grip told Wendy that he wouldn't give it back until her dad came and asked him for it. That's how everybody knew she wasn't just on her phone... she was sexting which means she was sending sexually explicit messages or pictures to Travis Wreck! That turned his stomach and the visual of those two together was enough for him to finally get over her. He wasn't looking for a new girl though. They were too much trouble. Somehow those pretty little things could cripple even a big guy like him without ever throwing a punch.

And now a new girl was wrecking his life. Gypsy had to go!

Family
Challenge

Life Lesson; The ones that are crazy enough
to think they can change the world
are the ones that do!

Chapter 7
Family Challenge Races

It's Thursday and the field is set for the Family Challenge Races this weekend in Raceland. Flash says, "Hey race fans! Flash G here to let you know who's who and what's what in Raceland's first race of the Spring season, The Facebook 5 lap Family Challenge. This is the first event of our annual summer series and it's sponsored by Facebook, the social media monster. There is a new format for this race. Only the final round of the tournament will be a match race for pinks, due to the wide range of racing experience that these racers have."

"Most of Raceland's best racers are coming, so we should see some very competitive racing this weekend. The family format is two racers with the same last names per team, single elimination. The racer that finishes first takes their team to the next round. It will require 5 rounds to get our winner, so be prepared to run both days. It's a great weekend for racing, and it should be lots of fun."

"I'm wrapping up my setup to call this big race, but I'll be back in this booth Saturday morning to bring you the dirty lowdown and rock this town!"

Oval Mile Racing 2 person teams

1. Saturday 10:00 AM Wheelers vs Changes

2. Saturday 11:00 AM Leadfoots vs McKays

3. Saturday 12:00 PM Redliners vs Speeds

4. Saturday   1:00 PM Coynes vs Malones

5. Saturday   2:00 PM McQueens vs Peppers

6. Saturday   3:00 PM Cools vs Lopez

7. Saturday   4:00 PM Turbos vs Tulz

8. Saturday   5:00 PM Hollenbuts vs Vixens

Flash had their profiles printed up as a program for this event.

Hello everyone, Flash G here. I just put together this little program to give you racers a little insight into your opponents, and to give the spectators an inside glimpse of who you are as a person and how you got here. If you don't like my summation of you, come see me after this tournament is over. If you don't like your rating as a racer, let your racing do your talking and I'll make changes before you race next. Good Luck and Race Safely

The Annual Raceland Family Challenge competitors;

1. Wendy Wheeler   - aka Wheels, a nationally recognized racing talent. She's smart, pretty and really cool. Tall and athletic good racer

1. Wally Wheeler   - aka Dub. hot rod genius, wears glasses, has braces and appears thin and uncoordinated, but very fast runner, avg racer

2. Lane Change   -originally called 'diaper', this Tennessee boy is height challenged and talks like he's some hip gangsta rapper and he has struggled for the 1st couple of years with fender benders, but he's one of Keegan's buddies, poor racers

2. Seasons Change -'Seasons' was a top recruit of HRH after winning a couple of big spins around the oval at Talladega. Seasons change and so did she, started smokin pot: free spirit so off she went to save the world, but she didn't change much very good racer

---

3. Larry Leadfoot - Goofy looking guy, but a tough competitor. Wins often on the Raceland circuit but not ready for Sunnyvale very good racer

3. Lisa Leadfoot - smart and witty, but not very athletic. She lacks confidence but she's a competitor

---

4. Kyle McKay -. Kyle's taller and better looking than his brother and very smart. He's detail oriented, faster and more charming than his brother and he's a totally fearless competitor. Good racer

4. Keegan McKay - Good looking, smart and athletic. Where his brother is fast and more practiced, Keegan is quicker and a more natural athlete He's a big picture guy, but he makes some mistakes by not paying enough attention to detail very good racer

---

5. Ricky Redliner is a highly rated amateur from the pro circuit's Preview class This is his second try at HRH. He's an excellent racer, but a little immature thus far. Explosive temper good racer

5. Rosie Redliner is Ricky's little sis. She's an outspoken advocate for the Greenies and Frannie Fueller's recycling team poor racer

---

6. Steven Speed Steve's a scholarship winner from So California. was tearing it up in Fontana last summer invited to HRH very gd racer

6. Samantha Speed aka Mustang Sammy. Steve's sister, she's very pretty, funny and cool, Kyle has a crush on her plus she's a great racer.

---

7. Cathy Coynes a beauty queen with a streak of mean. She's from the richest family in Sunnyvale and acts like it. She's more than a little spoiled and has a very quick trigger on a bad temper. Ok racer

7. Charlie Coynes Charlie's also a spoiled brat who comes to school with his sister every day in the back seat of a Rolls Royce Shadow. The best dressed boy at HRH but he's got a legend to live up to His dad won the coveted HRH Champion's Cup 4 years straight! Good racer

8. Miles Malone   he's half black, tall and thick with an athletic build plays tight end and first base very smart and kind hearted gd racer

8. Maria Malone   she's Miles' half sister and her dad is Puerto Rican. She has a great sense of humor and loves to laugh, strong athletic dancer's body poor racer

9. Maxine McQueen   is lean and mean and expects to be treated like a queen. she's got a fuzzy fro and loves her gangsta rap poor racer

9. Michael McQueen   is named after Michael Jackson call him Michael, wears his hair short but it's nappy and looks greasy poor racer

10. Pedro 'Chili' Peppers   is a great athlete that aspires to be a great racer. He is tall and thick for a Latino boy from Bogota, Columbia. His forearms have tattoos of naked ladies Kyle nicknamed him Chili. Brand new at this sport, but a great natural athlete good racer

10. Juanita Peppers   is Pedro's cousin. Her parents were killed in a drive-by in Compton and she is much younger than Pedro. Brown hair, brown skin great smile and enchanting eyes avg racer

11. Max Cool His name says it all. Always dressed right, bleach blond/white spiky hair clean freak with germaphobia good racer

11. Candy Cool she's sweet as candy, cute little dimples, short blond curly hair wants to be an actress and loves movies avg racer

12. Lupe Lopez is a Latino girl that dresses flashy and talks about being a famous movie star someday, but right now she's a Roller Girl at Pit Stop Two, a Sunnyvale burger joint. She's a Taft student but takes racing classes at HRH. Her mom is a top model and her dad is a pro football player that left his family. Pretty good racer

12. Viktor Lopez is an accomplished track athlete at Taft, so he knows how to go fast! He's Lupe's big brother and biggest fan. He's been taking racing classes at HRH with his sister for a couple years already but this is his first race good racer

13. Tommy Turbo does everything fast. He never slows down until it's bed time then he falls over and is fast asleep. His curly carrot top doesn't require much maintenance and doesn't get much very good racer

13. Tina Turbo is named after Tina Turner and she has a great soul voice. Thin with long, soft blonde hair. excellent voice poor racer

14. Stanley Tulz Jr Stan's nickname is 'Tools' because his dad owns a company that makes tools. He is Kyle's best friend despite being a bit younger, because he is very smart and knows a lot about cars, He's the best mechanic in Raceland ok racer

14. Sandy Tulz is the oldest of the three sisters Stan has. She has long brown hair and is pretty but plain. Doesn't wear makeup and is almost always in hightop Cons. GREAT basketball player good racer

15. Ben Hollenbut Jr. Not handsome. sensitive and intelligent not athletic. Talks in rhyme all the time. Only races for his dad poor racer scared

15. Shelby Hollenbut- The official starter in Raceland, she's tough as nails, and the prettiest darn thing in town her family is well to do So she's always in style great athletic figure very good racer

16. Valerie Vixen　　Val is the head cheerleader at Taft and Stik Vixen's half-sister. Val loves Motown music and plans to have a singing career, but she signed her and her brother up for racing classes at HRH because she loves to drive and needs a backup career because she knows the music industry is tough good athlete good racer

16. Stik Vixen　　Stik is the outstanding QB from Taft High. He's a very talented, 6-foot-tall thin black kid that loves Rap music and plays the heck out of a Sax. HRh racing classes good racer

---

Flash G fires up his mic. "Hey everybody, it's Flash G bringing you live action racing right here in Raceland. This event is single elimination, so the losing team goes home early, and the winners stick around and race again until they lose or it's over. They are setting up down there for the first race of the annual Family Challenge Race. Every round of this tournament is only 5 laps, so we should see some hot action right off the line. Our first race features Wendy and Wally Wheeler against Seasons and Lane 'pocket' Change.

The Change team was a late entry. Seasons has been away for over a year, but she got back here last week and ran a few practice races. She told me yesterday when they registered, that she feels like she's going to pick right up where she left off. She's the wild card in this heat!

All four racers are approaching the starting line. It looks like we're all set, and here comes our beautiful starter, Ms.

Shelby Hollenbut.

She's standing in front, and now in the middle, and...The pompoms drop and they're off! Pocket has the early lead and has taken the inside lane through the first turn; The other 3 racers are spread wide through the turn and are losing time. It's stil Pocket in front, then Wendy, then Wally and Seasons is way back after 3 laps. Wendy Wheeler is a very experienced racer and she is making a strong move on the outside. She overtakes Pocket with a lap and a half to go.

Wait a sec! What's this? Seasons is flying down the front stretch and is now just about 8 car lengths back going into the first turn. Now at the top of the backstretch, Seasons passes Wally Wheeler and is coming up fast on her brother Pocket. She passes him before the back turn and now is only about 2 car lengths behind our leader as they turn for the homestretch. This one is going to be close. And here they come, it's Wendy by a nose right now with only...Whoa! This one is going to be a photo finish. It's way too close to call. What a great race to start a tournament!

Due to modern technology, I'm already looking at the picture of the finish and it's very close but there's no doubt who won. In an upset of epic proportion, Seasons Change gets her first win ever at Raceland!

Our next matchup in the Family Challenge, pits the McKays against the Leadfoots. Larry Leadfoot went pro last year, and he already has a 3rd place finish in Talladega. He'll be a big favorite to win this match today, but you can never count out the Mac Brothers. They are heading down the backstretch and this is the 5th and final lap. With all 4 cars bunched in the middle of the track, this last turn will cost the 2 outside cars some time. Now entering the stretch run, Kyle puts his right foot down hard on the long skinny pedal and uses his Nitro-pop. Kyle *jumps out* to the lead, and barely holds off a hard chargin' Larry Leadfoot. crossing the finish line first and getting the best time of the day so far. Keegan took fourth.

Whoa! Stop the presses! We have an unprecedented problem here at Raceland. Wendy Wheeler just handed me an official protest! Boy, this is interesting because I know Wendy well. She's a good sport and a smart girl, so this isn't some poor loser just makin' a stink.

Will someone please find Wendy so we can see what this protest is all about. "Ben Hollenbut Jr. is Flash's apprentice, and he brings Wendy up to the booth.

"Wendy, Flash starts "why are you protesting your loss? I didn't see any bumping or boxing in, and the start was definitely clean or the red lights would have lit up."

"Well, Wendy said, "unless the rules were changed and no one told me, Seasons isn't qualified to even enter Raceland, let alone race in an HRH competition. She graduated last year and no one has seen her since. She ran off to save the world or whatever hippy chicks do when they finish school."

Flash responds, "So Wendy, you're challenging the Change team's win due to Season's age. Everyone knows that you can't come to Raceland after you turn 18 and graduate, so how do you suppose she got past the Strange sisters? Honestly, I didn't think it was possible for this to happen, so let's wait to have the Trackmaster review the HRH registration files and give us a ruling."

"Hi everyone! Flash G back at your service. Just a reminder. There's a whole lot more racing to get done today, so please have your vehicles on the track on time. The third pairing should be on the track now please."

Your third race of the afternoon features the Redliners against the Speeds. Ricky Redliner is a highly rated amateur from the pro circuit's Preview class. He left HRH a year early to see if he was ready for the bigtime, but he's back and enrolled at HRH again. He'll be partnered with Rosie Redliner, his younger sister. They'll be racing against the team of Steve and Samantha Speed, two scholarship winners who were racing in So Cal just a few months ago. Shelby gets them lined up and they're off!

Samantha Speed finished first, way ahead of Steve and he was almost a full lap ahead of the Redliners. Evidently, Ricky had engine trouble. Looks like Sam's practicing with Kyle paid off.

The crowd is waiting for the next race to start. It's the eighth and final race on today's schedule. Flash has been hearing the mumbling from the crowd ever since he announced that Wendy Wheeler had filed an official protest. That was the first race of the day, and the Change team is still listed on the scoreboard as the 'unofficial' winner. The mumbling has gotten louder with each race and Flash wants everyone to be listening to him. It's his job, ya know.

"Your attention please, Flash says just a little louder than normal. "We need the Hollenbuts and the Vixens to report to the starter right away please. Can we get Lupe Lopez down to the track to start this race please? I need your help, Lupe. Shelby is driving in this race, so she left her pompoms down there for you."

Flash G hates it when he loses the crowd's undivided attention, so he's been pushing Raceland's Trackmaster, Professor Birmingham for the protest results every chance he gets. Flash is sure that's the only reason his crowd isn't harging on his every word.

"Ladies and gentlemen, right after this race we will share the results of our investigation into that protest made by Wendy Wheeler earlier today, and I'll be announcing all the pairings for tomorrow's racing schedule. But right now, please turn your attention to the starting line, where you'll see our backup starter, Lupe Lopez is ready to start our last race of the day."

This race features two teams that don't like each other very much; the Hollenbuts and the Vixens. The Vixens attend Taft's High School, but they have been taking racing classes at HRH since the football season. Valerie Vixen is the head cheerleader at Taft, and she's very jealous of all the press Shelby gets for doing the same job at HRH. Her older brother is Stik Vixen, an outstanding QB and athlete. HRH defeated Taft in the playoffs last year, but Stik still has a year of eligibility and is reportedly interested in transferring to HRH for his senior year. HRH isn't just another high school, it's the top racing academy in the country and they don't just let anybody in here. There's only two ways to get in. If you're a resident of Sunnyvale, you're automatic but otherwise, you have to be invited. A win here would really help Stik's chances.

Flash says, "Lupe drops the pompoms, and the eighth race is finally underway. No surprise, Shelby Hollenbut jumps out to take the lead, followed closely by Valerie Vixen. Stik is tailing his sister but appears to have enough power to pass her whenever he chooses. He's got something up his sleeve, or at least that's how it looks from here. And last, and probably least-oops! sorry little buddy. I'll start that again. And last, but not least is Ben Hollinbut Jr. They are in front of the grandstand now for the fourth time and all four drivers are in the same order as they were after the first lap. I don't understand it. Valerie seems content to be second and Shelby seems to be just cruising because she's not worried about anybody but whoever's in second. The pace seems to have slowed down this lap, wait a second! Now I know what's up! Right then, Stik pounds that skinny pedal and pulls his Nitro-pop.

Suddenly Stik's car called 'Hater' lurches past his sister, and before Shelby notices his move, Stik is passing her in the final turn. Once she realizes what Stik was doing, she puts that hammer down and retakes the lead. They're running side by side now and the finish line is fast approaching. Shelby can't believe it, but Stik wins by a nose."

Wow what a race! Stik Vixen is our winner ladies and gentlemen. After their cool down lap, Flash says, "Come on up here Stik . " Flash says, "That was a very smart race Stik. How did you win today?"

"Well Flash, Stik says, "I just let Shelby choose the pace and get comfortable. Then when she had been cruising long enough, I surprised her from the outside and once I passed her, I knew I had the race."

"Well, congratulations young man and best of luck to you tomorrow." They shook hands and Stik left the booth to loud applause from a surprised crowd.

Flash continues, "Alright everyone, here are the results from today's races and the pairings for tomorrow; In the first race, there was a protest, so I'll update that last. The first race was unofficially won by the Change pair and if the initial ruling sticks, they'll be matched with the Vixen pair."

"The second race was won by the McKay brothers, and they'll be racing against the Tulz team, who narrowly beat the Turbo team today."

"The third matchup for tomorrow will feature the Speeds vs the Lopez pair. Both winners weren't really challenged in their first races, beating the Redliners and the Cool pairs respectively. These winners easily beat teams that had amateur drivers that were previously unsuccessful in the Preview class on the Pro Circuit."

"The fourth and final matchup for tomorrow will feature the Malones and McQeens. Both of these pairs were pushed to their limits by the Coynes and the Peppers respectively. These winners narrowly defeated teams with some success in the Preview class on the Pro Circuit."

The crowd hears Flash talking with someone and then he's back on his mic; "Now, ladies and gentlemen I finally have an update for you on Wendy Wheeler's protest. Professor Birmingham is the Trackmaster here at Raceland. Professor, will you please explain your ruling on his matter?"

The professor explains, "Well, I was surprised by this protest because Wendy Wheeler knows the rules here. If she was right that Seasons no longer qualified for acceptance into Raceland, then Seasons would have been denied admission by the Strange sisters. Those girls are fembots that the Company had programmed to manage admission to Raceland, and fembots don't make mistakes."

The grandstands are packed with kids that have all met the Strange sisters but NO ONE knew they were fembots. There is loud grumbling from the crowd and it's getting louder!

Finally, Flash speaks loudly into his mic, "Ladies and Gentlemen Please! Have a little respect for our Trackmaster. So, Professor Birmingham, please explain specifically what happened."

The professor said, "Well, I think all you kids know the rules around here. Once you have graduated from high school and have had your 18th birthday, you are forever banned from Raceland and all memories of this place will be deleted from your brain screen forever." Seasons Change was a senior here at HRH and when she had her 18th birthday on May 1st, she was now legally an adult and she had adults' rights. She left Sunnyvale that day to go travel the world, but she left before she completed all her courses that last semester. She was given incompletes for those classes and didn't graduate. HRH will only allow you until your 20th birthday to graduate, so Seasons has to complete all her courses before she turns 20 on May 1st. The semester isn't over until June 21st but because she was a good student prior, her teachers are accelerating her assignments so that she can complete her courses by her 20th birthday on May 1st.

Until she is forever banned on May 2nd, Seasons is an HRH student and can take any courses she chooses or participate in any HRH event. Subsequently, the Change team won their race today and will advance in the tournament."

The crowd here loves the Wheelers, so this decision got only minor applause.

Flash says, "Thank you for clarifying that rule. By the way, you're a professor and that takes years of college, so how'd you get by the Strange sisters?"

"I am only 17 years old but have an IQ of 190, and was given my accelerated doctorate, college and high school educations in the palace of the Queen of England, says the professor. I only took this job to spy on your racers and advise the queen of any potential Formula One racers!"

Flash is thinking, boy is this guy on drugs or something. He just blew a secret that has the crowd humming. The guy said the Strange sisters are fembots and then he admitted that he's a spy for Europe's Formula One racers. This guy's a loose cannon! He knew he had to tell one of the Three Kings right away, so when he saw Mr. McKay in the pits, he paged him.

Mr. Mac came up to Flash's booth right away, but Flash is announcing a race, so he had to wait until the race is over. Mac says, "Flash, what's so urgent?"

Flash tells him about the professor being a spy for the Queen and spilling the beans about the fembots. He can't help himself, so he goes on to tell Mr. Mac that the crowd was very unhappy to hear that the Strange sisters weren't human. VERY unhappy he repeats.

The Change team gets the win and will be paired with the Vixen team tomorrow. It's official. Following you'll see the final pairings for Sunday's races.

Some loud-mouthed clown in the front of the grandstand had a loudspeaker and yelled really loud, "The Strange sisters are FEMBOTS!!" The crowd booed loudly for a long time. Maybe many hearts were broken?

Mr. Mac heard the crowd for himself this time. Flash knew that they would have a new Trackmaster in the very near future.

9. Sunday   10:00 winners #1 and #8 Changes and Vixens

10. Sunday   11:00 winners #2 and #7 McKays and the Tulz

11. Sunday   12:00 winners #3 and #6 Speeds and Lopez

12. Sunday   1:00 winners #4 and #5 Malones and McQueens

13. Sunday   2:00 winners #9 and #12

14. Sunday   3:00 winners #10 and #11

15. Sunday   1:00 winners #13 and #14 Champions

Sunday morning the crowd is forming in the grandstand next to Raceland's Mile Oval as the Transportation Tube unloads time and again. This figured to be a great day of racing and all the competitors were already there taking warmup runs and having their motors tuned. By 9:30 the track was cleared and the stands were full. Flash G went over the rules again and explained the ruling on Wendy's protest and the crowd booed loudly again.

At 9:55 Flash G announcing; "Good morning, everyone and thanks for coming to the second round of the family Challenge. Let's get our first pair of racers to the starting line, and Shelby can you head down to the starting line?"

Now it's 10:00 AM and Flash asks the crowd, "has anyone seen our racers? We're waiting for Stik and Valerie Vixen and Lane and Seasons Change. If anyone sees them or knows why they're not at the starting line, please let me know asap. And where is Shelby for cryin' out loud?"

Flash G doesn't consider patience a virtue. He considers it a waste of time, so he's still complaining that the races haven't started on time. "Ladies and gentlemen, I apologize for the delay, but I don't have any racers! Those teams earned the right to race again today, and they didn't bother to show up? This is totally unacceptable and there's no excuse in the world for both of these teams to be late for their race! Will someone please reach out to them and get me an ETA asap?"

Ben Hollenbut Jr. aspires to do what Flash G does so they do every event together, but Flash does the mic work and Jr. is the understudy. Anyway, Junior always talks in rhyme so he says;

"Boss, no sweat I got your back

You need racers at the track

These guys must be whack

Or maybe they're smokin crack

But we aint got time to yack

got a race to run and that's a fact"

And then he's gone. Now it's 10:10 and Flash is getting worried. He asks the crowd to hang in there. Says he'll have an explanation for them shortly. Now it's 10:20 and he's losing his mind. Wait a second. He sees Shelby Hollenbut coming out of the tunnel, so at least he's got a starter. He says into the mic, "will Shelby please come to my booth immediately?" Shelby hears him and heads straight to Flash's office. She says, "Flash, settle down. It will be alright. The Vixens don't live in Sunnyvale and there are some bad characters in their town. They were on their way to Raceland this morning and some fools that had been out drinking and partying all night ran a stop sign and T-boned them."

"The driver was Travis 'train' Wreck. He and another S.C.A.B., Rocky Rhodes had been out all-night causing trouble and drinking heavily. Travis ran a stop sign and T-boned Stik and Val Vixen on their way to the races. The police got there before Travis and Rocky could break their car loose and bail. Travis was arrested for a DUI and they found a pound of white powder the cops said was cocaine. Travis said that stuff was Rocky's, so he was arrested too. Looks like they are going to be locked up for a good while because their dads don't have the bail money. That's great news for Raceland because the S.C.A.B.s are Train Wreck's crew that are always trying to mess with Raceland races. With Travis locked up, the S.C.A.B.s will be too scared to mess with HRH's new crew run by Chili Peppers." When Miles heard about this mess, he smiled. He realized he hasn't done that in a while.

Shelby continued, "Luckily, the Vixens weren't hurt but the police made them get checked at the hospital as a precaution. The Change family lives just down the street from Sunnyvale General, and Stik saw Lane driving Black Magic by there and waved him down. Anyway, to make a long story short, and Flash interjected quickly, "too late." Shelby ignored him and said, "Bottom line is that both teams are riding together and will be here any minute."

Flash G grabs his mic and announces, "Ladies and gentlemen, we just saw both teams enter the track, and we will have a race for you in just a couple of minutes. They were detained for good reason, but everyone is ok and this race is now officially scheduled to start in precisely 6 minutes."

Flash announces, "Ladies and gentlemen, Shelby has all 4 racers at the starting line, and she drops the pompoms. They're off and running! I got the signal that it was a clean start so this race is for real. Check them out! This race is entirely different than I expected! Yesterday, I'm sure you all remember that both Seasons and Stik stayed off the pace and made strong moves for the lead toward the end yesterday, but not today! Seasons has a big lead early, and Stik is running second. Then, way back in third is Pocket and Valerie is running last."

"Now they're in the backstretch on their last lap, with Seasons holding on to about 5 car lengths lead over Stik. But wait, Stik is making his move and closes the gap right before the last big turn. Seasons hugs the rail which forces Stik wide, and he loses a little time, but he takes the lead with a $1/8^{th}$ mile to go and he looks like he's got this. No way! Seasons bolts forward right on time and beats Stik by a nose. Way back, Pocket gets third and Valerie limps in for fourth place. Man was this race close or what? This one could have gone either way. Nice win Seasons!" Flash continues, "

The next 3 races went as expected with the McKays getting the win over the Tulz team. Kyle and Stanley battled head-to-head for the first three laps before Kyle opened up a big lead. Keegan McKay finished 4th for the second race in a row. The crowd's wondering what's up with that because Key's a darn good racer.

The Speed team handled the Lopez team easily, but notably, Samantha Speed was only 2/10ths of a second off the best time so far in this event, which was Kyle McKay's run yesterday.

The Malone team handled the visiting McQueen team, with an impressive victory by Miles Malone, who's getting a new PB almost every time he pulls up to that starting line. In fact, today he beat his Personal Best by an amazing 1.45 seconds!
The next two races will match the Change team with the Malone team and then the McKays against the Speeds. Immediately following those two races will be the final and the way things are setting up, that could be the best race of the year."

Flash tells Junior to cover for him so he can use the restroom, and he runs to the men's room down the hall. He had to go for a while but wasn't sure about leaving the mic with Ben Jr. Turns out he made the wrong choice. He hustles back to hear Junior talking into the mic...

"I work for dis lame called Flash

but he doesn't pay me no cash

So, when he gets all shaky and wiggly

cuz the boy, he gots to go peepee

I step on up and help myself to his mic

and I can say whatever i like

and you can"...that's as far as Jr. got before Flash grabs the mic and starts trying to cover his tracks with "Ladies and Gentlemen, Please allow me to apologize to everyone in the house for that very unprofessional interruption in my normally stellar performance..." But Flash's voice isn't loud enough to cut through the laughter. The crowd loved Jr's little rap and they're givin' him flowers. When the laughter dies down, Flash says, "alright, alright enough. I have to admit I heard Jr's whole thing there and it was pretty funny. Good job little buddy!" The crowd could hear Flash give Jr. a high five.

Flash continues, "The next two races will determine who will race for the championship, and they are both closely contested. The McKays escaped with a win over the Speeds but just by a nose, as Kyle held on for the win over a hard chargin' Samantha Speed."

Kyle really struggled with this race. He was still hurting from Sam dumping him and then getting lucky in their race. Plus, the way she said that story didn't include the fact that Kyle was way ahead before he smoked his motor. He really wanted to beat her bad, but he was also trying to build his brother's confidence, so he was trying to let Key win the race, but he didn't think Key was going to beat her, so he jumped up at the last minute to make sure Sam didn't win. It kind of worked out because he beat her with everyone watching and Key did too. That was cool because in their first two races in this event, Kyle won both but Keegan got fourth, so he was pretty bummed.

Flash says "And in the other match, the Change team handled the Malones with a wire-to-wire performance by Seasons Change. Miles Malone made a couple of valiant efforts to catch her, but she had too much speed for him today."

"So, everyone out there hold onto your seats! The next race is a match race for the championship and it will be starting soon. This race will feature the McKay brothers vs the Change team. Kyle McKay will be racing his royal blue 'Renegade' and Keegan McKay will be risking his fire red 'Ragin Cajun.' For the Change team, Lane Change will be racing his yellow 'Alienator' and Seasons will be racing her lt blue 'Perfect Guest'."

"All these racers are risking their cars because this is a match race for pinks like most RodKingz races. This means that the winners will get to take home the losing team's two cars, and these cars ain't cheap! Just look at these pristine, awe inspiring, real race cars! These cars are worth a whole bank's worth of cash, so the stakes on this race are humungus!"

Flash G starts using his pro announcer voice and says, "All four gorgeous cars are lining up and you can see right there just how high these stakes are! These custom imports are all Supercars! They're all set on the starting line and ready to go. Shelby drops her pompoms and they're off. Seasons has the lead going into the first turn and she is increasing that lead down the backstretch. Kyle is running a fairly close second, and Lane and Keegan are battling for third. There has been no change in the order as Seasons leads them into the last turn. Kyle is catching her but they're rounding the Big Crash turn and I'm guessing all four racers will use extra caution here now. That's exactly what happened and now all four cars are pretty even coming down the last ¼ mile. First it looks like Keegan has a slight lead, but Lane catches him, and then Seasons breaks out a little and has a clear lead but here comes Kyle on the outside. This one's going to be close!"

Flash brags, "I told ya! We have a photo finish. Hey guys, let's get that photo up here right away. We've got four HRH racers that all think they won this race, and the stakes are crazy high so let's get them their answer!"

"Thanks guys. Flash says, "I have the answers right here. Oh man was this a tight finish. There are pictures from every angle here and wait a minute! I just saw a ghost! I'm not kidding. That just can't be! Oh no! I have to talk to Major Coynes right away. This is very disturbing."

The crowd doesn't want to hear Flash's rant and they want to know who won, so they are booing louder and louder! Now they're throwing soda cups and things on the track. Junior shakes Flash and yells at him to get a grip. Flash shakes his fear off because he's a pro and he has a job to do.'

His voice is shaky this time when he says, "Ladies and gentlemen, here are the final results of the Family Challenge Raceland 5; Lane Change finished 4th, Seasons Change got third and the McKay brothers finished in a dead heat, also called a tie. Congratulations to the McKays! Everyone is welcome to stay and watch the cars previously owned by Lane and Seasons get delivered to the McKays' garages."

Flash wraps up his gig with, "That's the conclusion of our great weekend of racing here in Raceland. Thanks to all for coming and we'll see you again soon in Sunnyvale!" Then he turns to Junior and tells him 'Great job little buddy!'

Now, Flash is out on the track and finds the McKay brothers talking with Lane and Seasons Change. He pulls Keegan aside and tells him that he needs to get ahold of his dad quickly and tells him to call a meeting of The Company with Major Coynes and Mr. Hollenbut in the executive suite at the Sunnyvale Speedway as soon as humanly possible. It's an emergency! Flash says, "And Key, this is Top Secret!"

The

PHOTO

Life Lesson: There are no ties in racing

So leave your sister out of this

Chapter 8
The PHOTO

Mr. Kevin McKay, Mr. Ben Hollenbut and Mr. Major Coynes all arrived within the hour but none of them had any idea what this meeting was about. That is until Flash walked in.

Flash said, "Gentlemen I was studying these pictures of the finish in the last race of the Family Challenge because it was the tightest finish I have ever seen but look past the cars. There's an adult there, and I know who it is."

"No way!" Mr. Mac says.

"Yes, Mr. McKay there is a way. says Flash. "You weren't here back then, but I'm sure your partners here told you about him."

Major Coynes, interrupts their conversation by saying, "Mac, I'm sure we told you about Randy Rodd. We needed a mechanic when we first started because we were having trouble keeping the cars running, so we made a deal with a 17-year-old kid named Randy Rodd who was an ace mechanic. He had a baby boy with a Taft girl. She looked like trouble; short skirt, all tatted up and always a cigarette in her hand. The first time she saw a chance, his girl left town. We knew this 17-year-old single dad needed a job, so we hired him and paid him enough so he could afford a nanny and a roof."

"He worked hard and went home to his kid every night until one night he fell asleep in the pits at track 12. That was the first sign that the track had taken on a life of its own because Randy got stuck down there. When he woke, he tried to go

home but the track wouldn't let him. The track needed him so it wouldn't let him go. I agreed to house his boy, but I never imagined I'd have Ricky for 16 years. The Rodd report was originally his dad's and now Ricky runs it. He won't let that picture get printed with his dad in it. He can't. He collected on the life insurance his dad had through The Company."
"You know, when I started the Speedway project, we just buried Track 12 and built Sunnyvale's Speedway over the top of it. That wasn't legal for a lot of reasons, but it was the only way I could afford to build the Speedway. Well, all that cement we poured was enough that our ground floor doubled as a roof for Track 12 and Raceland had its start. As the construction of the Speedway continued, material kept disappearing. I had an idea that it was going toward a good cause, so we just filed insurance claims and kept building.

There was enough material taken to build 2 Speedways and that's what happened. I knew about it but could never acknowledge it to anyone because the insurance company would surely have come after me. There's a lot more to know but that's enough for now.

"Wait! Mr. McKay said, "who built it and who runs it and what do you mean 'a life of its own."

Mr. Hollenbut joined the conversation, "Hey guys, I've gotta get back so let's deal with what we have to get handled tonight and we can get together another night next week.

"Ok" said Mr. Coynes.

"I guess," said Mr. McKay

Ben Hollenbut took over the discussion. "So, the only problems I see are first, the pictures. Flash can you take care of that?"

Flash replied, "Yes sir. Mr. Rodd will not appear in the finish line photos from the Famlly Challenge. Got it."

Ben continued, "Other than that, we need someone to talk with these two Rodds, Ricky and Randy. Major, can you take care of that?"

Mr. Coynes said, "it will be done tonight. Gentlemen, thanks for coming on such short notice, but Flash you were right to call an emergency meeting tonight. Thank you. See you all soon." And with that, Major Coynes picked up the phone and started dialing. The meeting was adjourned.

But the problem wasn't solved. Heck no. There were lives in the balance and more secrets to be kept. All three of these men would find it difficult to sleep tonight.

Major Coynes left the meeting after promising to get a hold of both Ricky and Randy Rodd tonight. Once again, he bit off more than he could chew. The only number he had for Ricky Rodd was the one for the Rodd Report office and nobody answered it. He wasn't surprised, Ricky had no business being in HRH this late in the evening. Randy Rodd lived in Raceland and no adult could get in there, not even Major Coynes. Cell phones weren't an option either because Raceland was buried under tons and tons of concrete. No service available. Well it wasn't his fault, but talking to the Rodds was going to have to wait until tomorrow.

Ricky Rodd is the editor of the school paper called the Rodd Report. Everyone thinks he named the paper after himself, but the truth is The Rodd Report was named after its first editor, his dad Randy Rodd about 17 years ago. This afternoon, Ricky Rodd is in his office at HRH reviewing the photos he got from Flash of the incredible finish of the Family Challenge this weekend.

Kyle McKay enters and says, "So Ricky what's up bro? You know I'm always willing to help, so what can I do for you?" Ricky had asked Kyle to come by this afternoon because he wanted to ask him a few questions about the races. He picks out the photo he likes best and hands it to Kyle, and says "What's wrong with this picture? I ask because I'm confused about how this picture was taken. Now, you can tell me the truth. Did Flash or someone else photoshop this?"

Kyle replies, "I don't think so why?"

"Because Kyle, there is no way that you four people all ended up in the same picture at the end of a race. At the beginning? Of course. Ricky said, "but at the end? After 5 miles? Come on?"

"Look Ricky, Kyle said slowly, I get your point, but I really don't think the general pop. around here that reads your rag. I meant mag, really, I did, but they aren't as analytical as you."

Ricky replies, "Ok, so you're not denying that you threw the race. Ok. The only way I can print this pic is if you tell me, it was for a good cause. Can you do that?"

"Of course, Ricky." Kyle said. "Everybody knows that Key has been in a slump lately and I think he just lost some confidence somewhere so I was trying to let him win, but that darn Seasons was there too, and I couldn't lose to her. So, see, it was for a good cause. Just print the dumb thing, will ya? If you don't, the whole school will be here knockin' on your door because everybody is talkin' about it already and they all want to see the pic to believe it. It's up to you but I know what I would do. Make them happy Ricky!"

Now, Ricky is about to use the picture of the 4-car photo finish for the cover of this week's edition of the HRH news, when something about it catches his eye. He takes the photo to the window and holds it up toward the sun. Now he can see more clearly what had caught his eye. It's him! How in the wide world of sports is he in a picture that was taken at a race he didn't even attend? Maybe that was a picture of his dad? He's straining his brain to remember everything anyone ever told him about his past, but he has no memory at all of any parents. The Major had taken him in when he was only about a year old. He had his own room at the Coynes' mansion, and the nanny took good care of him, but it never felt like home. He remembers seeing his dad a couple years ago and getting to talk with him, but then the memory always just kind of evaporates in his doubts. He decides to use the photo for the paper just to see if anything comes of it. He knew it was a bad idea.

Ricky is about to send the picture to the printer when Flash drops in on him, telling him not to.

Flash said, "Ricky, I was in a meeting last night with the THREE KINGS also known as The Company. That's right. I met with Mr. Coynes, Mr. Hollenbut and Mr. McKay and I was told in no uncertain terms that I had to make sure that picture didn't get printed. I should have reached out to you this morning, but I slept in because that tournament was exhausting. Please don't get me in trouble with those three guys! A guy could get his whole family smoked for messin' with just one of those guys! You gotta promise me you won't print it."

"I have to print it Flash, Ricky pleaded. "The whole town's been waiting to see it. There's never been a 4-car photo finish that ended up in a dead heat at Sunnyvale or Raceland or probably anywhere else! Besides, it's my job to give people the news and this picture is most definitely NEWS!"

Flash is debating with himself in his head about telling Ricky why he can't print it. He decides that he shouldn't be the one making that decision, so he asks Ricky when the last minute is for the pic to be given to the printer and he can still get the paper out on time.

Ricky's not sure, so he calls over there and asks them that question. When he hangs up, he looks at Flash and says "9 o'clock tonight."

Flash is relieved and says, "Ok buddy, now let's talk with one of the Three Kings."

Ricky says, "Ok Flash. I'll talk to Major Coynes when I get home and I'll call you with a head up ok? Sort of a professional courtesy because I know you're a newsman too."

When Ricky got home from school, he went looking around the mansion for Mr. Coynes, and found him in his office.

He asks, "Sir can I have a minute of your time?"

"Of course. Mr Coynes says "What's on your mind?"

Ricky says, "Well sir, there's a lot on my mind, but there's one urgent matter. I was told by Flash not to print a picture of the Family Challenge's 4 car photo finish but everyone in town is dying to see it. You can't blame them. It's extremely rare to have a 4-car photo finish these days, and then to have it end up a dead heat. The odds have to be billions to one."

Mr. Coynes says, "That's probably true Ricky, and the public deserves to see the picture and it's your job to see that they get that chance. However, you probably noticed that there's more in the picture than just the four cars. It's important that you just frame the pic correctly so there's nothing to distract the viewer from the 4 cars. Do you understand me son?"

Ricky Rodd doesn't know what to say but he knows there's

an image in the background of that pic that is important and very well might change his life. Major Coynes has been very good to him though, and he has given him an incredible home and really raised him. He can't disrespect him. He decides to speak his mind. "Mr Coynes, he says, "I think I know what you're asking me to hide. That's my dad in the background, isn't it?"

"Yes Ricky, that is your dad," Mr. Coynes says, "and we can't let anyone see it because everyone in Sunnyvale thinks he's been dead for years. Most will react like Flash and think it's a ghost, and the fear that it might be a real ghost would keep all those people from ever returning to the track, and frankly, I can't let that happen. You don't want to fight me on this Ricky, I promise you don't."

"Of course, not Mr. Coynes," Ricky says, "so you know I'll do whatever you say. I wanted to print it to see if there's anybody out there that could help me find my dad, but now I know that you can. Will you help me Mr. Coynes?"

"Do you trust me, Ricky?" asks Mr. Coynes. "Because if you do, you'll crop that pic like I asked you and later this week, we will work up a plan that will get you your father back provided you don't tell a soul. If a word of this gets out, I swear that you, your dad and your newspaper will all disappear and be forgotten forever."

Boy, Ricky thought, this is a tough one. If I print the pic with the image of my dad in the background, everyone in town will see it and be talking about it and there's a good chance I'll find out how my dad can escape. Or I can trust Mr. Coynes to let him loose later next week even though he's the guy who imprisoned him there in the first place. Yeah, that's what happened. It has to be. There's no way my dad would have just abandoned me. Plus, Mr. Coynes took me in probably so he would look less suspicious. He was always kind to me, but he never made me feel like I was one of his kids. Cathy and Charlie always had big birthday parties, and I would just get a birthday card with a few bucks in it, and every Christmas those two would be opening presents for hours before they'd find one under their tree for me. Still, I don't know what to think. If he didn't kidnap my dad for slave labor in Raceland, then it was awful nice of him to share his home with me for all these years, and he's never beat me or neglected me.

I have to make a quick decision because it's 8:55 pm, so if this pic is going to make it to the printer by nine, I'll have to start uploading it now. He started the email he has to send and has the scanner ready to go. Then he looks down at the scissors on top of the picture and takes one more look at his dad's face. The picture is in the scanner now and in moments it is attached to an email and the email is sent.

Ricky sat back and pondered the decision he had just made. He was hoping time would fly now so that he could see how things were going to work out already, but time has a mind of its own and the next couple of days were going to feel like years.

This all started because Kyle was trying to let his brother win a match race. That photo finish caused a lot of problems, so Ricky sure hoped it helped Keegan.

This whole mess had Ricky so uptight that he almost forgot that Mr. McKay had asked him to do a photo story of all the local racers' garages. He said he wanted Ricky to post pics from all the guys' Race Spaces twice a year, starting with one right away. Mac wanted Ricky to arrange tours and to manage a bi-annual contest for the best Race Space. He would have to make ballots, have a secure ballot box and someone honest to count the votes. He was going to make enough on this project to be able to hire help, and Frannie would be perfect for this job. Frannie Fueller wasn't into the glitz and glam of expensive race cars and stuff. She was in charge of recycling in HRH and was kind of a greenie, but she was honest and wouldn't be impressed with any of these guys and their toys.

Frannie was in Ricky's office at the Rodd Report the next day, and she was willing to do this job. It was hard for him to see her because she was his girlfriend before. When Pocket got 'Black Magic' Frannie broke up with Ricky and was hanging out with the little jerk whose real name was Lane Change, but everyone called him Pocket. That is everyone but Ricky.

Frannie had some experience that applied here because she had run the student body elections. Ricky asked her to first go see and photograph each of the Race Spaces and then select the 12 biggest and best ones to create an easy-to-use ballot. He also asked her to use all the photos to make a photo wall to bring attention to the voting area. Photos of RodKingz micro-rods have to be perfect pictures. He couldn't help himself, so he asked, "How are things with Lane?"

"Not great, Frannie said. "He is always driving the McKay brothers around. He hardly ever takes me out anymore. I swear Ricky, if you had a car, I'd probably drop him to roll with you. Anyway, I'll do the best job I can for you and who knows what tomorrow will bring. I'll bring by some of the pics I take tonight.

Of course, right now the only picture other people were waiting to see was being printed and would be the front page of the Rodd Report tomorrow. He knew for sure that Flash and the Major were anxiously awaiting it, but Kyle had other fish to fry tonight.

First, he had to meet Frannie in Raceland and give her a tour of his 'Race Space' for some contest Ricky was having. Kyle had 39 RodKingz custom cars in his collection.

He had won most of them in match races. He learned something recently that was a game changer. He needed to take advantage of it before everyone knew about it so he planned to go to the Merch Mart after his meeting with Frannie. She was finished already so she saw her out and went straight across the mezzanine to the Merch Mart.

He checked the entire wall of cars, but there were only 9 cars there that he didn't already have. These were the micro-rod size and came in a cannister with a title and dice that you would use to race any available opponent. But, that's not what Kyle planned to do. Nope. He figured out that if he used one of these $5.00 microrods to access Raceland, the car and he would both morph and end up full size on the track. This time though he was going to leave the car behind when he left Raceland, because he knew that the track crew would just wash it and put it away in his race space while it was still FULL SIZED! He figured he could collect the whole set this way, and when he did, he would win RodKingz grand prize! This was exciting! He bought 3 of the 9 they had that he didn't. He didn't want to buy them all yet, in case his trick didn't work. He was going to try his plan now, so he went through the side door directly into the Chill Chamber. Sally didn't recognize him! What the heck? He knew this Sally wasn't his Sally, so the twins were probably already rusting away in the scrap pile in Major Coynes closet upstairs.

He needed a plan to save the Strange sisters immediately now that Professor Birming-buthead had sold them out to the whole world. What's wrong with that blockhead? He had to know that would wreck those two girls' lives, but that was the whole problem…were they really girls? Kyle thought about how he felt when Sally was around and he decided they were girls, or cool enough fembots that he didn't care what they were. He made the decision right then that he was going to save them.

Fixing
Keegan

Life Lesson; When you have a brother,
you might as well fix him
because he's not going away

Chapter 9
Fixing Keegan

When Keegan McKay was younger, he was the perfect big brother. He was good at everything he tried, like racing, school, football, baseball, even girls and everyone looked up to him, especially his younger brother Kyle. Somewhere, or maybe somehow, Keegan lost his confidence and that was the one thing that made him so good. In fairness, he had more than confidence. He was always a better than average student and athlete, but until a couple of months ago, Keegan McKay never lost at anything in his life and he was confident that he never would. But something happened. Something took his confidence away and he's been struggling at life ever since.

In fact, his little brother who has always worshipped Key and looked up to him, has lost faith in him. Kyle didn't get it. His BIG brother was afraid of the dark? What in the heck? Kyle was embarrassed about that, but not Key. Key went out of his way to tell everybody. Plus, Keegan lost his girl, Shelby Hollenbut a little while back, he got benched this year in football after he threw a pick when Sunnyvale was on the other teams 3-yard line, how dumb is that? And he got a B in his Acceleration class at HRH. That was the first, and probably the last, time that either of the McKay boys brought home a report card that had any letter other than an A on it.

That is, unless HRH follows the trend at some point and changes their grading system to numbers. Of course, that would be really dumb, but adults do dumb things sometimes.

Excuse me again, but this is another dumb thing that adults did. Why did so many schools switch their grading system from letters to numbers? Where I went to school at St. Benedict's in Seattle, we didn't even have the plus or minus deal. You got a letter grade and you never knew when you got a 'B' if you were one assignment short of an A or one paper away from a C…. but you lived with it. Now, most schools not only give you a number instead of a letter, they let you know how close or far away you are from a different number by using the decimals. Really dumb. It leaves nothing to the imagination. Plus, some schools messed it up even worse because at first when they started using numbers, a 4.0 was an A, the best grade you could get, but they had to mess with that too. Now, you can get a 5.0! Clearly those schools don't care about their graduates out there looking for jobs. All those people are submitting resumes touting their 4.0 gpa's thinking they're showing off that they got all A's. They're not still in school so they don't know that their resumes now say they were B students.

And how are you kids going to feel when they decide they're going to a 10.0 grading system? You know it's going to happen. Think about how many times people have asked you how you would rate something on a scale of 1-10. Happens often, right? Anybody ever ask you to rate stuff on a 1-5 scale? Nope. Me neither. The grading system will no doubt be 10.0 soon and you bragged to everyone you know that you finished school with a 5.0? Lots of those people will remember, and you're going to have to answer questions like…'Hey, how'd you ever graduate? I remember you bragging about having a 5.0 in school but my first grader just showed me her report card and a 5.0 is an F. You failed loser! But hey, don't worry about it because your kids are always going to think you're an idiot anyway. Adults do dumb things sometimes. Sorry for the interruption.

There's no doubt about it. Keegan has become pretty mediocre at life, and it keeps getting worse. Key told Kyle about Suzi Strange yelling at him. First, Shelby dumps him and now this computer-like girl who is ice-cold all day anyway, not only rejects him, but shouts at him in public for even thinking he had a chance. Poor Key! A year ago, he was a star athlete, a champion, and a really smart guy, that all the girls dreamed of dating, but man have things changed. Now, he's a bench warming loser with bad grades that can't even get a date with a computer!

Worse, he's not even getting props as the 'big' brother at home anymore. How could he? Kyle grew a bunch last summer and is now 3 inches taller than his 'big' brother. Plus, Kyle had a date just yesterday with a smokin' hot older girl that has everyone at school talkin'. And more importantly, on the scale of rating big brothers, Kyle was NEVER afraid of the dark.

Now, stop the presses for a minute. Before we all bury the guy, Kyle has decided he has to help his brother out. It's his brother after all and Kyle wants to fix him before Key embarrasses him again. Kyle thinks about the whole mess and comes up with a fairly solid plan to rebuild Key. He starts with his mom, and he finds her in the kitchen talking to M's. He joins the conversation and takes a seat across from the two women that are maybe accidentally, but pretty obviously, competing for the job of 'mom' in the McKay household.

He explains to them the problem and suggests that the solution is that everyone works together to rebuild Key's confidence. He even went so far as to give them permission to put himself down to lift Key by comparison. The example he gave them was 'like after the game tomorrow night, it's ok if you compliment him more than me. Maybe even say something like… "Wow Key, you hit the ball really well tonight, WAY better than Kyle." I might even strike out on purpose a couple times, just so you can say that! But don't worry, I'll make sure we're ahead before I pull any shenanigans. I don't want to get in Coach Doubles' doghouse because it's really hard to get out.

Reluctantly, the two women agree. They know it's really cool of Kyle to help his brother out, but his plan is not without risk.

The next day at school, he corners Shelby Hollenbut and just very bluntly blurts out, "Shelby, I know it's not my business, but Key's confidence is way down and he needs our help. Can you tell me why you dumped him, because I might be wrong, but I think that's when his troubles started."

Shelby says, "Kyle it's very personal, and frankly, it's none of your business. I know you're just trying to help your brother but screw him. I hate him, so don't ever even try to talk to me about him again. He's the biggest jerk in all of Sunnyvale!"

Kyle thought, Girls! What's wrong with them? They mess everything up. I can't even talk to her now. I'll never be able to fix Keegan.'

He knew he needed a new plan. He was out of his league with this stuff, but who could help him? He thought and thought, and he couldn't think of any way to get Shelby back on board with the McKay family. Heck, it wasn't that long ago that she was crying happy tears when he and Key were found alive. They had been presumed dead when they were left unconscious in the back seat of Pocket's caddy SUV called Black Magic. That's a story that's been told, but Kyle remembered how happy Shelby Hollenbut was to see Keegan that night.

What happened? That's the first thing Kyle had to figure out.

That afternoon he sees Pocket, one of Keegan's best buddies, in the hallway at HRH. Pocket's real name is Lane Change and he has a sister named Seasons because his mom has a sense of humor. She married into that last name and thought she might as well have some fun with it. Kyle nicknamed Lane 'Pocket Change' because he's small, but 'small change' sounds mean. Over time it just became 'Pocket'. Anyway, Kyle thought maybe Pocket could help, so he asked him if he knew why Shelby hated Key so much, but since Pocket finally got a girlfriend (Phil Fueler's daughter Frannie) he has been kind of out of the social circle and was no help at all. He offered to give Kyle a ride home after school though. Kyle would have loved to hang out with his buddy and get another ride in Pocket's new car that he named 'Black Magic', but Kyle has baseball after school and he still needed some answers to help his brother, so he has to pass.

Right when the McKays made it to the field, Kyle pulled Coach Doubles aside and asked if he could keep Keegan busy for just a couple minutes before the game so Kyle could have a private talk with the team. He explained that he was going to ask the team to give a little extra effort and support to help build Keegan's confidence back up. The coach thought about it. He has never liked 'players only' meetings because you can't let the inmates run the asylum, but then he remembered how shaky Key was in his last start. The boy was battling just to get the ball in the strike zone. Great defense is the only reason Key got a win that day.

Maybe a team meeting before Key pitches tonight will be good for everyone. He tells Kyle he thinks it's a good idea and helps him pull it off, yelling at Keegan to come to him. Kyle passed Key on his way to meet with the team. Kyle just asked the guys to try a little extra tonight to help get this win. He explained Key's confidence problem, and one of the older guys, Chili said, "aw, he just needs to get laid, and we can't help him with that! Nah, I'm just kidding. Key's one of us, so if Kyle says he needs us to pick him up a little, I say fellas let's beat that little white ball all over this park tonight!

The guys slapped gloves and hit the field.

The game started right on time, and HRH is the home team, so they start the game in their positions on the field, as the managers exchange lineup cards. Hot Rod High's starting lineup and batting order is;

1. CF Wally Wheeler

2. SS Kyle McKay

3. 3B Skyler Martinez

4 C Pedro Peppers

5. P   Keegan McKay

6. 1B Miles Malone

7. LF Steve Speed

8. 2B Wendy Wheeler

9. RF Ben Hollenbut Jr.

Kyle also asked his friend, Little Flash G. to come tonight to announce the game. Hot Rod High's baseball games didn't usually have an announcer, but Kyle knew that little Flash could really get the crowd going and somehow, the little guy just makes sports more fun. Flash is the Sunnyvale Speedway announcer so the whole town knows him and he's very popular. He has to bring his own equipment tonight because this level of baseball never gets the games announced and they're not really set up for it. Kyle had to promise a favor to get Flash to do this gig because Flash only performs for much larger audiences usually.

There's a couple of loud crackling noises and then you hear Flash say, "Welcome everyone to HRH's home baseball park. Starting on the bump tonight for Hot Rod High's Speed Demons will be Keegan McKay. One of the best pitchers in the state, Keegan already has 7 wins this season and has been almost unhittable. He'll be throwing heat all night with that cannon attached to his right shoulder. Catching those smokin' hot fastballs will be Pedro Peppers, who is new to the team but has already hit 11 homers this season and is leading the SouthEast league in 4 different hitting categories. Ladies and gentlemen, you're in for a treat tonight because you're going to see one of the best hitters in the country. The team has nicknamed Pedro, 'Chili' and he's the kind without beans! "

Flash continues, "The guys are ready to go so I'll give you the rest of the lineup as I get time. Keegan McKay toes the rubber, starts his windup and blows one by Taft's leadoff hitter. This batter looked scared up there and who could blame him, that pitch came in at almost 90 miles an hour. This batter missed the next two pitches by at least a foot and he's out on strikes. Keegan is on tonight. Taft's 2nd batter pounds a long ball to center field. Wally Wheeler was playing too short, and it looks like this one is going to land behind him for at least a double. Wait a second! We have to wait until Wally stands back up and reaches into his mitt. He's standing and reaching into...does he, have it? HE DOES! Wally pulls the ball out of his glove! An unbelievable catch and The Speed Demons have two away. Key strikes out their 3rd batter on 3 pitches and Sunnyvale's coming in to hit. Sunnyvale's leadoff hitter is the speedster, Wally Wheeler. Here comes the p tch. Wheels turns and lays down a bunt. He's gonna have to fly to beat the throw and he does. Close play. Sunnyvale has a runner on first base with no outs. Next up is the short stop, Kyle McKay. He steps into the box and here comes the pitch. It's low and hits the dirt. It gets by Taft's catcher and Wheels is safe at second easily. With an open base, they walk Kyle intentionally. That's smart. They have to respect his bat. He's hitting over .300 and has yet to strikeout."

"Next up and batting for Sunnyvale is their 3rd baseman, Skyler Martinez. Sky is new to HRH and the team, but he's a natural athlete that plays great D and can crush the ball. He takes a ball, low and away. Taft isn't going to give him much to hit. Here's the second pitch to Sky and it's ball two. Just low. Now they've gotta throw him a strike. They do and he swings through it. It's a deep drive to center and the Taft fielder is in hot pursuit and he makes a diving catch! Both runners tagged their bases after the catch, and these two guys are flying around the bases. Wheels scores easily, and Kyle does too! It's a two- 0 ball game already and Chili Peppers is just coming to the plate. He hits the first pitch a mile! Its 3-0 now."

"In the top of the second inning there's a ground ball hit hard in the hole to Kyle's right. This is the toughest play for a right-handed shortstop because his glove is on his left hand, so he'll have to catch the ball with his left hand by extending his left arm all the way across his body, but somehow Kyle gets to it, now he'll have to hurry the throw, and...it's in the dirt before first. Malone keeps his left foot on the bag and extends his glove...and he makes the catch! Great play by both these young men!"

Flash G says, "Sunnyvale's defense is pretty solid this year, although Hollenbut Jr. is a little scary with the glove out there in right field." Flash can't stop himself sometimes.

"In the third inning, Keegan McKay struck out the side on 9 pitches, and Taft's hitters are swinging way too late."

"Now, we're in the bottom of the fifth, and the Demons are up 5 to zero. The bases are loaded for Kyle McKay but there are two outs. Kyle takes the next pitch and he's behind 0 and 2."

Kyle backs out of the box and thinks for a second. He was thinking this would be a good time to strike out and that's why he took those first two strikes, but then their pitcher smiled. Kyle decided the kid was laughing at him. Ok, alright he thought and then the kid threw what would have been strike three.

Flash shouts, "Oh My! Kyle crushed that pitch and hits a grandslam! Wow! I just found out that Kyle hit a grand slam last week too! It's 9-0 now. I'm not surprised that Kyle is starting for HRH's varsity team, but I am impressed at how well he's hitting varsity pitching. He's seeing the ball exceptionally well, especially since he's the youngest player on HRH'S squad. Kyle is a star."

"This one's over ladies and gentlemen, and it probably was from the start. Keegan threw his first no hitter in a complete game shutout and had two hits, a double and a homer. He will be the favorite for MVP this season if this keeps up. But I have to comment on the defense behind him tonight. First, is the new catcher, Chili Peppers. They say this guy never played a minute of organized sports before, but he runs the defense from behind the plate like he's been doing it all his life. Plus, he's got the best average on the team and leads the league with 11 home runs. There's no doubt that Keegan McKay never would have thrown that no hitter without Chili Peppers behind the plate. Plus, Wheels made two running catches near the wall in centerfield that were pro level catches; Sky robbed Taft of at least two runs by leaping and snagging line shots. Then there's Wendy Wheeler breaking the sex barrier and playing great defense at second base. She's the first girl to ever play baseball in this league and she's having a great season.

Baseball is a team sport and Sunnyvale has one helluva team. Flash G out!

The guys made lots of plays tonight that were stellar, and Kyle secretly thanked them all, but that kind of worked against Keegan. Instead of getting all the credit for pitching a great game, the defense was getting all the credit. And darn it, Kyle hit a grand slam! The team mauled him at home plate! He was trying to strike out. He really was. He watched the first two pitches come right down the middle and get called strikes, so he figured this pitcher wouldn't throw another pitch there again and started swinging without really looking but the pitch was right down the middle again and Kyle hit it a mile. Flash and The Rodd Report were going to make lots of noise about that, which took away from Key too. Everyone was still huddling around Key on the mound and trying to make him feel like he just won the World Series. He seemed to be buying it, but it wasn't the one man show Kyle had hoped for. Kyle realized he might not be any closer to helping his brother, but he has another idea. He decides to talk to Shelby's best friend, Wendy Wheeler. He figures Wendy will help him because Kyle's the one who convinced Coach Doubles to make an exception to his rule of 'boys only' and let Wendy try out.

He finds her taking off her cleats on the far end of the bench in the dugout and she's alone. Kyle sits down next to her and says, "Wendy, I need your help. This is about Keegan. I promise I'll never tell anyone what you tell me here, but why does Shelby hate him?"

"Listen Kyle, I'm not really comfortable around Keegan anymore either," Wendy cautioned, "and why would he tell your mom that he was having kinky, weird sex with Shelby, when it isn't true? "

Kyle said, "Whoa! Wendy, I don't believe that he did. I know my brother and there's no way he said anything like that to anybody, but especially not my mom! There's absolutely no way."

"Kyle, I'm sorry but you're wrong about this I swear," Wendy replied. "Wendy, Kyle said, "that couldn't have happened because my mom has been in a coma since before Shelby broke up with him, and she's only been able to speak for a couple of days so she couldn't have heard or told that BS to anybody.

Wendy shrugged.

"Listen, I think you're wrong," Kyle said diplomatically, "but I also know that neither you nor Shelby just made this crap up, so I need your help getting to the bottom of this. Will you help me?"

She said, "I guess, but I don't think it can be fixed, so don't get your hopes up, ok?"

Kyle got up to leave, and said, "Thanks Wendy and sorry to put you in the middle of all this, but I swear to God, Key didn't say that junk to anyone ever."

Kyle went straight home and asked his mom to meet him in his room. When she came in, Kyle spoke first. "Mom, did you ever tell anyone that Key talked to you about doing nasty things to Shelby? Please say no. Please say no Please say no" Moms thought about his question longer than Kyle thought she should have to. "Come on mom this is a simple question.... did you ever tell anyone that Key talked to you about doing nasty things to Shelby?" There's no way he did that. He'd have to be out of his mind, and Key doesn't do drugs as far as I know. Come on mom!"

"Kyle, I'm trying to answer you, but you keep talking. So, take a deep breath and listen for a minute please," moms said, and continued "You know my memory has been compromised and I've been basically unconscious for months, right? Given my frame around your thought, I see two questions that you need answers for, and I will answer them as honestly as I can. The answer to the question you asked is...no definitely not. I never said anything like that to anyone and I'm 100% positive of that."

"Perfect! Kyle shouts. You just saved Key from a fate worse than death! He was about to be stigmatized as a social outcast at

HRH for his last 3 years of high school!" He's heading for the door and says, "thanks mom, I gotta tell Key."

Now, moms raises her voice, "Kyle stop! Did you forget I said you needed to ask 2 questions?"

Kyle responds with, "Oh yeah! "Sorry mom but I'm good. You gave me the only answer I needed. Thanks."

"Kyle, please sit down and pay attention. Moms said impatiently. "I don't have energy like I used to, so I'm not going to chase you, but if you don't listen to me, you will be really sorry. It's up to you."

Kyle was sure they were just wasting time now, but moms was making him stay and listen to more chatter when he already had his answer. He decided to hear her out, but who does she think called this meeting? She needs more mom practice or he might just get with Key and demote her. M's is dying to take her job anyway.

Because Kyle is still here, Moms says, "Wise choice. Now, here's the part you're missing. I didn't tell a soul that Key talked to me about doing nasty things with Shelby. That's true. But Keegan did tell me about doing improper sexual things with Shelby."

"Holy Guacamole beandip Batman!" Kyle whispers. "Oh no. my brother is a weirdo, perverted jerk of a guy. I'm so embarrassed! I'm never going to HRH again and I'm moving out as soon as I can. I don't want anyone to think I'm like him."

Moms says, in a much kinder tone, "Kyle you're overreacting. Don't forget that my memory could have filed that incorrectly or something. We need to talk with Key or Shelby because we need more information. Key's in his room, so it's easier to deal with him, but he will be embarrassed and may deny it. Can you get Shelby to come over or facetime us?"

Kyle said, "I'll try. You want me to do that now?" Moms shook her head yes.

Kyle called Shelby, but she didn't answer, so he tried Wendy, and she answered. Those two are together so Kyle says, "My mom really wants to talk to Shelby. Do you guys mind coming over? I know it's getting late and it's a school night, but I think we need to get together as soon as possible."

"Kyle, we can't drive and you're not close, Wendy said, "so how about we meet at the Palace in half an hour?"

The Palace is what they call this old automobile manufacturing plant that the Wheeler family owns. Mr. Wheeler has it set up like a shop class at school. There's a bunch of old cars that don't run anymore, and tons of car parts and tools AND an open invitation to friends of the family to come wrench there anytime. It's way cool and you can learn anything you want to about cars there.

Kyle says, "we'll be there" and hangs up before the girls can ask any questions. Neither wants Keegan to come, but Mrs. Mac probably didn't either.

Half an hour later, everyone that should be there is there, and some that shouldn't be are too. It's uncomfortable for everyone but really awkward for Keegan and Shelby.

Before anyone else can, Kyle stands and says, "Thanks you guys for meeting with us. My brother's name has been getting kicked around and I want to get that cleared up, so I'd appreciate it if everyone is quiet and listens to the whole story before you say something you might regret."

Kyle has watched a whole lot of Judge Judy episodes, and he thinks he's got this.

Kyle continues... "This story is messed up. Just listen to how bad it starts...Shelby said that my mom told someone that Keegan told her that he did a bunch of nasty things to Shelby. So now let's break that all down. "So, Mom did you tell anyone that Keegan told you that he did a bunch of nasty things to Shelby?"

Moms replies, "No I did not. Of course not."

Now Kyle says, "So Shelby, why did you say that my mom did that. Are you saying she's a liar?"

Shelby feels attacked and she doesn't like where this is going, so she says, "my neighbor 2 doors down is Andrea and she told me that she heard Keegan saying that to his mom. So, Mrs. McKay, did you ever hear Keegan saying he did nasty things to me?

Moms thought about this for a minute because she remembered Keegan saying stuff about him and Shelby, but she wasn't sure when that was or if it even ever happened. She said, "I'm sorry Shelby but I have had 11 surgeries on my brain in the last few months and I don't trust my memory right now. I can say that I remember Keegan saying things about his relationship with you, but I can't even remember what he said or when it was. I'm not trying to be evasive, but the only thing I know for sure is that I didn't repeat anything that he said to anyone. I know that for sure."

Keegan had been standing in the back, and out of the light, but he walked forward now and said, "I think I might be the only person that can explain this. But first, I need to ask Shelby a couple of questions if that's ok with you Shell."

"Keegan, she said," I'm not inclined to try to help you right now because what you said hurt my reputation and wasn't true."

Key replied, "I understand, but if you just answer a couple of things, I think you'll feel better."

"I doubt it, but go ahead," Shelby said.

"Thank you, Key says, "so Shelby is your neighbor Andrea's last name McAffrey?"

Shelby replies, "I don't see what difference answering those questions will make, but I'm not trying to be a witch here, so yes, it is, now tell me why you asked?"

Key asks another question, "Does this neighbor work for an Ambulance company?"

"Yes, Shelby says, "she does why?"

Keegan says, "Shell, patience please. I'm going to make a call now on speaker. I have never dialed this number before, nor have I spoken with the person that I hope answers regarding these issues."

"Everyone please be quiet," Kyle says. Now everyone can hear the phone dialing and now ringing. A male answers, 'Hello'.

Keegan asks, "is this Mack Davis the ambulance driver?"

Mack says. "Yes, it is. Who is calling?"

"You probably don't remember me, but I'm hoping you can help me." Key says. "My name is Keegan McKay and…"

Mack interrupts, "Hey Key, of course I remember you. You're a true hero buddy. I'll never forget you."

Key's embarrassed but pushes forward, "Do you remember where and how we met and what you asked me to do?"

"Sure do," Mack says. "That was the night of the Big Crash at the Speedway. Your mom was in really bad shape, and your left arm had a compound fracture that was pretty bad, I asked you to sit in the back of the ambulance and hold your mom's head up so her brains didn't fall out of her head. I wasn't thinking about your arm, and every time I checked the mirror, you had both your arms up in the air holding on to your mom's skull. Your arm had to be throbbing."

Mack continues, "I told you that your mom was seriously injured, and she probably wouldn't survive unless you could keep her brain working all the way to the hospital, and you were holding your mom's very life in your hands and that I still needed more from you. I told you to talk to her and try to get a reaction that shows her brain is still alive. I also said, "Please talk to her all the way to the hospital and anything you say that gets any kind of response from her repeat it and add to it and try to make each sentence you speak get even more response from her. She was in real trouble Keegan and you had to get her brain to keep working."

"When we got out of the ambulance at the Emergency room, and I saw your mom, she looked a whole lot better and her brain was much more responsive. I told you right there in the emergency room that you had done a great job and you may have saved her life. And I said thank you. Then I rushed her back to an operating table, where Dr. O'Connor took over. She looked at your mom and said, "this one's got a chance, so team, let's get to work."

"The next time I saw you, was about an hour later and you were looking for your dad and brother, but now you had a big cast on your left arm. I can't believe that your arm was that messed up and you never even cried. You're a tough guy, no doubt. I told you that your mom still had a long road to recovery, but if she's half as tough as you are, she's got a good chance of walking out of this hospital one day, thanks to you."

"I'm sorry for rambling, but seeing how you handled that crisis gave me new hope for my profession. I had delivered too many dead bodies this early in my career, but you gave me new hope.

I even came up with a mantra, "Maybe we can save some, and maybe some are worth saving."

Davis finishes with, "Anyway, what's this call all about Keegan?"

Key said, "Mr. Davis, I'm sorry to bother you, but was the nurse that was working with you that night named Andrea McCaffery?" he said, yes. Key said "thanks, and I'll call you with an update on my mom's progress in a couple weeks. Thanks for all your help." And he hung up.

Kyle is standing again and says, "So we now know where the story came from. The nurse overheard Keegan talking with his mother and decided that Shelby needed to hear about this private conversation. Very unprofessional if you ask me. You with me so far?"

"Ok", Kyle said "so apparently Keegan did say he did nasty things to Shelby, but he did it only to save his mother's life. Now, I'm going to guess that once he got into the ambulance, he started talking about a few things, probably sports, school and girls. His mom reacted most when the girl's topic came up, so now he has to talk about girls for the next 20 minutes that it will take to get to the hospital. Twenty minutes sounds like a small amount of time to me, so I took out my recorder and taped me trying to talk about girls. I was repeating myself after 3 minutes, and Keegan couldn't have that happen, or his mom may die. He had to talk continually and kinda 'shock' his mom to keep her alive, so repeats weren't going to work. Plus, Key's only love has been Shelby, so if he's gotta talk about girls he's going to talk about Shelby. She's the only girl he knows."

Kyle continues, "The only bad part left is where did he get the nasty ideas? He told me that the seniors on the varsity football team talk about doing really nasty stuff to their girls and that's where he heard it. Well, its Spring and the football team is playing Spring ball, so I went into their locker room while they were at practice and hid in an empty locker. I recorded the senior guys talking after practice yesterday and it is disgusting. Frightening even. I'll play that recording for you at the end of our meeting, so I can leave without hearing that junk again."

"I have told the whole truth and asked the hard questions and just shared with you what I learned. Honestly, that's all the explanation and clarification I think anyone should need, but I still have 3 things on my mind;

"1. I feel like my brother, Keegan got a lot of really bad press for being a kinky perv dude and is getting shunned by some only because he did what he had to, to save his mom's life and that's not cool. He's not some sicko perv guy."

"2. Frankly, I'm proud of Key and it sure sounded to me like the main ambulance guy was proud of him too. I don't blame Shelby, but I hope she'll step up and own her part of this issue."

"3. I think this Shelby's neighbor, Ms. Andrea McAffrey should get fired. She destroyed Key and Shelby's relationship and compromised my mom's right to privacy while in her workplace. She's a hater and intentionally caused Shelby pain, and made my brother's life miserable for the last few weeks. The only one who should be facing charges here is her, in my opinion."

On the ride home, Moms said, "Kyle, I'm really proud of you for going to bat for Key like you did tonight two different times!" She was trying to lighten up the mood. "You hit a big homerun in the game and another one in that meeting!"

Keegan said, "Thanks bro." He was embarrassed that he said that nasty stuff, but he's sure he had to at the time. And he knew before he said that stuff that it would probably bite him in the butt!

He's hoping that's the end of that rumor and that Shelby likes him again. But she didn't exactly come over and hug him after Kyle explained to her that he really wasn't being a weirdo perv guy.

Moms said to Keegan, "I'm really thankful for you Key. I wondered how I ever got out of those bleachers at the track. I knew someone had to have taken me out of that mess and Mr. Davis just confirmed it. You saved my life Key."

Kyle is deep in thought, just lying on his bed. He's trying to gauge how his Keegan reclamation project is going. Keegan had conquered his fear of the dark, with just some friends' support and that was a big step in the right direction because that particular thing was humbling and embarrassing to him.

So, Kyle planned to get to work on Keegan's two favorite things; sports and girls. He decided he'd work on sports first and he already tried two things in sports; first, he tried to give Key the Family Challenge race-instead they tied.

Then, he tried to make Key the hero in the baseball game, even tried to strike out- he hit a grand slam instead and Key had to share the spotlight again.

And as for girls, he tried to get Shelby back for him by clearing up the bad rumors, but even that didn't seem to work- she didn't apologize tonight even though Kyle proved Key was innocent.

And Shelby heard about Key hitting on Suzi Strange from Wendy, then everybody heard that the Strange sisters were fembots, making Key look extra lame.

Man, this was not going as planned! Keegan's life was getting better, but Kyle didn't think Key was getting his confidence back. He felt like every time he took two steps forward, life took one step back. He wasn't giving up yet because he wanted his big brother back. What did Key's ambulance guy say, "maybe we can save some, and maybe some are worth saving." Key is one of the ones worth saving.

Kyle had a restless night worrying about fixing his brother, but in the morning, he came up with a new plan. Key was on time at breakfast and looked well rested.

Kyle teased him, "Hey Key, looks like you had a good night's sleep. What happened? You give the monsters a night off?"

Key said "Nope, they're gone for good and have been for almost a month already. It's weird, but that seems like years ago. I can't even fathom what I was ever afraid of. It just shows you that your brain can convince you of anything good or bad. I'm so focused on the good now that I don't have room in my head for stuff like monsters, fake friends, phony girls or dead heats!"

On the drive to school, Kyle replied, "I'm glad to hear that you're getting your head straightened out. I was a little worried about ya big brother. But hey, what did you mean by including 'dead heats' in that list?" Keegan intentionally ignored Kyle's question, which had Kyle thinking he knows that I tried to throw the race.

Walking together in their HRH letterman's jackets down the hallway on the first floor in Hot Rod High, Keegan said, "You know Kyle it's been too damn long since we played down in Raceland, what do you say we go right now?"

Kyle said, "What have you got in mind?" But Keegan already entered the bump code and was heading down that dark hallway before he responded.

"Then menacingly, Key said, I'll challenge you to a 4-track match."

Kyle was stuck because they were already sliding up to the

velvet rope at the Chill Chamber. Keegan was trying to scare him. Key knew that Kyle didn't know squat about drag racing, would be intimidated by the Speedway guys going 200+ mph, and he'd have an advantage on the off-road course too because he tried it twice already!

Suzi Strange welcomed them and then said, "Hey guys! Thanks for coming in. How was your ride here?" Key replies, "Same as usual."

Suzi continues, "Oh. That doesn't sound so crazy. I guess lots of people get freaked out running the Gauntlet to get here. So, I take it you're a regular here."

Suddenly, Suzi grabs her head with both hands like she's plugging her ears. She turns and walks a few feet away still holding her head.

Key says, "Hey Suzi, are you alright?"

She walks back to the counter, but she's still shaking her head like she's expecting something to fall out of it. Finally, she looks back up at the boys and says, "Oh. Hello Keegan and Kyle. Great to see you guys as always. Are you two going to race against each other today?"

Before they can respond, Sally walks up and says, "Hi, you two are the McKay brothers, right?" Kyle was right. The twins were replaced with new fembots.

Suzi says, "Oh come on Sally. You know these guys. They come here all the time."

Suzi keeps talking and it feels like she's trying to control the conversation, or maybe she's just trying to keep Sally out of it. She says, "Guys, sorry. We're both just a little off our game. We heard that the professor told everyone that we're fembots, and everyone has been coming in here and trying to feel us and saying mean things. You guys know us. We're not fembots. If you're not sure, touch my skin or feel my forehead."

Sally says, "I know! check my pulse. Fembots don't have hearts so they wouldn't have a pulse right, so check my pulse."

She sticks her left wrist out and says "try mine." Kyle notices that her bracelet is gone. He says, "would you like me to get you a bracelet for your wrist."

Sally says, "No thanks Kyle. I really don't like jewelry." It wasn't the real Sally, but this one did have a pulse.

Suzi says, "Come on guys. You know us. That fembot stuff is just a big fat lie. Feel my hands, she says as she rubs her hands on Key's arm and they feel warm...

Sally says, "I can't believe that loser professor sold us out to the whole school! What an idiot."

Suzi corrects her by saying, "I think you meant he lied about us to the whole school, right? I mean he couldn't sell us out because we're not hiding anything."

They all say goodbye, but the hugs that were part of their exit routine for the last few weeks, weren't part of their parting today. These were absolutely, definitely, 100% undeniably not the fembots that the boys had come to know.

"Now let's get to the track and do a little racing," Key said.

The guys get off their Transfiguration Tubes without incident at blue Platform Six, the Drag strip.

Kyle stops Key at the end of the tunnel to talk about their friends, Suzi and Sally. They both could tell that Sally was anxious to get out of the conversation, but Key thinks "It's just because they're having a bad day. Who could blame them when everyone is calling them fembots and touching them and everything. I'm not surprised that they're stressed out."

Kyle says, "Yeah, I get that too, but why were they pretending they weren't fembots? We know they are, but their programs are just wearing out. I mean they told us that themselves."

Keegan acts very surprised. "When did they say that? I never heard them say anything like that before. They are twin sisters for crying out loud Kyle. You know that, and I know you have a little crush on Sally but one thing at a time. Let's race there Romeo!"

They had put their favorite cars in the pipe at the Grateway, and both cars are lined up on the drag strip; Kyle's Royal Renegade and Keegan's White Night. Now Kyle could tell that Key had done this more than a few times before. Keegan was way too comfortable and almost cocky. The lights turned green and both guys pounded the pedal on the right and held on tight. Keegan won easily. As he got out of the car, Kyle saw that look he used to see on his brother's face often. A look Kyle hated. A kind of sideways smile that said I'm better than you. Damn, Kyle forgot how that look made him feel, and he was hatin' his life right now.

They exited the Tube again. This time at the Road Course called Lost. As they lined up, Key yelled over, "I love this track!" And they were off! Kyle had never made a right turn in the Renegade, and he did it poorly, but now he knew where they could do some drifting. He'd be back here for sure. When he got to the finish line, Key was already seated over by the Tube. Damn, this was embarrassing, and he knew it wasn't over yet.

Kyle did better on the Speedway than Keegan thought he would. He was closer on this track, but Key still won. Not easily, but let's just say that Key never looked back.... Standing at the

Tube platform, Key said, "Had enough?"

That does it! Kyle thought to himself. Now that cocky jerk is mocking me! That son of a "Heck no!" Kyle said. "You're not getting tired yet are ya?"

Next thing he knew they were neck and neck approaching the finish line on the Mile Oval. Kyle had to win this race! He pounded that skinny pedal, pulled his Nitro-pop and even found himself leaning forward in his car. He won this one but only by half a car length. He got out of the 'Gade and tried to swagger over to his brother thinking, "bet I wiped that cocky grin off his face this time." But he hadn't. Key gave him that look again and said "Not bad little brother. Always feels good to win, right," and then after a pause added "but you gotta admit it feels better when the other guy didn't let ya."

Kyle is completely surprised, "You're not going to try to tell me that you let me win that race, are you? Because I" and Key interrupted him

"Little brother, I'll just say this. I won't next time." And then he said quietly, but still with that look, "Hope you won't ever again either." As he briskly walked away, Keegan McKay left his little brother Kyle behind to digest some of the humble pie he had just jammed down his throat.

Kyle was ticked off and confused but he needed to know something, so he went upstairs to his dad's office, and when he opened the door, he could see the 3 Kings in the glass conference room. He said, "Dad, it will wait. I'll talk to you at home." He went down to Major Coynes office and opened the door. He found the key in the Day-Timer just like Sally told him and he took it down the hallway to the last door and it had 222 on it. He opened it with the key, glanced inside. Then closed it quickly and returned the key and was gone in seconds! His heart was racing!

It was just like Sally had said. Their two fembot friends, Suzi and Sally were in the scrap metal bin in Major Coynes' storage room #222. Kyle couldn't believe his eyes! Two of the prettiest girls he'd ever seen were casually discarded into a junk pile. He had promised Sally that he would try to save them, and now it would be his top priority.

The
DANCE

Life Lesson; Dance like no one is watching because more than likely no one is. If they are watching you, don't worry about it. They're worse than you or they would have got asked first.

Chapter 10
The Dance

The next day at school, there were flyers everywhere. The 2nd annual Spring dance was officially scheduled for 2 weeks from Saturday. Once again, it will be held at the Coynes' mansion. The guest list had been written with care and included all of Sunnyvale's finest; the town's mayor, judge, dentist, both lawyers and all 3 doctors, the golf pro, all the teachers and administrators from Hot Rod High and Sunnyvale High, all the Major's business associates, the high society types, the power brokers, the most attractive couples, and the socialites, along with all of Cathy and Charlie's friends.

So, anyway the big party at the Coynes' mansion was only a couple of weeks away. The Major didn't really want to do it again this year, but he has some big plans for Sunnyvale's future, and he knows he's going to need some support to make big things happen in this town. He's hoping to get commitments from Mr. Hollenbut and Mr. McKay in a meeting he planned to spring on them at the party. The three of them were the big dogs in Sunnyvale and so far, they had supported each other on every issue. He hoped that would continue because he has big plans for Sunnyvale. Plus, there were some issues at Raceland that they needed to resolve sooner than later.

Other than all the flyers getting stepped on and kicked along the floor, it was just another day at Hot Rod High. All the guys were hanging out by the Secret Door and telling jokes and lies. Chili told a joke that had them all laughing their butts off. Chili said, "Bob was showering and his wife was just climbing in to join him when the doorbell rang. His wife wasn't wet yet, so she said she'd get the door. She wrapped a towel around herself, went downstairs and opened the door. The neighbor, Bob was standing there and he took a look at her situation and said, "I'll give you $800 to drop that towel. She knew she shouldn't, but she decided what the heck, she could really use the money and no one would ever know. She says "deal" and drops the towel. Bob looks her over front and back and hands her the $800. She tells him he better not tell a soul, wraps the towel around herself again and hustles upstairs. As she's getting in the shower, her husband asks, "who was that at the door?" "Oh, just the neighbor, Bob" she says. The husband says, "Ok cool, did he give you the $800 he owes me?"

Kyle noticed that their crew had grown this year. Besides getting taller, there were more of them. The McKays were always nearby, but these days, their morning meeting was attended by the Wheelers and the Speeds, Shelby, Pocket and Frannie, Miles, Ricky Rodd, Tulz and Dub, Cathy Coynes, Skyler, and Chili. This morning Chili's joke got everyone's attention and he had something he'd been meaning to say. He said, "Ya knows this group of rag tag kids, chicks and losers needs to develop a code if they ever want to be recognized as a club and respected on the street. He challenged everyone to show up tomorrow with a 4- or 5-line pledge, or code. Then they'd vote to decide the one they would all swear to AND have tattooed somewhere on their bodies. He would choose for them if they couldn't decide where they wanted it. As the group disbanded to head for class, each of them was caught in their own terror.

Some were afraid of needles, some were afraid their parents would go ballistic, some were afraid it would hurt, but they were all afraid to tell Chili 'No'.

The next morning at the regular time and place, the HRH crew is gathered and discussing possible pledges or oaths. Everybody had one and presented it now.

Cathy Coynes suggested this one;

We're better than all of you

we're cool and brand new

time you caught a clue

Cuz We're the HRH crew

We're good at everything we do

She got some applause and a few kudos, but Chili didn't like her cocky approach and said, "Girl, we ain't done nothin' yet. We gotta earn all those words before we say'em."

Nearly everyone had their turn, but so far nothing clicked. Wally Walker, who Kyle nicknamed Dub, was an aspiring rapper and it was his turn now. Dub's is a little shy and needs a push, so Kyle gives him an introduction; "This next guy's no fool, so don't treat him like a tool, or he'll take ya to school!"

Dub steps out to the middle of the circle and starts quietly and gets louder as he goes….

Dig the well deep before you thirst

And you'll never let a good friend fall

Put God, country and family first

And if you can, Save them all

Everyone is quiet now and waiting to hear Chili comment. Chili is just staring at Dub with cold hard eyes. Finally, he breaks the silence by starting to applaud. Then he claps louder and louder.

Now, everyone has joined in, and Dub is beaming. He says, "Mr. Chili, did you like it?" But Chili still has that cold stare looking right through little Dub and so it gets quiet. When you could hear a pin drop, Chili says "No Dub. I didn't like it." Now the silence is painful. Chili speaks again and says "no little man I didn't like it...I loved it! You have written the best club code I ever heard!"

The crew bursts into applause as Chili tosses Dub up on his shoulder and danced a bit. The man was smooth. The celebration ended abruptly when Chili stopped dancing and said, "Ok everybody, I expect each of you to have Dub's code tattooed on your body somewhere by next Wednesday. It can be big or small and, in any font, you like, but it has to be a permanent tat and under it, you should have the tattoo artist write HRH '98. Any questions?"

Key spoke up, and said, "Chili, the bottom line you're adding sounds like the thing real clubs do that tells the world what year the club was founded."

Chili replies, "I know that Key."

"But Chili, we didn't start our club way back then," Key says.

"I know that," Chili starts, and then says "do you think all those other clubs put the real year when they started? Don't think so cuz that wouldn't have been cool. They made up a year that made them look like they'd been around awhile. They didn't want to look like they just thought of this club thing. Now, if anyone challenges us on that, you tell them the club president came up with the code back in '98 when he was in prison. If they push any further on the issue, you tell 'em to talk to me about it, ok? Make sense now?"

The group is quiet now, so Chili says, "Next Wednesday then." And walks away.

Little Stanley Tulz says, "Keegan do we really have to get Dub's code tattooed on us? You're not really going to do that are ya? That's like gangster stuff."

Keegan replies, "Guys, I know that our parents aren't going to like it, but we have to do it if we want to be in the club. I'm going to have it done small on the back of my left shoulder and try to hide it for a couple of years. I'd recommend you all do it the same. It is a cool code and I think our parents won't be too mad if we tell them that the club is going to do good things at school and in the community. Like we could have a bake sale in the summer to raise money for the poor people. Then maybe a car wash next fall, and we wash the cars by hand, the football team in their trunks and the cheerleaders in bikinis. We'll come up with some good fundraisers and that will make everyone happy."

The next Wednesday everyone in the club was in the regular meeting place when Chili asked, "Did everyone get their tattoos done?" He pulled up the left sleeve of his t-shirt and showed his off. He had it done pretty big, but he does have huge shoulders. Almost everyone had taken Key's suggestion and got the tat or the back of their shoulders. Cathy Coynes had hers put on her lower back. The tat guy told them that was a 'tramp stamp' but that's what she wanted.

The two little guys, Dub and Tulz didn't have them yet because they said they didn't have enough money. Chili said he'd give them another week but if they didn't get them done by then, they were out of the club.

The Spring Dance is only a week and a half away and some of the girls haven't bought their dresses yet. Every girl will want a new dress for the dance, and they have been busy shopping for that special one for weeks. Finding that dress is a whole lot more important than coming to your game, or anything else you ask her to do. She's too busy. It should be easier than ever to find a dress with online shopping, but it has to fit her perfectly too! There are a couple of problems with that part. First, she can't try it on online, and second, high school girls' bodies are changing almost daily, so they're trying to hit a moving target. Retailers know that very few dresses will stay 'sold', and they have to add staff to handle all the returns and exchanges. Eventually, she will decide that one of the dresses will be 'fine'.

That word stinks. Even if she said it was 'perfect', there's still a good chance that she isn't done shopping, but she didn't say it was perfect. She said it was 'fine.' If you say something is fine, you mean it will work or it will do, and you will keep that something and never complain, but that's not what she means. Nope. Any time your girl says something is 'fine', you can be pretty darn sure that she's not happy with that something. What 'fine' really means is she's tired of or bored with her search...for the moment. Of course, now she has to help her bestie with her search. During this exercise in futility your girl will inevitably run across a dress that she thinks she likes better than the one that she thought was 'fine'. This will cause her to start her search all over again. To which you will say, "fine." But that's not what you mean. You want to scream at her, explaining that she has not spent 5 minutes with you since she started searching for this dress weeks ago.

But you say 'fine.' That word is a lie. It really is. When mom dropped you off at school today, she said tonight we're having cheeseburgers and fries for dinner. You didn't say 'fine' did you? No, you probably said 'awesome' or 'my favorite' right? If you had said, 'fine' she would have probably made something else for you because she knows you didn't mean it was 'awesome'.

Or, when you're walking the girl you like home from school, and you offer to carry her books before you see that she's got so many. You stack hers on top of yours and in about a block or so, you stop to change hands because it feels like your arm might fall off. She can see the pain in your face, and she says, "Oh, I'm sorry. You want me to carry mine? And you want to say, heck yeah, but instead you say "it's ok, I'm fine." But you're not fine. Your arm is probably going to fall off and you're just hoping it waits until you're out of sight.

Or, when you are on the playground and the school bully walks up and slugs you in the stomach hard. You almost puke it hurts so badly. Then, a buddy comes over and asks, "are you ok"? You say, 'I'm fine' but you're not even kind of fine. It hurts really bad. That 'fine' word is never fine. In fact, it's always a lie.

Finally, the day everyone's been waiting for is here. It should be a huge event that will have everyone pumped up and ready for summer. Everyone who wants to be anyone is going to the Coynes' big party. The whole McKay clan was on their way in their blacked-out Cadillac SUV. M's was with them, and would be making her first social appearance in Sunnyvale. She was impeccably dressed and looked "really pretty". At least that's what Kyle said when he saw her all done up today. She surprised herself this morning, when it crossed her mind that she might meet someone today and she was excited about it.

This was going to be the 2nd Annual SPRING DANCE at the Coynes family's mansion. It was a big event with tons of fine food and drink, valet service, live music etc. Everyone who is anyone in Sunnyvale is in attendance and dressed in their Sunday best! From the house's entry, you could see the huge ballroom with a live band warming up, and to their right, the dance floor opened out to three Olympic sized swimming pools and numerous waterfalls and Jacuzzis.

M's said, "everything is so beautiful, this feels like a Hollywood party for the stars!"

Keegan had to admit that the setup looked really cool, but it seemed like a bad combination to him. He wasn't going to swim in his slacks and jacket, nor dance in his wet trunks. Still, Key couldn't argue with his grandma M's. The place was beautiful, but if you were only going to use one word to describe it, Key thought the word 'amazing' would have been a better choice. What the heck? Keegan realized he was being critical about things he really didn't care about. He knew better and made a conscious effort to chill. It's just that he has never liked dressing up or fancy affairs. Ok, what was really bugging him was he knew Shelby was going to be here and she was probably going to be hanging with a new guy. She hasn't really forgiven him and they have barely talked since that night at the Palace. Today was going to be fun though, or at least he was going to look like he was having fun because he couldn't let Shelby ruin his day. Actually, she was probably going to ruin his day, but he couldn't let her know she ruined his day. How did his life become all about appearances? This sucked. He and Kyle would spend most of the day in the pool and playing catch. So, he told himself to get in a better mood.

So far, the pools haven't been used yet, and they knew it would be rude for them to be the first ones in, so the McKay brothers have spent their time thinking they were carefully dodging dance invitations even though no one was dancing yet. They liked the dresses and seeing the girls all dressed up, but they were going to school at Hot Rod High, not Janet Jackson's Dance School! Neither of them had ever even thought about learning to dance, but if they were ever going to try dancing, it sure wasn't going to be here, with everyone's parents seated around the dance floor and watching!

They were positioned in a spot that had reduced visibility, and they were watching each other's backs, and so far, it was working out. No one had asked them to dance yet. They thought there might have been a couple of close calls, but so far so good. Then,

Key let his guard down for just a second and Cathy Coynes caught his slipup and asked him!

No one else was dancing yet, but this was her party, so he really couldn't turn her down. With everyone watching them, Keegan and Cathy Coynes walked timidly onto the dance floor. When the music started, they both began moving, awkwardly at first, but then Cathy took the lead, and she was swinging Key around all over that dance floor. On the second song, Key started to bail, but Cathy wasn't havin' it. She started swinging him around again, but this time Key took over and started swinging her. He would pull her close and then let go with one hand and kind of spin her as he swung her away from him. He was doing pretty good and he made it through the second song. They even got a little applause. Now, Key was feelin' it, and showin' off a little, but he didn't really know what he was doing and this time he swung Cathy a little too hard. She spun right into the swimming pool in her brand-new dress. The crowd reacted with a loud collective gasp followed by an awkward, nervous laugh.

Cathy was horribly embarrassed, but things were about to get much, much worse. The music had stopped with the mishap, so everyone was just standing there watching Cathy climb the steps out of the pool. When she had emerged completely from the pool, she turned toward the now crowded dance floor, and there was a loud collective gasp! Cathy Coynes had no idea that her dress was now completely see through. There was another loud gasp from the crowd, and this time people were pointing at her and talking loudly. She heard someone say, "Oh my God" and someone else yelled "look, she's naked". Cathy looked down and discovered that her brand new, very expensive dress was completely see-through when wet. She started to cry and raced through the crowd upstairs to the privacy of her bedroom. She saw herself in the floor-length mirror on her closet door, and just collapsed to the floor.

Cathy Coynes had turned 13 just last week and her body had changed quite a bit over the last year. She was still just getting used to those womanly changes, when she accidentally showed them to the whole town! She was horribly embarrassed and just buried her head in her pillow and cried herself to sleep.

After half an hour or so had gone by, Major Coynes began to be concerned about his lovely daughter. He went upstairs to check on her and found her pretending to be sleeping. He needed to talk to her, so he sat down on the side of the bed anyway. He was a big man, and his sitting caused the whole mattress to roll like a big wave all the way across her bed. She gave up on the sleeping act just before the wave tossed her against the wall. She sat up angrily and yelled at her father. "I hate you" she said. Then louder, "and I hate this party, and I hate dancing, and I hate this dress!"

She took a breath and then continued her childish tirade. She was almost yelling when she said, "and I hate Keegan McCoy for throwing me in the pool! What a ! I swear I'll never speak to him again as long as I live."

Mr. Coynes had seen his spoiled daughter get mad before, but this time was different. Her eyes were glazed over, and she was almost spitting the words at him. Then with the rest of her rage, she yelled "and I hate you too!"

Yeah, this time was different alright, and he was afraid she might not calm back down ever! Poor Keegan McCoy! She called him a . She didn't talk like that normally, and he made a note to talk with her about that later. Right now, he had to do something before his daughter went back down to the party and gave Keegan a piece of her mind...very loudly!

Major Coynes knew Keegan and his family very well. He had been watching Key play sports for Hot Rod High for a couple of years now and thought the young man was a good athlete and a strong leader. In fact, Mr. Coynes privately had hoped Keegan might marry his daughter someday. He couldn't let Cathy's temper tantrum ruin his plan, so he had to calm her down somehow, but before he could say another word, his daughter jumped up and raced out of her room. He heard her flying down the stairs and he took off chasing her. He was big and slow with zero percent chance of catching her, but he had to try.

Cathy went straight up to Keegan and started pushing him as hard as she could in the direction of the pool, and she didn't stop pushing until Key was falling backward right into the deep end. When he surfaced, she was standing right there and shouted, "I hate Keegan McKay and this whole damn town!" Then she turned around and ran as fast as she knew how, until she reached her bedroom again. Once inside, she locked her door because she definitely didn't want to talk to any of these losers again.

Keegan probably wrecked his shoes, but he had been anxious to get them off anyway. He headed straight for the men's room by the pool, stripped his wet clothes off and put them in one of the guest lockers. He had planned for a quick change, so he already had his trunks on. He wasn't gone five minutes, but as he dove in the pool, he thought he saw Kyle and he thought, no, that couldn't have been Shelby. As he surfaced in the warm, clean pool, he spun around to look at the spot where he had seen his brother and possibly Shelby Hollenbut, but neither of them was still there. He could touch the bottom, so he sort of did a slow 360 keeping a lookout for his two favorite people. He spotted Kyle, who was pointing at the pool behind him. He turned just in time to see Shelby shooting up from the pool's bottom right next to him. He caught her as she was coming down and suddenly, they were face to face, and man one of those faces was downright beautiful. They kissed like it was the first time, and Keegan thought his heart might burst. They stayed like that, with their faces close enough to feel each other breathe, and for a few moments just stared deeply into each other's eyes. It looked to Kyle like maybe they both had found their way home.

Kyle knew now they wouldn't be playing catch today, so he took the football and headed to the third pool. It was further away from the house and not as deep as the other two. He knew he'd find someone to throw the ball with back here. As he was walking that way, someone jumped out to scare him. He caught her and pulled her close, but he didn't kiss her (he remembered how she felt about PDA's). Instead, he just whispered, "I've missed you" and let go. She had started to walk away when she heard what he said. She stopped, turned toward him and said, "me too." Kyle couldn't help thinking that God made Samantha Speed just for him. Sam felt his steady gaze on her and threw caution to the wind. She kissed him like she had kissed him in Raceland, and Kyle wasn't really sure what was happening to him, but he felt parts tingling and growing and guessed he was falling in love. He thought to himself, "what happened to only seeing each other once a month and not letting anyone from school know about us?" That was a question he knew instinctively not to ask. He thought of the theme song from a tv show his grandpa used to watch called Rawhide. It said something like 'don't try and understand 'em, just grab a rope and brand 'em'. Kyle thought, "If only it were that easy.' He knew he was going to try his butt off to hold onto Samantha Speed this time, and he knew it was going to be the most difficult thing he would ever try to do.

While his boys were having fun in the water out back, Mr. McKay was seated in Major Coynes office discussing the Rodd situation with the Major and Ben Hollenbut. These three men were known as the Three Kings by many of the business owners in Sunnyvale, which was a sarcastic biblical reference. This was a difficult discussion because their decision would have a huge impact on not just Randy and Ricky Rodd, but all of Raceland.

The Major said, "The way I see this is, Raceland is for kids cnly, but we need a top mechanic full time down there. and the r ght guy for that job is the guy that's been doing it for years, Randy Rodd. There have been zero sightings of him in Raceland in all these years because he's been content to work behind the scenes.

Now Ricky sees his dad and he has every right to know his dad. Do we can Randy? I mean we'd give him a healthy retirement package for sure, but who's going to replace him? Give Ricky special access? Can Randy even get out of Raceland?

Kevin McKay says, "Guys, I have a suggestion. Why don't I meet with Randy and find out what he wants to do? If he wants out, we have to let him go. But if he can't get out, we have another discussion. But this seems like the best place to start. I'll also meet with Ricky and fully disclose the situation and tell him that we're discussing options with his dad."

Ben Hollenbut says, "Kevin, I think that's best and thanks for handling this for us."

The Major says, "I agree. Thanks Kevin."

By the time her dad reached her room, he could hear Cathy in there, but he decided not to make another attempt to talk with her today. He knew he wouldn't get anywhere with her right now. Some nerve! She caused a scene and embarrassed him in front of all their guests and most of Sunnyvale, and for the life of him, he couldn't understand why. He must not have seen her coming out of the pool! The good news was that he knew the polite nature of Sunnyvale's finest would likely carry the day, and sure enough, everyone was sympathetic and supportive as they said goocbye. The Major saw M's on the dance floor and approached her in the middle of a song. He cut in before he noticed that M's had been dancing with Ben Hollenbut. The Major was glad he cut Ben off because that was his only competition for M's attention, and he wanted all of that. He had been single forever and M's was a breath of fresh air that drifted into his plans when she walked into his party this afternoon. He thought, 'thanks again Kevin.'

Before they left, Keegan went upstairs and knocked on Cathy Coynes' bedroom door. She very quietly said, "Who's there?"

Key said, "It's just me Cathy, Keegan. I'm really sorry about the whole pool thing and I want you to know I feel like crap about it and I'll buy you a new dress, ok? I'll take you shopping next week, promise."

Cathy was surprised at Key's apology, and she really appreciated it. She said, "Key I'm sorry too. It's ok. I know you're a good guy. I don't want another dress, but thanks for offering. Can we maybe have lunch next week?"

Key said, "Thanks Cathy. Lunch sounds great! See ya at school."

Their dad was driving the McKays home now, but moms could tell his mind was far away. After a while she decided to say something, so she playfully said, "A penny for your thoughts".

Mr. Mack finished her little song, "a nickel for a kiss. A dime if you tell me that you love me. Oh, I'm sorry honey. Hey thanks for coming today. I was very proud to have the prettiest woman at the party as my date. And my meeting with those two bears went better than expected, so I am now handling the Rodd situation for The Company. It might require some late hours over the next few days but I'm committed to doing the right thing for Randy and Ricky, and I may need the whole family's help. This is a huge responsibility because if the press gets ahold of it The Company will be destroyed, along with the Speedway, HRH and Raceland. Right then, his phone rang. It was Ricky Rodd. When he hung up, he turned to his wife and said, "I may be out late tonight."

He pulled into the garage and hurried into the house to get a cup of coffee. As usual, Karen and her mom unloaded the troops and deployed them to their rooms. When they found Kevin, he was sitting at the kitchen table and writing notes on a small tablet. They both kissed him goodnight and headed to bed. The whole family was going to bed early after a long day in the sun, except Kevin. His night was just beginning. He called Ricky back and made plans to meet with him at his RodKingz office at the Speedway. He told Ricky to be sure to bring the pictures, and he hit the road.

Hey Ricky, thanks for coming. I met with Mr. Coynes and Mr. Hollenbut today and they have put me in charge of helping you and your dad work through this mess. Would you rather tell me how you want me to resolve things first, or for me to tell you how we got here first?

"Well, Ricky replied, "Since you may not be able to resolve it how I'd like you to, maybe it will help me understand everything if you go first."

Mr. McKay replied, "That's fine Ricky. Now keep in mind that I wasn't here when your story started, so I'll only be able to tell you what I've been told, but I think for the most part I know the truth. Ok, so your dad was in school here and he got a Taft girl pregnant. They had a baby and a month later your mom was last seen heading out of town on the back of a local thug's Harley. Your dad's parents were devout Catholics and disowned Randy and threw the two of you out on the street. It was winter and it was too cold for a baby to be outside at night, so he took you to the church and left you with a priest. The priest helped arrange a foster home for you. Randy wanted to keep you, but he was a 17-year-old unemployed homeless kid. Raceland was just being built and Randy loved cars, and he was already a master mechanic. Major

Coynes hired him as the only mechanic in Raceland and paid him enough to be able to get his own place and hire a nanny for you so he could still work. He worked his tail off 7 days a week and spent 7 nights a week loving and raising you. One night Randy was tired and fell asleep in his garage on the track. He woke up a couple hours later and tried to go home to you, but he was trapped inside Raceland. Mr. Coynes was having insurance issues, so his insurance company installed an electric barrier that came on automatically every night at midnight. They wanted to keep thieves out, not your dad in, but when he woke that night, it was after midnight and he tried to break out to get with you. He was hit with more than 200 volts of electricity. He tried again and again, even though it hurt worse each time, until he couldn't try anymore. Well, that restraint system had a new feature that allowed it to retain the image of any offender that tried to disable or escape it more than twice. The system had loaded your dad's image throughout the whole place and there was no way your dad could get past it ever again. Mr. Coynes tried to get the insurance company to remove the barrier system, but they threatened to shut the whole project down. Major Coynes and your dad made an agreement that The Major would take you and raise you in his house, get you a great education and a foundation for a better life, if your dad would stay in Raceland and handle the track's mechanical needs until your 21st birthday. It maybe wasn't the perfect solution but both men agreed that it was the best thing for you.

Well, there were a couple things that no one would have seen coming, like;

1) your mom coming back to Sunnyvale 9 years later and suing Mr Coynes and Raceland for her damages of pain and suffering. She wasn't trying to get you back. She was only trying to get money from Raceland to get her latest boyfriend out of prison. It caused a lot of trickle-down damage

2) your dad is not aging. Your dad is still about an 18-year-old version of himself. There is something very strange about time in Raceland. It just doesn't exist. If you and I go into Raceland at noon on Monday, and we race for two days straight, when we exit Raceland, it will still be Monday at pretty close to noon.

Ricky interrupts, "Yeah, Mr. Mac. I've seen that with my own two eyes, so I know you're telling the truth, but how is that possible?"

"Ricky, we've had lots of brilliant scientists visit and investigate, but we still don't know exactly." Mr. Mac said. "Your dad was the first to get the transportation tubes to transfigure people and things, so we think he may be able to help us control the morphing, so that we can go backward and forward in time. We have been learning along the way. For example, Key got stuck in a tube last week and came out approximately 100 years older and we were able to run him backwards through the tube to get him back to normal. That's a lot of progress."

"Sorry Ricky, I got off point for a bit there," Mr. Mac said. "I was explaining some of the challenges we didn't anticipate that have brought you and I together tonight, and the aging issue greatly impacts you and your dad's relationship. At this point, you two would have to reconnect as brothers. I imagine you would like to have a dad, but Ricky your dad's not even 2 years older than you. How's that going to work?"

Ricky's got tears running down his face, and says, "Damn it! I really wanted to finally have a dad like everybody else."

"I get it Ricky but be fair. Mac says "Let's say we can get control of the morphing process. What would you want us to do? Make you 6 months old again? Or take 20 years off your dad's life. You think he'd be ok with that? When you think about it, there just isn't a perfect solution possible, so I'm hoping that you and your dad can work together to bring me a wish list. You know, a solution that you both are ok with. Once we know what you guys want, I'll have plenty of challenges to work through, but with a wish list, my mission will be clear. But first, we need you both to agree 100% on what you want. If you two can figure out a way to go forward from here, you have my word that I will do everything humanly possible to make your wishes come true. Deal?"

"Heck, Ricky says, "Mr. Mac I don't think I know what to say. I'm not angry at anybody anymore and I understand why nobody ever fixed this. I'm still sad and mad, but not 'about' or 'at' anything or anyone in particular. Does that make sense?"

Mr. Mac says, "Honestly none of what's happened makes enough sense for us to understand it or forgive them, but we don't have to today. For now, we just have to close the wounds and learn to live with the scars and try to be better humans tomorrow."

"Ricky, Mr. Mac says while looking at him right in the eyes, "thanks for taking the time and you have my number now, so please feel free to call with any ideas, fears, anger, plans or whatever anytime. This is one adult that will stick with you all the way to the end, and I promise to fight my butt off to get this resolved exactly as you want it done. You're a fine young man and I'll be happy to see you through this. Take care and we'll talk soon."

Ricky said, "Thanks for everything Mr. Mac. You're alright for an adult!"

It was pretty late when he sat down at the news desk and put the finishing touches on the next edition of the Rodd Report. He was still committed to his free speech ideals, but now he understands the other side too. Being a newsman wasn't just about printing facts, now it was more about telling stories where the telling is as important as the facts. He had lots to think about for sure. And on top of that, he couldn't ignore his personal life. After talking with Mr. McKay, Ricky believed he had a chance of spending a lot more time with his dad. He wasn't sure how he felt about his dad being almost his own age, but the guy looked like he might be pretty cool, so maybe they'd just become friends? Maybe he had enough friends already. But he's already mostly grown and he got this far without one, so did he really need a dad now? Maybe Ricky would be better off without this guy in his life at all...

His dad's busy with Ricky tonight and Keegan has homework, so Kyle finally has a chance to try the trick he thinks he learned about Micro-rods. He's already at the Grateway and he puts one of those 3 micro-rods he bought at the Merch Mart, right into the pipe by the doorbell. It gets sucked in so he heads to the Chill Chamber and watches these two fembots pretend they know him. It wasn't long before the doors on the Transfiguration Tube opened up, and he anxiously walked right out onto the track. Sure enough, that micro-rod was now a full-size racecar. The first half of his test went well. Now, he's going to skip racing and just go home. If he's right, the new car he used in the Grateway will be delivered to his race space tonight and still be a full-size race car. This would be really cool. He figured he would just buy all the cars he was missing in his collection for $5.00 each and then run them through the morph tube. In no time he'd have a full collection and he would be a RodKingz grand prize winner! This was going to be so cool! He couldn't wait!

School
Shooting

Life Lesson; You can't shake hands
with a clenched fist

Chapter 11
School Shooting

Kevin McKay slept in a little bit on this fine Tuesday morning. He had a big meeting planned at 11 o'clock with Mr. Coynes and Mr. Hollenbut. Yeah, the Three Kings. He didn't know if he liked that moniker or not, but if it was a biblical reference he knew for sure it wasn't appropriate for these three businessmen. They weren't bad guys really, but probably like all businessmen, they've made decisions along the way that were maybe not always for the greater good. Sometimes it's a hard balancing act trying to be successful and doing the right thing. Still, Kevin McKay felt like, of the 3 of them, he was the most committed to family values and to Christian morality. Of course, that was probably why he was the least financially successful of the three men. He realized that he was brought into The Company to be the social rudder responsible for navigating their group through the filthy sewer water that society was becoming largely due to growth, greed, and a general relaxation of law enforcement.

The challenges were far more complicated than any one human could control or even understand, but Kevin is part of the moral majority, and he tries to keep Sunnyvale in step with that mindset. His opinions regarding the following social issues are that we need to stop the direction we're heading;

1. Drugs are everywhere now, even in grade schools and the laws that were voted in by a social majority to control drugs have mostly been removed or relaxed. There are now legal pot stores in most of our cities. And there's a new drug called fentanyl that

is killing kids in record numbers.

2. Gun shops and smoke shops are popping up in neighborhoods across the country. They combine to be the fastest growing retail channel. Gun control is out of control and smoking, even with vapes, is not healthy for our kids.

3. Today, it's even common to change the gender you were born with, and many states will use tax dollars to pay for your sex change. There is no doubt that some people were born with the wrong body parts, and a social acceptance of those people is the right thing to do, but it has become a trend with kids making these choices before they even understand them. It's also not right to make people that don't agree with them pay for them.

While his partners agree in principle with Kevin's opinions, he believes their decisions are made solely on their personal financial benefit. Kevin believes that his partners might even finance some of these business ventures if the profit was enticing enough. He likes to think he has higher standards than they do, but it could just be that he hasn't had those opportunities presented to him.

Many conservatives might change their positions on these issues if the possibility of substantial personal financial gain was an option. I know that I would struggle with some of these decisions. For example, what if you were making $40,000 a year in your job with port security, and you had a chance to make a million dollars a year, and all you had to do is look the other way once a month when a gun or drug delivery comes in...would you do it?

What if you took it and you're driving an expensive new car and living in a big new house, and one day your brother's 11-year-old son gets shot in a drive by, or ODs on fentanyl? Social responsibility holds people to a very high standard and I'm not sure that any of us measure up all the time, but that's what Kevin

McKay expects of Kevin McKay.

The meeting today is regarding two pending issues; the Rodd's and the fembots, and both these decisions would end up on Kevin's to do list, undoubtedly.

Halfway through his breakfast, there was a firm knock on the door. And then again. Mr. McKay was on his way to the front door now. He opened it and was surprised to see detective White on his front porch. He invited the detective in and offered him a cup of coffee.

After he delivered a black coffee, Mac asked his friend "what brought the 'detective you' here so early on a Tuesday morning."

Detective White said something that caught Mac by surprise.

Mac said, "Detective, seriously? I know you're serious by the time of day that you're here. I wouldn't have believed you were ever out of bed before noon until now. And you have some questions for my mother-in-law? Damn this is going to be good. I'll get her out here pronto, and I'm sure we can straighten this all out in time for you to get home for some more sleep today."

Mac made the introductions and sat down. He wasn't going to throw M's into this meeting cold, so when they were all seated, Mac said, "Mary, the detective thinks you may have some information about a stolen a car." "Yes ma'am, the detective said as he handed her a picture, "Isn't that you driving that silver BMW X5?"

"Well, yes, it is, but I certainly didn't steal the car. That's the car I drove home from the Big Crash. It was Miles' dad's car. We left the track that night after most everyone else was already gone. Miles lost both his parents in the wreck, but he had taken the keys out of his dad's burned pants pocket before the Morgue took his body. Anyway, he said he had the keys to his parents' car and if I didn't mind helping him, I could drive and drop him at his house and drive their car to my house. He said he'd get an Uber and pick it up later that same day. I parked it down the street and left the keys on the visor just like he said. It was a crazy night, and I barely remember getting home, but I did walk to the market later that day and I went right by where I had left the car and it was gone, so I assumed Miles had kept his word and retrieved the family car. I assure you that I had nothing to do with any stolen car. Is that the car you're asking about?"

"Mrs. McKay, Detective White said, "when was the last time you saw Miles Malone? And how would you describe Miles' condition when you saw him last?"

"You know, detective, I rode with my son to the track that day, but I couldn't find any family members after the wreck," M's said "and there were no more ambulances, or I would have gone to the hospital in one of them. Uber declined to even give me a time estimate for pickup. Then I recognized Miles. I watched him play football the night before and he was sitting with us watching the races. I knew he was a friend of the family, so I was comfortable enough to approach him. Anyway, I drove him home and then I used MapQuest to get to my son's house. I know that's not what you asked me, but I didn't want you to think I was some old Cougar chasing young boys. Anyway, the last time I saw Miles was when I took him home. He was heartbroken and sad, and I think he was pretty numb. He may have lost his whole family that night of the crash, although he only mentioned his parents to me. Was he hurt or is he missing or something?"

The Sunnyvale PD didn't have the staff to investigate anything, so Kevin couldn't help wondering why this guy was interrogating his mother about a possible stolen car. Kevin thought, if she stole a car, the only place for her to put it would be in their garage.

He got up and left the room to check and returned quickly with his report. "Detective White, Kevin says, "my mother hasn't even left the house for days and I checked the garage and found no vehicles that weren't mine."

"If you aren't going to arrest her, then our conversation is over." Mac says. "Have a nice day!" And he is back at the front door opening it for the detective, who takes the hint, and stands up to leave. At the door, he turns back toward M's and says, "Please do not try to leave the state until further notice, because there are signs of foul play regarding the Malone family. Have a nice day!"

Kevin felt like the detective was fishing and he didn't have any reason to be doing that here. Maybe he was just bored. There is so little crime in their little community that boredom is often an issue. Kevin has been to the Police Department occasionally over the years and has often found the cops and detectives playing poker in the lunchroom, which is why he voted against hiring another one last year. The locals all thought they didn't even need a police department and voted against adding to it every time it was on the ballot. Like Kevin, they will regret those choices by the end of the day.

Mr. Mac wanted to understand why Detective Bob White was questioning his mother-in-law, so he took a drive down to the Sunnyvale PD. When he walked in, he thought he heard 'Chewy' Chavez,' Taft's sheriff. It was Chewy and his voice on the answering machine was booming through the station, "Hello! Is anyone there? Hello damn it! I need help! Pick it up!" After a pause, he starts yelling again, "Damn it! Where are you guys? Hello!"

Sunnyvale's sheriff, Steven Speed picks up in the other room, so the call is still coming through the answering machine and being blasted on the PA system. Steve says, "Easy their b g fella! I was in the bathroom!"

Chewy says, "Sorry Steve but I need you and every able-bodied man on your team up here at Taft High pronto! There's been a school shooting here! A couple of kids are dead, there's some injured and the two perps are heavily armed and still out there. They called in a bomb threat before they started shooting kids, and we have reason to believe there may be some explosives in the cafeteria."

There was a sudden burst of gunshots that had to come from an automatic weaponl Then Sheriff Chavez continued, "I need all the help you can bring so please hurry bro, I gotta go."

Steve paged the dispatcher, Louise from the lunchroom. Caught her in the hall and told her, "There are two shooters at Taft High. Chavez is undermanned against '47's and there's potentially some bombs about to explode, so I need everybody we've got to get their asses up there yesterday, you got me?"

"Yes sir!" she said and she was on her mic immediately chasin' down her boys.

Charlie Jones and Steven Speed run out of the police station and are speeding now toward Taft. Steve calls the station and asks for Kevin McKay to try to borrow Gordon, his bodyguard. Louise answers, Sunnyvale PD, can I help you? Steve says, "Louise is Kevin McKay still there?" She says, "I haven't seen him."

Steve says, "Louise I just left there, and I saw him, please page him for me."

Now she tells her officer that "Mr. McKay can't be disturbed." That's it! He knows she's not the sharpest cheese in the tray, but this is ridiculous. Steve says, "Please let Kevin know it's an emergency." McKay picks up and hears the fear in Steve's voice. He readily agrees to send help immediately...

Mr. Mac looked at his cell phone and hit number two on his dial. It didn't ring twice before his personal bodyguard, Gordon picked up. "Yes sir?" He spoke.

Mr. Mac tried to control his speech. He needed to give Gordon clear instructions and quickly. He said calmy, "There's a school shooting still in progress at Taft High. Those Taft boys may be over their heads. Can yo.."

Gordon interrupted,"Handled!" he said and hung up. Kevin knows Gordon is an explosive weapon and he's capable of mass destruction. He hoped he didn't light the wrong fuse.

Next, Mac called Keegan. His timing was perfect because the kids were between classes. He told his son about the Taft problem and then said, "Son get Kyle, Chili, Miles, Sky and anyone else you can round up and get up there NOW. Try to find Sheriff Speed and tell him you guys want to help if they need it. Do what he says and don't be heroes. Be careful but make sure those creeps don't get away!"

In less than 5 minutes Pocket had the whole crew (except Miles) loaded in Black Magic and was flying up the hill to Taft High. Keegan was giving the crew instructions when,

KAAAAABOOM! There was a loud explosion, and thick black smoke was billowing into the sky. It looked like it was coming from the general direction of Taft High. This could be really bad.

Jones and Speed arrive on the scene at Taft. One of the Taft cops hustles over to debrief these guys with the latest status; "Guys, most of the students are trapped in the lunch room and the perps have indicated that the whole lunchroom will blow sky high if any authorities come near. We just had an explosion that appeared to have been in the lunchroom. We'll have an update shortly."

"The perpetrators are two white teenage boys that are on a mad mission. They have already shot 11 students, leaving two dead; Viktor Lopez and Cathy Cool and are holding two other student hostages; Lupe Lopez and Valerie Vixen are bound together, and have obviously both been beaten."

The Taft cop continues to debrief the Sunnyvale cops, "Most of my guys are down at the lunchroom. OK. Our guys were able to extract a bomb and detonate it in the woods below the high school. No casualties are reported. Now, we have to hope that bomb was the only one these jerks planted here."

"The remaining students and teachers are escaping using the students' upper parking lot. It's safe for the moment, and they can be picked up without getting near the shooters. The teachers are helping coordinate getting the kids' parents to get them home safely asap."

The Taft cop continues, "The two perps are avid gamers. This type averages like 30-40 hours a week alone in their bedrooms playing first person shooter games where they get points for killing innocent people and stacking up the bloodied bodies. Looks like these two just decided to play their game for real today."

Keegan's crew found Sheriff Speed and told him they wanted to help. He told Key that it wasn't safe and he sent them to help the teachers. It wasn't far and they could see that the extraction was moving along very well. The teachers were pretty organized and were getting kids out of there as fast as possible, but he sent the crew up there to replace the teachers so they could get out of here too.

His phone rang and he almost didn't answer because he didn't recognize the number, but on second thought he said, "Hello, this is Keegan."

Gordon said, "Key I'm on location at Taft. I was able to detonate one of the bombs in the woods below, but there was another one in the lunchroom and it just blew up. Listen and do EXACTLY what I say. The two jerks that are the problem here didn't expect their bomb to go off when it did. They got knocked around a bit and decided to get out of there. They are heading to the upper lot right now. Warn the teachers quickly and have them get in the cars with the kids and get the hell out of here. Get your crew in Magic and have Pocket pull it up between the perps and the teachers. I'm hoping that will discourage the bad guys from going all the way up there. To be safe, have your crew get out of Magic and help with the evacuation. You and Chili stay in Pocket's ride and be ready to fly out of there if those jerks keep coming your way. Do it now! I'm on my way."

Everyone else has left with the Taft parents' last load of kids. Except Kyle. He's coming their way when he suddenly leans down, picks up a large rock and wings it over Black Magic. He and Chili had been hiding behind the truck and didn't see the two shooters coming up at them. Kyle hit one kid in the head. It was a great shot, and the kid went down hard. His buddy freaked out because now he was alone. The injured perp started moaning, so the upright jerk pointed his gun at his best friend and cursed him. Then he shot him 4 times in the face. He was crying and still cursing his now dead friend. He swung his rifle around to kill himself but was having a hard time reaching the trigger with the barrel in his chest.

Gordon, who was coming up from behind him but was still too far to be able to get to the kid before he could kill himself, pulled the glock out from his belt and made a perfect shot. It hit the kid's shoulder, and the gun fell to the ground. Holding his shoulder, he bent down to retrieve his rifle and never saw Kyle coming. Kyle was flat out movin' because he had to get to the kid before the kid got to his weapon. The kid reached it and was lifting it up when Kyle left his feet and dove full speed into the kid's side. He heard the kid lose his breath and in less than a second, Kyle rolled the kid on top of him and put him in a choke hold with his legs wrapped around the kid's waist.

Kyle yelled, "This jerk is wrapped up and he ain't getting loose. Not today. Not ever. Kyle squeezed the kid's throat hard until he went limp. Kyle could have killed him easily, but he didn't. The lack of Oxygen caused the kid to black out, so Kyle rolled him over and he stood up. Gordon got there in time to remove the rifle. Now, everyone was safe and since no one else was watching, Gord raised the rifle up and swung it down really hard on the kids left knee. He raised it again and destroyed the kid's right knee and then he was gone. Somehow, he was just gone. Maybe he just evaporated, Kyle thought.

It was over. Kyle took a deep breath and let his eyes wander across the mess below. A second bomb went off and this one was in the cafeteria in the middle of the school. Most of the kids that were trapped in there had escaped already, thanks to the Taft police force. This bomb exploded and spread debris all over the grounds, and unfortunately some bodies were found in the cafeteria later. The Taft police force was hiking up the hill and so Kyle turned and bolted for Black Magic. Key saw him coming and the local authorities behind him in hot pursuit, so Key jumped in Magic and spun her around so Kyle could jump in the passenger seat quicker. Kyle was in now and he grabbed Chili before Key took off just as Sheriff Speed reached the hilltop. He didn't ask, but Kyle knew his brother wanted to ask, so he said, "I know, I know. That was probably an evasion citation, but I just didn't feel like answering any questions. Especially questions about that punks' knees."

Key thought about it and said, "Well, I don't think we'll have to wait until the mail comes to find out how much trouble we're in!"

It wasn't that funny, but they needed a laugh, and they laughed hard.

The boys made it down the hill without seeing any police pursuit. Relaxed a little now, Kyle called Gordon who picked up almost before it rang, and Kyle put his call on speaker. Gordon said, "Hey buddy, that was a great midfield stick! You were horizontal and flying for at least 10 feet before you planted your shoulder in that punk's ribs! Your dad would have been proud! But ya know

Kyle interrupted and said, here it comes. I know and I'm sorry but...

Gordon interrupted and said, "I don't have any idea what you could be sorry for. Now me, well I know I'll be sorry when I get the call from Taft's finest to discuss with me what happened to that fine young man's knees, and you know by then he'll be a 'fine young man' to those damn liberals."

Key said, "What are you talking about? But Gordon wasn't answering, so Kyle said," Well, your honor, I don't think I remember seeing Gordon anywhere near Taft that day. I acted alone and I didn't mean any harm. It seems both knees just exploded when I tackled the punk. Oops your honor, I mean when I apprehended the suspect. I mean I was just standing there when he tried to stand up. It sounded like a small explosion and they both just kinda blew up!"

Key said 'no way' and busted up.

Now, Gordon was laughing and ready to talk about it. He said, "Do you have any idea how many perps I have delivered to the police unharmed, and they have been found not guilty of crimes that everybody and their mothers know they committed?"

"It happens WAY more often than it should, so for the last couple of years I've made sure that jerks like that guy pay for their crimes. That punk killed and injured a bunch of small kids that never did anything to him, and some high paid attorney will prance into town and get the punk off on some technicality. You watch. That will probably happen in this case, but this punk won't be walkin' anywhere scot-free. Nope. I made sure he wouldn't be walkin' anywhere ever. This one's gonna pay for his crimes. The truth is, I'll probably visit him again down the road. I knew one of the kids he killed. He shot my next-door neighbor's 6-year-old son in the back. I found him on the steps to the cafeteria and held him until he took his last breath. He was a great kid, and his mom will be devastated. He was her world, but just a target to this punkass piece of crap."

"Oops! Sorry about my language, but I'm not tellin' you the whole truth. See, in my line of work you can't have anyone or anything that is a weakspot for you, so guys like me have no family or loved ones that can ever be found. So, for the record, I hardly knew the neighbor kid and seldom spoke to his mother. But, off the record my neighbor and I live in townhomes. A town home is one of two homes that have one shared wall. We removed that wall when we moved in so basically, we live together."

Key guessed, "Your girlfriend?"

"No fool! She's my baby sister."

"Oh crap! That kid was your nephew?" Kyle asked.

"Yeah guys, that punk took my only nephew's life before he even got to his 7th birthday." Gordon said quietly, "Tommy would have turned 7 tomorrow. My sister's going to grieve for the rest of her life, but I'll be there for my sister. OOPS! She's just my neighbor from here on, ok? Your dad doesn't know I have any family, or he wouldn't have hired me. No vulnerability is permitted when you're a hired gun! It's a lonely life and it just got lonelier."

"But hey, I consider you two my younger and better-lookin' brothers, and I'm very proud of you guys. You were amazing today. I forgot to ask, why'd the first punk go down. I was watching my footing on the way up and I looked up just in time to see the end of his fall, and him get shot."

Keegan said, "are you kidding? You missed one of the greatest throws ever?"

Gordon said, "well I saw the damage your throw did and that was a pretty long shot..."

Key interrupted him, "Gordon, you missed one of the best throws I've..."

But Gordon interrupted him again, "Come on buddy. It was a helluva shot, but one of the greatest ever?"

"Gordon," Key said, "please let me finish. I was saying that was one of the greatest throws I've *ever seen*."

Gordon said, "Wait a minute! Then who threw it?"

Key said, "That's what I was trying to tell you. Kyle was at least 50 yards further away and he picked up the rock on the run and winged it without setting up or anything!"

"Whoa!! Damn Kyle!" Gordon said. "That had to be a hundred yards! That **was** one of the greatest throws ever! Little dude, you've got a cannon hangin' from your right shoulder! That was an amazing throw. Amazing!"

"Thanks guys, but I got lucky." Kyle said. "Key's the one w th a cannon. Did you hear about our last game?"

"Come on guys". Gordon said mockingly. "I work with your dad, so I hear about every one of your games- usually more than once! So yeah, I heard about Keegan's no hitter 5 or 6 times and Kyle's grand slam at least 3 times. Hey, your dad's calling me. We'll talk later." and he was gone.

Kyle said, "Wait a sec. we need to check in with dad. They called him and gave him the lowdown and finished with, we'll be home for dinner.

Their dad said, "Great job today boys. You guys are amazing. Thanks for all your help. I'll see you here 'shortly." Then, before he hung up, he asked, "Hey guys, you never mentioned Miles today. He was there though, right?"

Keegan said, "Actually, no dad. He hasn't been at school much lately and he's missed our last 3 games. I was worried about him and called and left a... Oh crap, I forgot. Last time I called him there was a recording saying, 'you have reached a number that has been disconnected' so I couldn't leave a message. My bad. I called him from the field to remind him we had a game that night and then the game started, and I spaced it completely. I'll call him right now and update you at dinner."

The boys were rerouting their trip because their dad made plans for the family to have dinner at one of the best restaurants around. Now, they were all heading to Houston's for dinner.

The restaurant had to get another chair for their table because their dad forgot that Pocket was with them. Heck, without Pocket this day would have been way different. They had taken his car, Black Magic, to Taft High, and his car was instrumental in their success. Of course, Pocket wasn't exactly the physical fighter type kid, so he had been hiding in the back of the truck from the moment they stopped the car in Taft's parking lot until they pulled into Houston's.

At dinner, Key told his dad that he called again, and Miles' phone was still disconnected, and they talked about checkin' up on him tonight. Then, the boys told their parents all about their day. Moms couldn't believe that one of the two shooters today shot his partner in the face 4 times. She thought that this act of violence was worse than all the rest. She said the others were random, but this one was planned and really horrible.

This was the first time Pocket had heard what was going on outside his car. Hearing those details and matching them with everything he heard the boys say in the middle of the battle, he now had a clearer picture of what actually happened up there.

He blurted out, "Kyle you're a real hero. I heard everything, even everything Gordon said, and both you guys were amazing but...Kyle! That throw took one of those guys out completely and you threw it a mile and hit the target square in the head! And then, you tackled the other guy right after he just shot his friend! You, my friend are an amazing athlete and my hero!"

M's suggested they all change the subject and order dessert.

The **Dessert** was awesome, and the ride home was quiet. Moms turned on the local news to see if there was any coverage of their local massacre. They caught the end of the national news........." school shootings have become an epidemic in the United States. They quoted data from CNN, the United States averaged just over 87 school shootings each year from 2013 to 2021, resulting in an annual average of 28.4 dead and 59.6 wounded. That qualifies school shootings as an epidemic.

They followed up with a report from a local news station in a city that had a school shooting today-the Taft news channel was doing interviews with parents of students from both Taft Middle

School and Taft High School.

Everyone expressed surprise and outrage, but many were aware of the nation's school shootings epidemic. They just couldn't believe it happened here.

Then the FOX News reporter happened upon Charlie Winston, whose son was arrested today. Charlie yelled at the news team, "You want a story? That's why you're standin' around out here isn't it? Well listen up cuz I got your story right here. Maybe I'm an old fool, but I'm convinced that all the killin' my boy has been doin' on the tv screen for the last several months, is what caused my normal, regular kid to try to kill all those kids he used to play ball with. I'm tellin' you my boy was addicted to killin'. He'd come home from school and head straight to his room and wouldn't come out until the Mrs. told him dinner was ready. He was normal at the dinner table, but when he was done, he didn't want to spend any extra time talkin' to us or his sisters like he used to. Instead, he was right back in his room killin' folks again. I'm tellin' ya, it's these games that got my kid in all this trouble. He was a good boy."

Now the reporter, took the mic back and introduced one of the Taft teachers, Miss Violet. She asked Miss Violet if she had noticed any changes in the two boys that had instigated the shootings today, but the teacher said both boys were good students and were always polite. She said she couldn't believe these two boys could have done anything like this massacre.

Next, they interviewed Mr. Smith, the high school social studies teacher, who sounded very smart and had an obvious point of view. He said, "We all should have seen this coming. These school shootings have been happening all over the country, so this isn't just about these two boys. Technology has made video games so real that they are addicting, and that's probably OK when the games are football or baseball, but the bestselling games are very real first person shooter games where people are attacking you in waves from all sides, and they are all trying to kill you, so you fight back and kill them first and you're rewarded, so you keep doing it. And as the years go by the killing gets more real all the time until the line between gaming and reality becomes too faded. I'm not saying these boys didn't do anything wrong, I'm just saying that maybe they didn't know that this time the targets were real people. I'm deeply saddened that we all lost two normal young men today, and a bunch of innocent targets in their game."

I'm just wondering if kids get so used to killing people when they're gaming, that it's a short walk in their heads to killing people at school. Maybe it feels like you're just playing the game. You pull the trigger and blood spits out and the targets go down just like in your room when you're gaming. It looks the same and maybe it even feels the same. You don't know those targets you kill at home and maybe you don't know the people at school either, so they're just more targets. Or, maybe you know the kids at school and you're mad at some of them, and that makes it ok to kill them.

Moms turned the TV off because they needed some positive conversation today, but she heard the fax machine receiving something and went to check it. She returned with an advance copy of the HRH newsletter;

THE RODD REPORT

Hot Rod High's weekly newsletter

Ricky Rodd, Editor

There was a school Shooting and bombing this week in Taft between the high school and middle school. The two shooters were both Taft High students. These atrocities have reached epidemic status, and they need to stop.

The Taft and Sunnyvale Police officers responded and apprehended the two killers. None of the officers were injured. However, one teacher was shot in the face and died in the hospital. The shooters injured 11 students and killed 2.

The bomb that went off in the cafeteria killed 14 students and injured 27 students. So, the totals are 17 dead and 38 injured.

Ricky wrote, 'There's a really fine line that the press has to walk regarding these shootings. That's the line between informing parents and inciting kids. At the same time, I want everyone to know about the incidents because that's the only way to get funding to stop them. The government is suppressing the press coverage of mass school shootings because 1) they don't want kids to think they can get famous or get the attention they crave by shooting kids at school, and 2) they are afraid that parents won't send their kids to school if they know how often these tragedies occur.

But I think parents deserve to know the odds of their children getting killed when they drop them off at school. I'm inserting a couple of statistics here to give our readers a better understanding of the epidemic that is sweeping the country. I'm adding a little product placement notice because it's interesting, so...'

In related news, there is a new product that is flying off the shelves around the country. It's a *bullet proof backpack.* This product is selling out in all the major US retailers, and following you'll find out the reason why!

From 2018 to 2023, 1,073 people were wounded or killed in school shootings according to US NEWS

In 2023 alone, there were 346 school shooting incidents across the country meaning the U.S. averaged nearly one incident every day according to K-12 school shooting database

A 2018 CNN feature tallied 288 school shootings in the United States between 2009 and 2018—the country with the second-most school shootings during that period, **Mexico, experienced only eight** shootings during that same time period.

According to data from **Everytown Research**, the United States averaged just over 87 school shootings each year **from 2013 to 2021**, resulting in an **annual average of 28.4 dead and 59.6 wounded**. That qualifies school shootings as an epidemic.

After the Rodd Report was read, or at least looked at, Moms said "I don't want to hear another word about shooting or death tonight." Grandma agreed. She sensed that her daughter was not ok having her sons in the middle of all that danger, so she changed the mood by challenging the whole family and Pocket to play another game of **King of the Road**.

Within minutes, the game was well underway, and things were returning to normal in the McKay home, but it wouldn't last long.

Deal
Done

Life Lesson; Love your neighbor
but don't take the fence out

Chapter 12
Deal Done

The phone rang and stopped the action on the game board while Mr. Mac took the call. When he hung up, he told the family that he had to run over to HRH to talk with Ricky Rodd before he published his view of the school shooting today. He thought he'd be back in time for bed.

Ricky Rodd was already working on his front-page story for next week, when Mr. McKay showed up in his office. Ricky asked if everyone from Sunnyvale was ok. When Mac confirmed that none of the HRH kids were ever really in harm's way except for Kyle, and his exchanges with the two perps both went his way, Ricky was relieved. He was glad he wasn't put in those situations, but he was very proud of his friends that were. Seems the HRH crew always handle whatever problems come up.

Mac continued, "I came over because it's been a couple of days since we spoke last. Have you had a chance to meet with your dad? Or to consider what option would work best for you? I don't want to push you, but my partners are concerned any time that there are loose ends in the business."

"Can we talk about it?" Mac asks, "Because I have lots of options for you, but many of them are going to require 5 signatures and I need to make sure I'll have enough time to convince my partners that the way you want this to go is the best way. I already promised that I'd help you any way I can, and this is part of that. If I don't keep the timing right, Coynes and Hollenbut may not support our choice and frankly, I'm a junior partner and I'm not powerful enough to keep my promise without at least one of them on our side." Ricky says, "Honestly, Mr. Mac, it's all I've thought about since we last spoke, but I'm struggling to make this call and really feel that I need some input from my dad, and some parameters from you first."

"Well, Mac says, "How about if all we figure out first, is what your ideal solution is. Then I have the starting point I need. How about if you just answer questions for me for a while? Like, where do you want to live? Do you want to live alone. Where do you want to work? What do you want to do for a career? How much money do you need to make a year? Have you considered changing your age in the Tube? Older or younger? Changing your dad's age? Would you want him to get younger or older? Have you thought about maybe a trial period? I think that would be best, but it will probably be the hardest option to get approved, but you let me worry about that. So, Ricky, please answer as many of those questions as possible."

Ricky says, "Ok Mr. Mac, here you go…. I want to live in Sunnyvale. I'm comfortable living alone, but I'd like to try living with my dad for a while if he's ok with that. I'd like to work for Hot Rod High, or at least keep the Rodd Report going. And I'd love to learn how to fix cars, so I'd like to try working with my dad in Raceland, if he's ok with that. I'm thinking that Raceland will need to keep my dad and if he can teach me, he could get some time off. If we're going to work together, we'll always be relieving each other so we won't get much time to spend doing cool stuff, so I'm going to recommend we initiate a training program and use HRH students that love racing and cars. My dad can train them, and Raceland will always have a qualified mechanic on hand. They would be students, so free labor. When we get them trained up enough, my dad and I can get some time off together. Having free help should help bring down the labor cost, but I'd like to see you pass the savings onto my dad and I. He's already worth a lot more and I will get up to speed quickly, so we'll earn our wage, but the increase will allow us some luxuries, like travel and dating. I don't know much yet about minimum wage or the cost of living, out we will be the best mechanics available in Raceland, since it has to remain a secret, so I'd like to make enough to have a middle-class lifestyle. Ideally, a 2 bed 2 bath house with a yard and a puppy and 2 cars in the garage so we can date. Regarding the age thing, I thought about what you said, and as much as I'd love to get a dad out of this, I couldn't ask him to take 20 years off his life, so I'm up for us just trying to live as brothers with him being the older, smarter brother. If it doesn't work and we both end up wanting him to be a dad, couldn't we bump him up 20 years row but stop the aging process there so I will just keep catching up a year at a time? And lastly, I think a 90 day, no commitment trial period would be smart. Mr. Mac, you have a big smile over there, what's up? Am I being too needy? Too lame? What's the deal with that smile?

"That's easy Ricky, Mac says, "That smile is one of great joy. I think you answered every question I asked EXACTLY as I think you should have, so with every answer, my smile got a little bigger because I knew you and your dad were getting a little closer to making a deal that will change both your lives for the better forever and in every way. I'd be happy to present your proposed life/career plan to my partners right away. But first things first We need your dad's approval. Are you comfortable discussing your ideas with him, or would you be more comfortable having me do that step?"

"Oh Mr. Mac, Ricky said, "I'd be terrified of being rejected. That would do irreparable damage if he said no to me. I'll put my faith in you to get the deal done, or if not, to protect me from any hurtful reasons why not."

"Ok Ricky, wish me luck and know that I will explain your wishes exactly as you expressed them to me," Mr. Mac said in a very kind, calm voice and then he gave Ricky a daddy like hug and he was off because he needed to get some rest. As he left the Rodd Report office, he checked his watch, and there went his sleep plan. His watch said he had enough time to do one more thing. Now, he was off to Raceland to find Randy Rodd. He found him out on the side of the Speedway smoking a vape. It smelled like blueberries.

"Hey Randy, I put together kind of a rough outline of how I think we can do the right thing by you and Ricky, while keeping up the maintenance in here, and making my partners ok with everything. Can I run it by you before I share it with Ricky, Mr. Hollenbut and Mr. Coynes?"

Randy said, "Please do Mr. Mac. I'd love to hear your suggestions but don't be disappointed if we disagree, ok?"

"How about if you keep an open mind? Mr. Mac replied, "Or better yet, how about if you tell me what you would propose to The Company to resolve the age differences, the living arrangements, the incomes and the long- and short-term employment plan, time off and some life outside of Raceland?"

"Damn Mac," Randy replied. "It's all those decisions and then some isn't it.?

Mac said, "No. it's not all those decisions and then some. It's all those decisions and one helluva lot more."

Randy was nodding his head, while Mac took the wheel, "Randy, I've taken everything I think I needed to, into consideration, so please hear me out. I'm proposing…. "And he went over the whole plan that he and Ricky had just put together. He closed with, "Whaddya think?"

Randy was a pretty seasoned journeyman after bustin his tail in this grease pit for 20 plus years, and he didn't like talkin' about feelin's and stuff especially with strangers and double especially with male strangers, but that story got to him. The Company was finally going to let him have a life? AND they were going to make that life more than comfortable for both he and the son he never got to know? Randy, had a single tear slowly rollin' down his unshaven cheek and for a change he didn't brush it away in a big hurry. He was feelin' somethin' he wasn't sure he'd ever felt before, but man, did it feel good. He gave Mac a buddy hug and said, "Sir, if you were able to just do half of all that for me and my boy, I would kiss your feet every day for the rest of your life! No shit, I would."

"Well, Mac replied, "I'll see if I can't make that happen because my feet have never been kissed before, and they don't ever need to be, but if I can do anything to make you that happy that you'd be willing to kiss 'em, I'm going to be damn near as happy as you are. I'll be back here as soon as I get the answer I want, but that is likely to take some time, some serious BS'n, some horse tradin' and a lot of butt kissin.' Wish me luck!"

Randy purposely said, "Good Luck Sir!' and he meant it like he never thought he could.

Mac thought to himself as he fell asleep, "halfway there." He slept good last night. Real good.

The whole family was having breakfast and planning their day. Mr. Mac had a 9:00 meeting at The Company's corporate office that overlooks the Sunnyvale Speedway. This was a big one, and his wife could tell he was anxious about it.

Moms said, "Hey Kevin how can you be worried about meeting with a couple of professional businessmen, when your boys are chasing down cold-blooded killers with fresh blood on their hands?"

Kevin replies, "Honey, don't get it wrong. Our boys were dealing with a couple of rogue kids that were likely still bedwetters, and I'm swimming with professional sharks wearing a flesh flavored swimsuit! Nah, I don't think they'd want to switch with me! Seriously, I have to get the guys to approve my Rodd family recommendation because I already convinced Ricky and Randy and they are both down for it so it will be very embarrassing if they veto my proposal and I have to take the deal the Rodds want off the table. I'm pretty sure that deal will stick though. The one I'm really concerned about is the fembots meeting that's 2nd on the morning agenda. Boys, do you have any ideas on how we should handle that issue now that Professor Birmingham screwed that all up?"

Keegan said, "What's wrong with their program. They're doing their job every day and are very professional."

"But wait Key, Kyle says, "Remember they said that they hate it now that they have to work every hour of every day because their programs are wearing out finally and they want to be normal now. Before, when the program was new, it had complete control of their every move and every thought. Now, that it's starting to fail, they can think and it's frustrating them because they want to do some normal things."

"Guys, these things are computers, not girls." Dad says, "It's not like they were girls first and then we programmed their brains to just do these jobs. These fembots are just made to look human, if you touch their skin, it's probably always ice cold. I think we just send them to the scrap pile out back and replace them right away, with new Fembots programmed for life, so we don't have to go through replacing them again."

The boys clearly don't like where their dad's heading on his topic, but he seems to be pretty firm on his position. So, Kyle takes another approach." So, dad, can we have them after you get the new ones? They would be kinda' like pets but you don't have to feed them or walk them and they can talk to you. I want one!"

M's says, "This decision is above my pay grade, but I want to be perfectly up front here...I'm not picking their poop up off the floor!"

Keegan says, "M's these girls are really pretty. They don't poop. I want Suzi! Come on dad! You would be our hero if you brought Sally and Suzi home."

Kyle says, "Come on pops! Your business dudes were just going to throw them in the scrap pile anyway! You have the opportunity of a lifetime to make your boys worship you forever! If you toss Suzi and Sally, I'm running away. I'll try to find them first and maybe they'll run away with me! Yeah, that's what I'll do!"

Their dad says, "Enough already, you weirdos! Get your butts in the car because I can't be late for my meeting."

The McKay boys went straight to the Secret Door because it has kind of become their homeroom or something. It's where the Crew starts their days whenever possible, and everyone is here this morning. Most of them were talking about the school shooting yesterday. They all lost some friends.

Ricky said "Two of the shooting victims were Viktor Lopez and Cathy Cool and they were both in our Family Challenge this year. There is a basket in my office for collecting donations for their families because burials are expensive these days. There were also 2 girls that the perps had taken hostage at the beginning and dragged them around with them."

Chili interrupts, "Crew, those punks tied these little girls up and they were seen actually slugging and beating these girls. Both girls are alive, but they are in Sunnyvale General, rooms 232 and 233. These girls are friends of mine and they didn't deserve this crap, so please let's all get over to the hospital and make sure they have everything they need. Their names are Lupe Lopez and Valerie Vixen, and I'm going to let them know that me and my crew will make damn sure that they are never assaulted again. These are little girls! Man, I'll make sure the punk that lived gets raped in prison, and I usually don't wish that on anyone."

"One last thing that has to be mentioned here. Kyle McKay you are one seriously bad assed dude for a skinny white boy. No, I can't even dis ya like that. You were an American hero yesterday my little buddy. I am glad you're on our team, cuz you, my man is off the freakin' hook. That throw and that tackle were both down bro, the stuff of legends big time. Congrats. You're makin' our crew proud."

Kyle is an incredible athlete, but he gets uncomfortable when he's complimented. He says, "Cool. Thanks." And then he went back to Coynes office. He knows he has some time because he's got Tulz down at the special parking lot for the execs and Tulz will buzz him when the Major gets back. Kyle gets the key to 222 and wheels the laundry cart to the door. He goes into the room and in the back in the scrap metal bin. Sure, enough Sally and Suzi are in here. Sally's still wearing the bracelet he bought her. He stuffs one in each of the oversized laundry bags on the cart and rolls them out of there, leaving everything else exactly as it was when he came in. When he puts the key back, he looks around for Gordon's number. Finds it and writes it on his hand. Then, he gets the heck out of there as fast as possible. He rolls the laundry cart back into the empty football locker room. Pocket agreed to help him get the baggage into the palace tonight. They are meeting in the locker room at 11 and Pocket will help him get the girls into the Palace. Of course, Kyle told him he was just going to fix some of the team's football gear for next season.

At lunch, Keegan forgot all about meeting Kyle to race, he needed to find out what was up with Miles Malone and Pocket was going to take him over there. It was ok though because Kyle forgot too and was busy on a mission of his own...

Keegan directed Pocket over to State Street on the poor side of town. Key was looking for address 2214. When Pocket pulled up to the curb, Keegan got out and told Pocket he better stay with his car, or it might not be here when we get back. Key heard some angry voices when he knocked on the front door. A few seconds later, a fat, dark skinned, middle aged, tatted up woman opened the door, looked Key up and down, and said, "You lost fool?"

Key replied, "Maybe. I'm looking for a friend of mine, Miles Malone. Is he here by chance?" "Damn boy! I was hoping you were lookin' for me. Let me introduce myself, I'm Gypsy Malone, Miles' aunt. Why don't you come in and I'll go downstairs and see if I can find him for ya."

Key said,"Sure." and stepped through the doorway. 'Whoa!' he thought. 'Oh crap. I never should have come here alone.'

There were nine large black men all standing around this big round metal table that had a few freight boxes on top. The boxes were those wax covered cardboard with plastic straps around them and large type letters forming words in a different language. A smaller man with a large hunting knife had cut one of the boxes open, now he put his knife inside the box and when he pulled it out, it had a pile of white powder on it. He dabbed the pile with his pinkie finger after he had wet it in his mouth, then he put his powder covered finger back in his mouth and licked it clean. Then he put the blade up to his nose and snorted that whole pile into his left nostril, shook his head rapidly and then steadied himself and started staring at Keegan. Finally, the man broke the long silent pause and said to Key, "Son, you're that pitcher for HRH. Oh shit! Just turn around and run as fast as you know how back to school. You were never here, and you never saw any of these people, right? I told you to run, right?"

Key nodded, "Yes sir." He said and he knew he should be running right now, but instead, while pointing at the boxes on the table, he said, "Mr. Malone sir, none of this stuff is any of my business and I don't care about it. I just came down here because I'm worried about my buddy, Miles. I can see that now's not a good time, but will you please ask him to call me when you see him?"

It seemed like the whole house was holding its breath in the dead silence following Keegan's request. Finally, Mr. Malone said, "Yeah kid, I'll tell him."

Keegan backed out the door, spun and leapt over the set of stairs and jumped into Black Magic and yelled at Pocket, "DRIVE!" They sped all the way back to school without either boy saying a word.

As soon as he saw coach Cheeks, Keegan told him they needed somebody else to play first this afternoon, because Miles wouldn't be here. Coach looked at him like he smelled bad, and said are you on drugs? You're late for batting practice, but you can head in there now and follow the guy at the plate right now. Key turned and started to run in, when coach said, "Oh, and by the way Keegan, when you figure out who is hitting right now maybe you'll get why I asked you about drugs. Key was so deep in thought that he couldn't really focus on the batter, until the guy hit a rocket that went right past Key's head at about 3 billion miles an hour. This team has some big sticks but there's only one guy that hits laser like line drives like that one, and that's Miles Malone.

Miles takes two more pitches yard, and then steps out of the box. He and Key do that bro hug thing, and Key asked, "Did your dad tell you that I came by?"

Miles said, "You're losin' it buddy! My dad died in the big wreck remember?"

Key thought he saw trouble coming fast, "Does anyone else you know answer to Mr. Malone?"

"Nobody I know," Miles said. My dad's dad died years ago and my dad never had any brothers. Why do you ask?"

Just then, Key saw the man with the knife that was at Miles' house sitting in the grandstand right behind home plate. "No reason" Key said. "Nope, No reason at all."

"Hello everybody and welcome to Sunnyvale. Flash G here this afternoon to call this exciting matchup between two of the best baseball teams in the SE conference. The Hot Rod High Speed Demons have the best team they've ever had, ever. No kidding. HRH has the lowest enrollment numbers in the league because it isn't for everyone. This school has high academic standards and it exists to build the best race car drivers of the future, which means that their athletes already have full schedules after school. Even with their restricted enrollment, the HRH teams have always been competitive, but the expectations have never been as high as they are this season."

"Since the McKay brothers arrived in Sunnyvale and enrolled at HRH, they have made the Speed Demons competitive with the top teams in the league. We're going to find out today if they're good enough at baseball now to compete at the top level because they are playing the only other undefeated team in the SE region, The Talladega Titans. Both teams are 16-0 and the winner of this game will go on to the regionals in Tallahassee. The loser will go home. Both teams have their aces healthy and ready to battle, so we're likely to see a pitcher's battle between Keegan McKay and Seth Johnson. Seth is a senior and 3 time all SE Regional All Star that is being heavily scouted by the big-league teams. It should be a helluva game!"

"Hot Rod High's starting lineup and batting order is;

1. CF Wally Wheeler

2. SS Kyle McKay

3. B Skyler Martinez

4. C Pedro Peppers

5. P Keegan McKay

6. 1B Miles Malone

7. LF Steve Speed

8. 2B Wendy Wheeler

9. RF Ben Hollenbut Jr.

"The Speed Demons have had the same starting line up all season because they have been very fortunate healthwise. In fact, they haven't had a significant injury all year!"

"Keegan gives up a hit in the first inning but strikes out the side after that, so now the Speed Demons will get their chance. Wally Wheeler strikes out, and he looks like he was scared up there today. Here comes Kyle McKay, who has been having an exceptional year. Seth Johnson's not going to scare Kyle. He throws a fastball for a strike and that pitch was movin'! Flash gets the team's manager to show him the reading on the Jugs gun..WHOA! Ladies and gentlemen, that last pitch was timed at 98 mph. That's big-league speed for sure, but Seth isn't going to intimidate Kyle McKay.

Seth's in his windup and he delivers another fastball, but Kyle took the first pitch just to get his timing right so he's ready for it. Kyle takes a big swing and hits a shot between left and center. He smoked that pitch and the left fielder can't catch up to it. The ball rolls all the way to the fence. Kyle's one of HRH's fastest runners and he has already rounded second, when the left fielder finally gets to the ball. He's got a strong arm and slings the ball to the cutoff man, Danny Clark the shortstop."

"Danny went out further than normal because the ball got all the way to the fence, so he's got a long throw to the plate. Kyle's around third and halfway home when Danny releases a great throw to the plate. It's just a little high and to the catcher's right. Kyle slides headfirst as the 'Dega catcher makes the catch and turns for the tag. Tommy Stinson swings the glove as quickly as he can. It's going to be close. We're waiting for the plate umpire to make the call and he's waiting for the dust to settle. Now, the ump stands up and makes the call by swinging both arms in a crossing motion and then barks, "Safe!" The HRH crowd goes wild!"

"The game has gone as expected, with a pitcher's duel. Both these young guns are throwing big league pitches, and the hitters have only managed to get 4 baserunners for each team. It's still 1-0 at the top of the ninth, and the Titans are at the bottom of their order with their number 8 batter coming to the plate. Timeout! Coach Martinez is bringing in a pinch hitter. Key gets him swinging for the first out. Then, he throws 3 straight fastballs by the 9th hitter for the second out."

"With two outs, the Talladega Titans are back at the top of their order. Danny Clark takes a breaking ball for a called strike. He laces the next pitch to right field where Junior tries to use that glove that's been hanging on his left hand. He manages to knock the ball down, but by the time he gets the ball to the infield, Danny slides safely into second. There are two outs, so Danny is going to be running as soon as the ball is hit."

Coach Cheeks calls for an intentional walk. That's a great move because it puts the force out back in play and you take the bat out of Joey Tudor's hands. The problem you have now is that Jim Swanson is coming to the plate with 2 runners on. He's the Titan's best hitter and is second in home runs behind only HRH's own Chili Peppers. Key pitches him carefully and now he has a full count. He looks at the on-deck hitter and decides he'd rather face him. He throws the next pitch low and Swanson takes it for ball 4.

The bases are loaded for Greg Virant. Coach Cheeks calls a timeout to talk with his ace. Key is smiling and shaking his head up and down. He likes whatever it was that Coach Cheeks called. Key goes into his stretch. He glances over his back, then he whips the ball sidearm to Skyler at third for the pick off, but Danny's cleats knock the ball out of Skyler's glove and Skyler can't find it. Danny takes off for home and Sky still hasn't found the ball.

Kyle was behind Skyler backing up the pick off play. The ball came straight to him out of Sky's glove. Kyle lines it up and throws a strike to the plate. Danny slides headfirst with the tying run, but Chili has the plate blocked perfectly. He makes the catch and swings his glove right at Danny's incoming hands. The umpire is in perfect position to see the play, and when the dust clears, he signals the runner is......out! HRH gets a win and will advance. Keegan outduels Seth Johnson in a great pitcher's battle.

HOORAH! For the HRH Speed Demons!

Coach Cheeks is elated. This will be the first time in his 30+ years in coaching that he will be bringing a team to the SE Regionals, and he knows he's got a good chance to win it all. He says, "congrats guys. Great win. I'm buying pizza for everybody, including the fans and parents. Hell, I'll even buy Flash G some pizza!"

Every player is giving Kyle props for scoring the only run in the game, and they're all giving Key his 'flowers'. Kyle notices that Keegan doesn't look very happy for a guy that just outpitched the stud that Sports Illustrated picks to go first in the MLB draft this year. Kyle's trying to get his brother's attention to congratulate him, but Key is staring at the stands. Finally, he notices Ky and they slap gloves. Kyle says "Hey K...

He's interrupted by Seth Johnson the opposing pitcher, who says, "Hey Keegan, great game dude! You are as good as all the scouts have been saying. I'd be proud to switch jerseys with you if you're down with that." Key quickly replies, "Oh heck yeah! Seth, you're every bit as good as they say you are dude! I'd be proud as heck to do the jersey swap thing. As they change jerseys, Keegan says, "Are you excited about the draft? And you got a team you're hoping drafts you?"

Seth is getting called away, but he replies to Key, "Yeah, I'm excited. Just hope those owners listen to their scouts. And, I don't really care which league or team, but I would like to play for a team in the SE just because we're spoiled down here with weather and the sunshine's a lot better for your arm than the cold. You take care of that arm and I'll see ya in the bigs man."

Keegan says, "Good to meet ya and best of luck in the draft."

Keegan should be glowing with pride, Kyle thought. He just got major props from a future big-league star. Kyle wanted to say,

Hey, what about me dude? I scored the winning run and made the play that clinched the game for us? But he understood. pitchers' kind of have their own brotherhood. He couldn't believe that Key was so casual about the compliments Seth Freakin' Johnson just gave him. He's still lookin' at the stands. Something's bugging his brother but he'll wait for Key to bring it up.

Keegan can't help wondering who that guy was at Miles' house, and why was he at the game today? Key felt like the guy was stalking him. Plus, Miles showed up for the game today, but where has he been the last few days? And what's going on with the stolen car story? And at his house? He had lots of questions but so far, no answers. Both boys rode with their parents to the pizza place. M's was in the car and Key asked her about the Malone car again.

This time she said that Detective White had received some intel that the car in question was involved in a drug transaction but she really had no idea what that was all about.

Kyle asked his dad what happened at his meeting this morning, and Mac was expecting to be quizzed. He replied, "we agreed to terms with the Rodd guys, so they are going to get a new home and a couple of cars, and Randy is going to teach Ricky how to work on cars. Randy is also going to continue to be the only adult in Raceland, and he's going to start up a school to train guys how to be mechanics so he and Ricky can get some time off together.

I met with them this afternoon and when I told them, they got very emotional. Ricky is thrilled to have a dad, even one that's only a couple years older. And Randy gets his son back, keeps his job and gets a house where he can live with his son. The Major is going to build the house for them next door to HRH."

"That's great!" Kyle said, "but I was asking about the fembots.

To tell you the truth, all I've been thinkin' about is you bringing Sally and Suzi home for me and Key."

New
Fembots

Life Lesson; When you're young, you want to be rich
when you're rich, you want to be young

Chapter 13
NEW FEMBOTS

You know, Mac says, "you guys have been awfully quiet about the Strange sisters lately. What's up with that? Don't tell me that you guys didn't notice the difference." Mac says almost tauntingly.

Kyle replies, "What are you talking about dad? I mean maybe they changed a tiny bit. Yeah, I noticed a little change. They're not complaining about their hours and stuff as much, but I figured they probably got in trouble for that too."

Mr. Mac says, "What do you mean, too?"

"Well, Kyle says thoughtfully, "it seemed to me that just a couple of days after Professor Birmingham told the whole world they were fembots, the girls stopped being quite so friendly. To be honest, I think they were replaced or got new programs or whatever. Didn't you notice anything different Key?"

Keegan is unsure what Kyle is trying to do with this conversation, so he replies very suspiciously, "Dad, they definitely changed right about when Kyle said. They stopped flirting with us completely and there were a couple of days when they kind of recognized us, but didn't remember any of our conversations before. Now that I think about it, it was like we had to start over with them, and it never really has been like it used to be. I just figured that they got in trouble for getting so friendly, but I really miss the way they were. They made Raceland a whole lot more fun."

Kyle said, "Yeah dad. Can't you guys let them go back to how they were?" They are back to how they were before they became our friends, but it sucks because they made Raceland personal with their personalities. Now, they don't have personalities. I'm glad you brought this up dad because I think you're admitting we got new ones. We did, didn't we? But why..Oh I get it. You didn't tell us because you know we really liked them, and we wanted you to bring them home if they got fired or replaced or updated or whatever. I'm right, aren't I dad?"

Mr. Mac said, "Yeah guys. I thought we'd be having this conversation a week ago. I'm surprised you guys didn't notice and complain right away. A lot of your friends did, and you're right. Everyone wants the old ones back and I've been trying to talk Mr. Coynes into having our programmer just tighten up the old programs instead of using the new fembots. The rub is that those things cost one whole heck of a lot of money. Just one of them costs us more than double what our house cost! And Gordon Doucette doesn't have a return policy, which means we are stuck with the new ones now."

Both boys look very disappointed and seeing them sad gets to him every time. Kevin McKay is a great dad, and he loves his boys as much as any dad anywhere in the world has ever loved their kids. He wants to fix this so bad it hurts, but he's stuck. Coynes spent $3 million dollars on these new improved fembots and he can't get his money back. Mac doesn't know what to do. Finally, Mr. Mac said, "boys, you know I love you and would do anything for you, but I'm not the only boss at Raceland and Mr. Coynes has already told me to 'drop it.'

They look like they're going to cry.

He can't take it. Damn it! "Alright, listen, I'm willing to

try to find some middle ground, but it's not going to happen overnight. I'll need you two to think this all the way through like you own The Company, and make a presentation to me that gives me ammunition to go fight for you. If you can prove there's a reason to throw away $3 million dollars just so our hostesses can be a little more flirtatious, I promise I'll present it and I'll fight for you. Deal?"

And he walked out. Mr. Mac hates to see his boys this sad and he just couldn't take the looks on their faces for one more second. He stopped in the middle of the hallway, turned back to say, "We don't have much time before this is irreversible, so you guys better get on this today!"

Keegan looks at his brother with some hope quickly replacing the sadness in his face. "Kyle, Did you hear what I heard?"

Kyle says, I'm just guessing here but, he starts singing "A child, a child somewhere in the night?"

Key says, "That was pretty funny, but no, dad said *"before* this thing is irreversible" which to me means that it's still reversible right?"

"Sounds right to me, so let's reverse it!" Kyle says. But how are we going to do that? Wait a sec Key. I have an idea, and I think it's a good one. I'll be right back."

With that, Kyle takes off after his dad and finds him in the kitchen. He says, "Dad if you want us to create a story for why we want, what we want...well that's one thing. But if you want us to give you a proposal to take to Mr. Coynes for how to get what we want based on the financial restrictions and the social implications, well, we will need more information. I think we need to pick your programmer's brain. Think you can arrange that?"

"Wow Kyle!" Mr. Mac said. "That's a very mature and smart way to approach this problem. I'll see what I can do."

Kyle didn't think he should mention that he had Gordon Doucette's number already and had been talking to him daily for a week or so. The cool thing is that once his dad gives him the number, Kyle won't be so stressed out about getting busted for his previous contacts with GD. That was the only way he could have got caught for kidnapping Suzi and Sally, except.. Kyle's thinking to himself...

Well, come on man. I had to tell one person. I needed a lookout to cover me when I went into Mr. Coynes office, so I asked Jr. to hang out in the executive parking lot and to page me if Mr. Coynes showed up. But that wasn't really a concern because Jr. didn't even ask me why.

I did tell Pocket though. How else could I move the bodies? I couldn't do that by myself. I don't have a car, so I needed Pocket to help me get the girls to the Palace. I told him we were moving football gear, but I don't think he believed me. But he can keep a secret, so I'm still ok right?

Oh, well and I had to tell one other person. I couldn't help it. I had to tell Dub, Wendy Walker's little brother because the Walkers own the Palace, and I needed their permission and a key. I knew my buddy, Dub would come through with that stuff, and he doesn't talk to anybody, so my secret's safe with him for sure, right?

So, ok. I told two, maybe three people. Oops! Hold on. Hold freakin' on! How was I supposed to take Sally and Suzi apart? I didn't have the tools, but I knew somebody that did! So, I had to tell my little buddy, Stanley Tulz. He's quiet as a mouse, so he's never going to tell anyone right?

So, ok look, no big deal. I only told 3 or 4 people, but I knew I could count on them to keep a secret, right?

Ok, so something went horribly wrong here. It seems now that pretty much everybody at HRH knows something's going on with the fembots, but there's no way that anyone suspected that I was behind it, I've always been a good kid. I never get in trouble or anything right?

Ok, well at least people don't think I stole the girls, right? Everyone would naturally assume that I was just working for The Company, right?

Well, all of those questions were answered at once when Keegan said, "Hey Ky, we still need to race on the oval again. Let's meet at the Secret door today at lunch, and you'll find out that I let you have that one! Key started walking away but stopped, turned and looked Kyle straight in the eyes and said, "Oh yeah and say Hi! To Suzi for me!" He chuckled as he walked away.

That changes everything! He was hoping that he could get Gordon to make them human and he and Keegan could each have one at home. Think about it. An absolutely gorgeous girl, that's smart and fun, cool and athletic, playful and intelligent, etc. that will grant your every wish! No more cleaning your room. No more homework. Someone to scratch your back when it itches. Someone who'll do all your shopping for you. Someone to play video games with. He and Keegan were going to have life made and he couldn't wait. But now what?

He was going to get busted and probably be on restriction for a whole year! No sports. No TV. No Raceland. He had to come up with a plan to integrate what he has done so far into the presentation he was making for his dad.

He called Gordon Doucette and he answered. Kyle started in with how he and Key both had crushes on Sally and Suzi and he was just warming up when GD cut him off. "Yeah kid, he said "Your dad told me all about it. I actually flew down here today to help you, but I'm delayed at the airport. For some reason, my plane was towed through a dark hangar on the way to the gate. This happened the last time too, and I learned my lesson. I'm not asking any questions. I asked what this procedure was for last time, and I was detained by airport security for hours. I've flown around the world and never have seen this equipment anywhere else, but this airport doesn't show up on any flight logs or anywhere so I'm happy to be here and Gordon, your dad's bodyguard is taking me to the Palace, so I'll meet you there asap. Well, that call was good and bad. Now he knew that his dad knew that he had stolen the fembots from Major Coynes' office. There were going to be some serious ramifications for that for sure. But help had arrived to save the fembots.

The McKay brothers got back from racing in time to hear the bell ring for their next class, but they ran into Ricky Rodd in the hallway. The dude was floating on an invisible cloud and cruising through Heaven. He grabs both the boys at once and hugs them. Ricky says, "You guys have the best dad in the world. Any chance I could have him adopt me? He is really an amazing man. You have no idea how smart he is and the dude gives a damn about the little people and all kinds of other cool crap. I hope you two appreciate what you have!"

"Wow Ricky, that's nice to hear. I'll tell him you had kind words for him today," Key says. "He told us that he had to battle his partners to get you what you wanted, but they ran out of excuses after a while and ended up going the extra mile for you and your dad. They are building you a really cool pad right next door to our school here. And I have a secret that nobody knows but me. My dad signed a deal yesterday with Professor Birmingham's landlord. I guess he's getting canned for spilling the fembots deal, and he'll be gone by the weekend so you and your dad can move in right across the street starting day after tomorrow. Act surprised because he hasn't even told his partners he did it yet. He said he paid for it personally because he knows his partners are too cheap and he felt like you deserved everything they can do for you. He's not an easy hand to read, and harder to impress but he had high praise for both you and your dad. Hope you make his choices come out good because he does a lot of cool things for people and they forget who got them started sometimes."

"Guys, Ricky cheerfully says, "I'll never forget what he did for me and I thought about it long and hard and I'm going to nominate him for Sunnyvale's citizen of the year this year because I can't find anything, anywhere that he's ever done in his life that wasn't 100% for the right reasons. He's totally earned everything he has and still works his butt off to do things the right way."

"He spent lots of late hours last week meeting with me and lots more hours with my dad just to learn what *we wanted* to happen, and then he went to the other two kings and he fought for us and finally got us everything we asked for and much more. He's a prince and now I know why you guys are turning out to be such great guys. I hope you're proud of him" he said as he kind of wandered away. If Ricky had turned around as he was leaving, he would have known from their glowing faces, cheek splittin' smiles and how they were both standing a little taller, that Keegan and Kyle McKay were very proud of their father. He did hear them both say, "Thanks Ricky."

Ricky never really noticed before, but both his boys have

Mr. Mac's style, confidence and strength. Damn, I'm jealous he thought! And thanks to their dad, he was finally going to get to know his dad, and man he can't wait.

Keegan spotted Miles down by the Secret Door and said to Kyle, "Hey bro, I'm going to take Miles out to Raceland. I could use some help with him because I'm afraid we're losin' him, and we really need him for the game. We'll probably race a time or two out there. So, can you join us?"

Kyle replied, "Um, I see a friend of mine down the hall that I kinda lost my connection with. Mind if I bring her along?"

Key turns around and is scanning the crowd down the hallway until his eyes light up when he sees who Kyle's talkin' about. Key says, "Sure bro, but you know she's a couple years or something older than you, and she is smokin' hot. You really think she'll come with you?"

Kyle says, "Maybe. I'll let you know shortly."

Just a couple minutes later, the four of them were talking with the Strange sisters. Kyle thought, 'This would really be awkward if these bots were really Sally and Suzi. The fembots that replaced them have zero personalities. They're just a couple of crusty, computer headed lames, but they do look almost exactly like the Strange sisters.

As soon as they all got back together after their Tube rides, Keegan started ribbing Kyle, "You're not runnin that old, run down, knuckle draggin Royal Renegade out there again today, are ya? If you do, I'll bet I beat ya like a drum."

Miles said, "Hey, you should be thinking about what car you're racing today, Keegan, or Sammy and I might beat ya both."

"Come on Miles! You know better than that," Keegan

says. "Racing is a dangerous game. I've picked my car before I even know who I'm racing brother, but I don't usually tell my competition in advance which car I've selected to humiliate them with on that particular afternoon. But since you're obviously concerned about it, I'm going to make an exception for you. Of course, it's only going to make you sweat a little early, but ok buddy. Today my three opponents, you will be looking at the tail end of the **Dark Night** out of Electric City in the great state of Washington! She's a goer and it'll be tough for any of you three to even be in that picture when she crosses the finish line this afternoon."

Miles says, "Bad news for ya buddy, but that boat you're going to embarrass yourself in this afternoon, ain't even gonna be in the game today son! You won't be able to see us except each time we lap ya out there. I'm going to be holdin on tight to the steering wheel just to keep from flyin' out the back of this beast. This afternoon, you'll be chasin' the electric orange "Sons of Anarchy" hailing from Oakland, C.A... Like the Sons say, "If we can't beat ya, we'll beat ya up!""

Sam pretends that she's Flash G, and says, "This ain't the first time the rookie record holder for this distance, will be showin' off against the local boys. Ladies and Gentlemen, please welcome the incomparable legend, Ms. Samantha Speed. Thank you, thank you. I'll be flyin' around that oval out there today behind the wheel in "Knockout" straight outta Knoxville, Tennessee." She bows!

"Well, the three of you are gonna regret all the bs that's been comin' out your mouths here this mornin' so I'll just let my superior racing skills do all the talkin' today," Kyle says. "You three will just be racin' for second this afternoon. But don't worry! It will be over soon. I'm just gonna get out front far enough that I'll be able to coast the last ¼ mile today, so don't waste any time lookin' for me. I'll be driving 'Elusive' out of Dodge City, Kansas. I don't want you to worry about why Sunnyvale invited Marshal Dillon down here to present the trophy to the winner today, but rumor has it that he is planning on taking that hardware back to Kansas with him. Good luck out there today!"

Now, our friends walk out to their cars that are all lined up on the starting line of the Mile Oval. They get a nice round of applause from the excited fans here at Raceland. Kyle, grabs Sam and spins her toward him. When they are face to face, he whispers "Good luck today pretty girl. I'll wait for you at the finish line!"

She breaks free and says, "We'll see." as she slides into her car.

It's a weekday morning, so Flash G won't be calling this race but Jr. needs the practice so he'll be doing the honors. And without Shelby, our racers will be starting using the lights, and they're off!

Little Ben Hollenbut Jr. starts with, "Wow! Looks like those 4 are in a hurry this morning. They will be passing by us 5 times today, before I can announce the winner, but if it ended right now, Ms. Speed would be your winner, ladies and gentlemen. Now, they are coming down the homestretch after a quick lap. Samantha, with what has become a good lead, seems to be having it her way so far today, but they've still got plenty of time to catch her. I'm guessing these guys know that you can never let a leader have an easy lead or you're done. Here at Hot Rod High, they teach you that one of the racers has to get up and push the leader or this race is over."

"For some crazy reason, these drivers have let Sam set the

pace and cruise comfortably. No one has pushed her at all and she looks like she's going to win this one wire to wire, as they are all on the backside straightaway on their 5th and final lap today. Oh, now they're waking up! Miles just shot up and has already caught Sam. Now, Keegan has pulled up near the lead as they start around the far turn, with Kyle still off the pace. Now, heading for home, they are all slammin' that skinny pedal down and whoa! Kyle McKay has jumped out in front now by a couple of lengths with a ¼ mile to go. Now, Sam is pulling ahead. Now Kyle has the lead. Oh my! It's too tough for me to call. Kyle had the last clear lead, but the finish had all 4 cars bunched up at the wire."

"Hold on. We'll have the photo of the finish up here in the booth any minute. Here it is. I'm taking it out of the envelope, and we have a clear winner ladies and gentlemen by less than half a car length. And the winner is Kyle McKay." From there, it looks like it goes Samantha Speed, Keegan McKay and last, Miles Malone in a very close finish. I swear there are 4 cars in the picture, and no one is ahead by more than ¼ car length. Great race guys!!"

Kyle gets out of his car and he's pretty sure he got lucky and won, but he didn't hear Jr.'s call so he tentatively heads toward Samantha. She's pissed off about something and is very animated in her chewing out of Kyle. Then, she stopped and did she just? No. That didn't happen. She was pissed off a second ago, but then she gave Kyle a kiss and they are heading toward the crowd arm in arm. They get there, and Kyle takes the customary bow, and Samantha stands next to him applauding. Those two have big smiles as they head back to school. Congratulations Kyle McKay on a great win aboard Elusive!

Keegan and Miles catch up to them at the Secret Door and

congratulate Kyle.

Miles gives him a high five and Key said, we left her out there alone with the lead for just a little too long, but you timed your jump perfectly bro. Nice Racing! And he whispers now, "Saw that kiss too little bro. What's up with that?" Kyle smiles and heads to class with his arm around her.

Miles and Key are waiting out front of Hot Rod High for Pocket Change to pick them up. They have already been upstairs to meet with Mr. Mac and Gordon and now, they are going to pay a visit to the phony Mr. Malone at Miles' house. Pocket pulls up to the curb and says, "This better be important Key because it's not like we're going to Raceland. I'm missing my Acceleration class and Seasons tells me that's the stuff I need to work on if I'm ever going to win a race in Raceland. Do you guys think I've got a chance? Ever? Even a really slim one?"

Miles, rolls back in his seat and laughing loudly he says, "Oh, hell no Pocket!" "Win a race? No. No, that ain't gonna happen sport. Finish a race? Maybe. Probably not soon, but you know someday, maybe. No promises though." Pocket looks like he's going to cry. Keegan comes to his rescue, "He's just messin' with ya little buddy. Heck, you probably could have beat him today! He came in last, and a girl beat him!"

Miles sees how fragile Pocket is on the subject so he tries to smooth it over. "I was just teasing Pocket. I think you have your work cut out for you, but I believe that anybody can do anything if they want it bad enough to work hard for it. So as Jimmy Valvano says, "Don't give up. Don't ever give up.""

"Who the heck is Jimmy Valvano?" Pocket asks.

Miles fakes like he can't believe it, "Oh man! You never heard Jimmy V.'s speech? Where the hell you been boy? Listening to motivational guys like that is exactly what you need. Pull over. I'll play the end for ya."

They are parked now, and Miles says, "Pocket, this man was one of the winningest college basketball coaches ever, and he's dying of cancer. From the hospital bed he starts a foundation to raise money for cancer research that is still doing a phenomenal job today. Anyway, so now the guy is at the end. He knows that the next breath he takes will be his last, and he uses that last breath to give hope to other people battling cancer. His last words were, "Don't give up. Don't ever give up!" I'm gonna get it on YouTube for you right now. He gets it cued up on his phone and hands it to Pocket. He and Key are completely quiet watching Pocket Watch Jimmy V's famous speech. Miles knew he was going to be wrong on some of the specifics, but Pocket is sucking up every syllable Jimmy utters. When it's over, Pocket has tears streaming down his face and he's too moved to even try to hide 'em. "Wow!" That's all Pocket could say. And, they silently get back on the road en route to Miles Malone's house.

Keegan breaks the silence, "Pocket pull over for a sec, will ya?" Then he turns to face Miles, whose sitting in back, asking him, "So, what happened to your house bro? I mean, I spent the night there with you just a couple of months ago and the place was spotless and everything looked normal. Now, it's obviously a drug house. I mean the guys I saw were killers dude and they might have had a million dollars' worth of drugs stacked up on the table."

"Come on Key, that's not my fault. Miles says, "I didn't exactly invite them in ya know."

"I know Miles, Key says "but how did those druggies know your dad was gone, and there was no one to keep them out. And I don't think all those huge guys got the same wrong address for the local gym. Jus sayin."

"Keegan you don't understand it and I hope you never do. Miles says "You got to grow up in the hood to understand the hood, ya know? I mean the street rules are simple…you take whatever you want and make the owner try to get it back. You hurt anybody and everybody that gets in your way even if you're not goin' that way. You know you can't win so you cheat and win and you dare em all to say anything different. Everything you see no matter where you are is yours for the taking and you're gonna just take it as soon as you're sure you want it. Then you'll destroy anybody or anything that tries to stop you.

I admit that both my parents were killed in a newsworthy event. But I gotta be honest, most homes in my neighborhood are not equipped with 84" big screens in every room. No. Most people don't have a tv of any size that works because poor black men have a habit of puttin' their fists through the damn things, but even if the tv works, the people there more than likely don't have cable you getting this? Because these brothas aren't getting the newspaper delivered, they haven't paid their phone bill, the cable bill, the electric bill, let alone rent. etc. so most news isn't easily shared in the hood. If it ain't easy, it ain't getting done.

Now, here's the part that's really messed up. Regular news isn't shared in the hood, but BAD news is a whole 'nother matter! That stuff everybody will hear within an hour. I have lived there from jump but I'm still not **sure** how it happens, but I know if somebody got evicted 5 minutes ago there will be 100 'sifters in their house right now going through their stuff. Somebody abandons a stolen car on your corner, there will be 9 families livin in it before those spinny hubcaps quit spinnin.

My best guess is it's those 6–11-year-old delinquents with the long afros and oversized sneakers with big holes in their jeans, that never get off their little brother's old stingray bike with the banana seat and the ape hanger handlebars that you run into everywhere you go. Now, I don't know if it's just one guy that just flies around and never stops movin' or if there's a whole fleet of these crumbsnatchers that have blocks that they're responsible for. I just know bad news travels damn fast on the street.

I was a little off my game when that wreck happened at the track but after I helped you I finally found my parents and they were both dead. Dude, it felt like some huge hammer hit me in the stomach. I lost my breath and just fell to the ground. I laid there next to my dead parents crying for hours. That is partly how all those bangers got the jump on my house. Shortly after I stood up, I saw your grandma and she needed a ride. I had already taken the car keys out of my dead dad's pocket. Then I offered to help her get home. I knew that the word was out already, so there would be bad people in my house. See my mom's baby sister Gypsy moved in with us a couple months before and she is an addict and a ho. She was already livin' in the basement and had all kinds of lowlife, lazy unemployed types showin' up and sneakin' in down there.

Those street creatures are like cockroaches, when one of them hears you comin' and starts to run BOOM they all get the news and every last one of 'em is hiding before you can smash one with that shoe you have in your hand. So, I knew Gypsy would hear the news and I was pretty sure that she would have already moved into my parent's room and taken over the house.

So, I told your grandma to just drop me off and she could

drive the car to your house. I knew it wasn't the gentlemanly thing to do. Heck, I knew she was new in town and didn't even know her way home yet, but bro I also knew better than to take her home first and then park that car at my house. It would have been stolen before I made it to my front door.

I figured it would be safe by your house until I could come get it the next day, but I didn't make it the next day. When I went into my house my aunt Gypsy was entertaining. I worked my way through the party and passed people shootin up and some smokin' that fentynol, and one girl was completely naked dancing like some kinky hooker. I finally got to my room and there was some fat dude passed out in my bed. I couldn't wake him so I went to my little sister Maria's room. She was curled up in the corner while some couple was having sex on her bed. I whispered please don't cry and grabbed her and started running. I ran out of my house and down my street and I kept running and I ran as far as I could. We fell asleep on a park bench. Are you getting the picture? Cuz I'm tired of painting it."

Keegan doesn't respond at all. He's stunned and maybe for the first time in his life, he can't think of anything to say.

Miles takes over and tells Pocket, "Get us to my house as quick as you can big guy. We're supposed to meet someone there.

When they get there, they all jump out. Pocket starts to come along. Key says, "Lane" and Pocket is listening as hard as a person can listen now because Key hasn't called Pocket by his real first name forever, so he knows Key is serious. Key repeats, "Lane. You need to stay in the car because this situation is extremely dangerous and we may need to escape in a flash, so keep it running and the doors locked until we come out, ok?"

"Yeah, yeah. I know I'd just be in the way." Pocket says,

feeling sorry for himself. Miles, it turns out is a big softy and he says "Ok. Ok, you can come with us but stay behind me with your key fob in your hands, alright?"

Miles is leading the way and they're going in, even though Keegan knows that it's a bad move.

As soon as they all get in the house, our team knows they're screwed. All the drugs are still there on the table and those giant black men without their shirts on are accidentally flexing muscles bigger than our boys have ever seen. This time, Key notices that everyone in the room is packin', except of course, our three minimusketeers. His stomach is getting really upset and he feels like he's about to be sick. Then, the littler kinda' Spanish looking dude who called himself Mr. Malone last time Key was here, turns and slugs Miles's square in the mouth. His legs start wiggling. Oh crap! He knows this feeling and it's all bad. Miles collapses on the floor and in less than a second, Key and Pocket are knocked out next to him.

When he comes to, Keegan is tied to a chair and one of those black guys is actually peeing on him! His stomach can't take it another second so Key turns to face the bully that's peeing on him and he lets it rip. He pukes up what has got to be at least a month's worth of junk food because it buries the one guy's penis and it's still coming out, so Key stands up as much as he can while he's tied to a chair, and starts spraying all these bullies with puke. His stomach is emptied, so he closes his eyes and braces for the punches he knows are coming.

He can hear Miles crying and it hurts his soul. He tries to get the chair off his back by slamming his body backward against the wall. On his second try, the chair busts into kindling and he starts throwing round houses at the big men still there, and he's connecting. He has knocked two of them out and the rest seem to have left the building. He gets his balance and steps out into the daylight on the front porch and he can't believe his eyes.

Every one of the men that were in the house when they arrived is face down on the sidewalk with their arms tied behind their backs. Key recognizes the two Sunnyvale cops who were at Taft last week. They have their weapons out and pointed at the men on the ground. Somehow this doesn't look right.

There are two young cops with their guns drawn standing over 10 men, and 9 of them are huge. He can't quite figure out how this went down, but his answer is about to come. He sees Gordon, his dad's bodyguard and international martial arts legend standing at the end of the line of bodies. G asks Key if he's ok. He says "fine, but where are Miles and Pocket?"

G tells Key that Miles and Pocket are both resting comfortably in the back seat of Black Magic, and Keegan finally relaxes a bit. Now, he asks Gordon which two of the guys on the sidewalk are the ones he knocked out.

Gordon doesn't mean any disrespect because it was awfully brave of Key to face these grown men, but he can't help laughing. He finally stops and asks, "Key what are you talking about?"

So, Key tells him what he remembers. He says "I came to and I was tied to a chair face down and one of these bullies was peeing on me. I started puking and spraying all these guys with it. I managed to get up, so I slammed backward into the wall a couple of times until the chair kind of exploded against the wall, and I started throwing roundhouses at those bullies. I know I got two of them because I felt two connect. Then, I guess I went out again because when I opened my eyes everyone was gone."

G says, "You sure one of those guys peed on you? Because I don't see any wet parts of your clothes, and come to think of it, none of these punks has any throw up on them either."

Key looks at all the guys on the ground and asks G to help him roll a couple over. They do, but there isn't any vomit in sight.

Then G says, "Key take a look at the back of my left arm and then at the left side of my back next to my tank top. Do you see any marks at all?

Key says, "Yeah, there's a couple little red marks in both places."

G says, "Buddy that's where both your roundhouse punches landed. When I came into the house all three of you were out cold and were tied to chairs. I cut you all loose and went to work. After a couple minutes, I was just finishing their last guy and I felt you hitting me in the back. I just ignored it and started dragging the bodies out. I saw you lying on the floor again and just let you sleep while I carried out the 10 tough guys."

Key is confused. He did throw a couple punches but everything else he just imagined? He says, "G, how could that have happened? I remembered my part of the fight differently than what really happened. I'm glad that some of what I thought happened didn't happen though because I was really ticked that one of those guys peed on me."

"Keegan," G said, "You were sleepwalking. Your mind wanted you to be knocking those guys out, so it told you that you did. Your mind is a powerful weapon. Think about it. You were still unconscious but got up and threw punches! I'm impressed. Of course, it would have been a little cooler if you had hit them instead of me, but I intentionally put my body between you three and those guys so you guys wouldn't get hurt anymore. Speaking of that, you got popped pretty good and you have a pretty ugly black eye to show for it. When your adrenaline slows down, you're going to have a helluva headache, but I'm proud as all get out of, ya man. You faced the enemy, knew you were outmanned and fought hard, nonetheless."

"Next time, wait until I get there will ya?"

Author's interruption: Today is Monday December 16th and just a couple of hours ago, at 11:00 AM EST, a young girl walked into a study hall at her small K-12 school in the NE corner of the US and opened fire. She killed a substitute teacher and a teenager. Another teacher and 5 other students were shot, and two of those victims are still in critical condition. This is the 9th time that a female student has committed a school shooting since the massacre at Columbine in 1999, but there have been many hundreds of these school shootings committed by males in the same time period. I have been tracking these the best I can, but our press has to walk a fine line between informing parents and inciting our kids. The government is suppressing the press coverage of mass school shootings for good reason. They want them to stop. We don't want kids to think they can get famous or get the attention they crave by shooting kids at school. Another real concern is if the national press released the details of all the hundreds of school shootings since 1999, parents might stop delivering their kids to schools. I'm not sure we can safely educate our kids anymore, and I'm not sure kids can learn when just by going to school, they are risking their lives. To imagine being a kid in that classroom today makes me sick. I can't describe how bad I would feel if my kid was in that classroom today. How can any of those kids ever even come back to school? This is a horrible epidemic that isn't going away. But pardon my interruption.

200 volts

Life Lesson; The most important, difficult and rewarding
thing that you can
ever work on
is you

Chapter 14
200 VOLTS

Keegan and Miles were riding back to school in Black Magic, and Pocket was driving. Pocket says, "I wasn't afraid of those big dudes. I really wasn't. Well, at least I wasn't scared until someone turned the lights off." Miles asks him, "Have you looked in the mirror tough guy?" Pocket says, "No. Why?" Miles says, "Well look." Pocket checks his face in the rear-view mirror, and he nearly runs into a parked car! "What in the heck happened to my face?" Pocket's nose was definitely broken, and he had two very big black eyes. He says, "My mom's never gonna believe this one!"

"That's because you're never gonna tell her 'this one' you hear me?" Miles asks.

"Please guys this is so embarrassing." Miles says, "I really don't want to hear everyone talkin' about Miles' druggie house, ok? Just make something else up."

Keegan asks, "Hey Pocket, could you drop us off at school before you go to the Doctor?" Pocket asks, "You sure I need to see a doctor?" Key replies, "Yeah, I'm sure. He'll need to reset that cauliflower that used to be your nose!" Pocket says, "Yeah, well look who's talkin'. Have you checked out your ugly mug lately?"

Key remembered that he hadn't seen his blackeye yet and looked immediately in the mirror. He yelped, "Ohhh Nooo! I have a date tonight with Suzi Strange! I can't show up looking like this! What a bummer!" Miles says, "Hold up homey! Did you say you had a date with Suzi Strange?" Are you some kind of sicko or what brother? That's not a girl. That's a computer!"

Key says, 'I know she's a computer and I plan to write her a new program tonight!" The fellas chuckle but it is pretty weird. Pocket dropped them at the curb in front of HRH and heads home. He uses his handsfree phone and says, Hey Siri, Call home." He thinks to himself, this is way cool as he hears his mom answer.

Keegan and Miles are in front of HRH, and Key asks Miles, "So where's Maria? Is she somewhere safe?"

Miles says, "I hope so but I don't really think so. I took her to her dad's, and he was with some skank that looked like a drugged-out hooker. He loves his daughter, but he needs to love her more than the drugs and tramps, and I'm not sure about that." I wanted to keep her with me, but I'm crashin' at the mens Shelter in Taft, and the counselor dude there told me, "Look here brotherman, you cain't have no female of any size in this here stallion stable because not one of these crazy ass niggers can be trusted to keep they in they pants, but you ain't heard that shit from me, right my nig?" "I'm guessin' her dad's place might be better than the mens' shelter in Taft, but I'm not very comfortable with my choices."

"Oh man, that's not going to work Miles," Key says, "Do you mind if I try to help?"

Miles is out of options, so he says, "Please do. And I might need your help with another problem too. Got a minute?" Key says, "For your bro? I always got a minute. What's up?"

"Ok. Miles starts, "There's also the issue with my dad's car. Your grandma didn't steal it. I rode my bike to the place your grandma said she left it. It was there, so I opened the trunk to put my bike in it, but it was jam packed with kilo bags like the ones on the table in my house. I slammed it shut, and looked both ways and there was a banger just sitting in his junky old ride. He stood out big time, so he didn't care who saw him. He was squatting on that rock in the trunk."

"I rode away on my bike and then ditched it in your yard and snuck back there. I borrowed a knife from your gardener and hid in the bushes until that ugly toothless banger fell asleep. Then I quickly cut the valves out of all 4 tire stems and ran. He woke up and started to chase me, but I was already in my dad's car and drove right by the loser knowing he couldn't follow me."

"The problem I have now is that those boys that we got arrested today are Cartel, which means there's lots more where those came from. And they know I have a trunkful of their drugs. I thought about calling the cops but then my dad's car, which could otherwise be mine and I need one desperately right now, even just to sleep in, will be taken by the police as part of their investigation and I'll never get it back. If I could get ahold of the Cartel, I could tell them they can have their drugs, if I can keep my dad's car and they'll say 'sure' but they'll mean 'not a chance in hell gringo snitch dead man walking beyatch.'"

"Wow, my friend, Key says, "We have a couple of huge problems! This is the kind of junk most guys would run from. But we know that doesn't work, so we've got to put a couple of plans together that will get your sister safe housing and get you your dad's car back with an empty trunk. Let's skip class today and work on our plans. By the way, are you hungry? "

"No, not at all, Miles jokes, "Homeless people are never hungry."

Key says, "How about we walk over to the Pit Stop Two and grab some lunch. I bet we'll think better with full stomachs."

A couple of weeks had passed since the last Rodd Report, but a new edition came out today and both the guys picked one up and were checking out the picture of that amazing photo finish that was on the cover. It had been cropped so there was nothing in the background. Ricky had done the right thing, just as he said he would, and in the next article it would seem that Mr. McKay had made good on his promise earlier than promised.

The article read, "The Trackmaster in Raceland this last year, Professor Birmingham was fired this week after disclosing some confidential information that was self-incriminating. He acknowledged to a full house at the races on Sunday that he was actually a spy for the Queen. She had commissioned him to Sunnyvale to study all the young racers at Raceland in hopes that none of them would ever be good enough to challenge the likes of Max Verstappen in Formula One racing."

"The Queen loves Formula One racing and wants very badly for it to continue to be ruled by European racers. She really wanted one of her sons to take up the sport as youngsters, but be William and Andrew were far too busy chasing girls even at a young age, to ever achieve any success in such a demanding sports endeavor. That was very obvious. If there was any chance that an American racer had the skills necessary to be competitive in open-wheel racing, she suspected correctly that they would be found racing at Raceland and she expected Thomas Birmingham to find them and deliver them to England by whatever means necessary."

This wasn't in Ricky's article, but Mr. McKay purchased the home across from HRH that Birmingham was living in and had personally cleaned out all of Birmingham's belongings to prepare the house for the new tenants. After he was terminated, he was deported immediately without so much as 10 minutes time to collect his belongings, so they now were Mr. McKays' property. Birmingham mistakenly left behind his racers' ratings that he had painstakingly collected and analyzed for his report to the Queen. He had rated both the McKay boys and the Speed kids as definitely capable of great success in Formula One racing. But his report went on to say that the McKay boys would never consider a move to Europe, so he intended to focus his energy on recruiting Steve and Sammy Speed. It appears some initial feelers were put out to these two, and he was planning to present a formal offer to them in the next couple days. He was terminated and deported before he could present that offer.

Mr. McKay had formally invited Randy and Ricky Rodd to his home for dinner tonight to share some news with them that wasn't in today's Rodd Report. He needed to find out if Randy could walk out of Raceland, but he had told his partners when he was negotiating the Rodds' reunion that any hold that may have been programmed into the track's security to keep Randy in Raceland would have to be released the moment he asked for it. To be sure that happened the way he planned, he told Randy that he'd meet him at the starting line on Track 12 at 7:00PM sharp and Ricky that the two of them would meet him in his office at 7:10. The brothers had talked about this plan and neither one of them believed there was a snowball's chance in hell that anyone could make that happen, but they agreed to be where they were asked to be. It was true that this was a longshot, especially since Randy had tried so many times before. But they didn't know Kevin McKay very well yet.

Mr. Mac was at the starting line at Track 12 when Randy casually approached. Randy said, "Listen Mr. Mac, my son and I really appreciate your efforts, but we know there are things about this whole complex that are beyond your control. I was here when Hollenbut and Coynes built this monster, and I know that they made deals with the devil that you never would have approved of. That's why I can't ever leave, so thanks for trying but we understand."

Mr. Mac replied, "Randy, you're right about how this place was built, and I get why you think I can't do what I said I would, but trust me, I'm smarter than most and my word is the most important asset I have, and I gave you my word. Walk with me through the exit and you'll see. Reluctantly, Randy went along until they came to the spot that always shocked Randy and threw him back on the ground, leaving his skin burning and his head throbbing.

Mac said, "Give me a moment Randy." And then he called Major Coynes. When Coynes answered, Mr. McKay told him 'This is the moment' and he hung up. He found Randy smoking a cigarette over by the grandstand railing, and said, "Hey, I thought you quit smoking."

Randy replied, "And I thought you said you could get me out of this prison. I told you there are secrets that would take this whole complex down if they let someone like you get any control."

Yeah, Mac said, "And I told you to trust me. Now's the time Randy. I know you're scared. I've never had 200 volts of electricity slam into my body, so I'm scared too. If you're right, this is where they will take me out. But if I'm right, this is where I take you out, out of Raceland, never to be stuck here again for the rest of your life." Come on man, it's gotta be worth one more try. Just follow me.

This is the most afraid Mac has ever been. He knew that the other two kings were different than him, and they had dark pasts, but he believed he was sent here to save them and this town. If they were ever going to turn on him, this was their perfect opportunity. He had good reason to be scared to death. He turned and looked Randy straight in the eyes, and said it again, "Just follow me." He did and he was crying in relief when he hugged Mac on the other side.

After an outstanding meal, specially prepared for the Rodds by M's herself, the three men adjourned to the library where they discussed the jobs The Company had in mind for them and what they wanted to be doing and what they thought were fair salaries. They discussed the details, and Mr. Mac took notes. Randy noticed that Mac left his notepad, with the notes he just took, in the library when they left. In his lobby, Mac said, "I guess it's time to take you guys home."

It looked to both guys like Mac was dropping Randy off first because they were headed toward Raceland, so Ricky said, "Mr. McKay, do you mind taking me home first, I'm tired and I still have lots of homework to do tonight."

"Oh shoot, Mac said "I'm sorry. Don't worry I'll get you home in no time, but let's drop Randy off first, ok?" Doing these things for people always made Mac feel good, and even he was excited about their next surprise. He had hired two painting companies two days ago, one for the inside, and one for outside, and he told them they had to be done by 6 o'clock the next evening. He did that so the place could get aired out for a day. He also asked Rosa, their housekeeper, if she could take the next couple of days off from her regularly scheduled clients, to deep clean and redecorate his new home. She asked him to give her a budget, but he gave her his black American Express card instead.

Randy said, "Mr. Mac, no disrespect, but did you leave your notes about our contracts at home on purpose?"

Mr. McKay anticipated this question, and answered honestly, "Yeah, I did."

Randy whispered to Ricky, "I told you he'd never get the other two to sign any real contract with us."

Now, Mac pulled into the driveway of a great looking house

directly across the street from HRH. It was weird because neither of the Rodds remembered ever seeing this house. Even Mac was impressed when the three of them walked into Professor Birmingham's old place. It was impeccably decorated and appointed with the finest furniture money could buy. As they toured the house, both Ricky and Randy were smiling ear to ear. They loved it! Randy still doubted Mac, so he said, "Mr. McKay, who owns this house?"

Mac said, "I do." To which Randy replied, "So how much are you going to charge us for rent? And how long will the rental agreement be for?" Then he nudged Ricky and whispered, but loud enough that Mr. Mac could hear, "I told you."

When they ended the tour, they were in the empty garages, and Randy waves his hand over the large empty spaces and said, "See Ricky." again just loud enough for Mac to hear.

It's quiet for what feels like hours, until Mac breaks the uncomfortable silence, saying, "I know guys that I promised you would each have a car, and so far, I know you feel like I'm not very good at keeping my promises, but you're wrong. Way wrong and" he pauses to hear his Porsche pulling up the driveway. Mac loved the sound of that motor the way every Porsche owner loves that sound. He says, "Give me a minute." He hits the button that opens the garage, and in walks Mrs. McKay. She says "Hi" to the Rodds and then, "You two are never going to forget tonight and you better always remember who did this for you."

She kissed her husband and handed him two large manilla envelopes and said "Honey, you are incredible. Your partners signed your docs without a single word of protest. They are learning quickly; just how incredible you are. See you at home." She walked right past the Porsche and was gone.

After a brief pause that allows Karen McKay's comments to settle in, Mac says, "I said you were way wrong about me and I'm about to prove it."

Mr. McKay opens both large envelopes and pulled out a smaller thicker envelope that he hands to Ricky.

Ricky said, "What is this?" as he was opening the envelope.

Mac replied, "That's my spare key to the Porsche in your driveway, and ten grand in cash. I figure you two should do a little car shopping and test driving tomorrow. You'll find that you'll get the best sales guy everywhere you go when they see you drive up in my Porsche. When you find the cars you want, put a $4000 deposit on each of them. That will leave you each $1,000 cash for gas or food for the weekend. I'll meet you back here at six o'clock tomorrow evening and we'll go purchase the two cars you've chosen. I will pay them off as they give you your keys and they will issue the registrations in your names. You will own both cars free and clear. OK so far?"

"Sure." Ricky said Randy said, "Well, maybe you got one thing right."

Mac says, "it only gets better." You asked me who owns this house, and I said 'I do' and that's true, at least until you each sign this document. I'm selling it to you two for just your signatures.

He hands them a real estate contract, listing the house they are all standing in. It shows that it is being sold by Mr. Kevin McKay to Ricky and Randy Rodd for the sum of one US dollar. They both sign this paper quickly and hand it back, saying "thanks." He pulls the dollar bill that was paperclipped on the back of the real estate contact and puts it in his pocket. He says, "That deal is now complete. I didn't want to hold up our business transactions just because you two might not have a dollar on ya. It's now official. You two own this house free and clear of any financial encumbrance."

Ricky says, "Wow! That's freakin' awesome! Thank you very, very much!

An older couple had walked in quietly behind Randy and Ricky Rodd and the Rodd guys didn't even notice, but Mac did and he chose not to address them. Maybe they were the realtors, or possibly they were there to notarize all the documents.

Mac says "Yeah. You have cars and a house with no payments ever, but I have to admit, this was the easy part because I didn't need anyone else's approval to give you the cars and the house. I paid for those things out of my own pocket to show my partners how important it is to me that we get this thing right. Since these are gifts from me, no one can ever take that stuff away from you. Now, your future is secure and you don't really need to work ever again. That means you don't have to have any employment contracts."

Randy says, "Sure we don't have to work, but that wasn't the deal. I want to work, and I want to work in Raceland."

Ricky says, "Yeah, I want to work too! Plus, we'll need to eat and buy gas, etc.."

Mr. Mac interrupts him, "I'm really glad to hear that you want to work for us, because your employment contracts were the hardest part to get done because I needed my two partners to sign them. Both men were against me making this deal with you guys initially and it was a battle to change their minds.

Once we have their signatures, you only need to add mine and you'll be officially employed by Sunnyvale Speedway Inc., which is the parent company that owns all the tracks and seats and everything else across the street. Including Raceland. An employment contract with Raceland wouldn't be any good because to most people and all bankers, Raceland doesn't exist."

"And Randy, I didn't forget to take the notes with me when we left my house, I left them there, right where I told my wife I would. When we left, she took the notes to her desk and typed in the information you guys gave me, that was on the notepad to complete the agreements and then she raced off to Major Coynes' place where he and Mr. Hollenbut were waiting to sign them. Surprisingly, I got both my partners to sign an employment agreement for each of you that gives you everything you asked for. You need three signatures, and you have the difficult two already, but I'd like each of you to review your agreement and make sure it's perfect before I sign.

Mac hands Ricky his contract and turns and hands Randy his. Please read them now, so we can make any necessary changes tonight. This will complete the employment contracts that I promised you just three weeks ago.

I think you're seeing that every single thing you asked for... you got. Oh, except one, I changed your vacation benefit to..."

Randy interrupts with, "I knew you couldn't get this deal done. I told you Ricky. Mr. Mac, that vacation time's important to us. Damn it."

Mr. McKay has had just about enough of Randy Rodd's attitude. He has had to battle his partners for hours and hours to get these guys what they want. And now Randy is ungrateful, rude and unapologetic. Mr. McKay has the patience of Jobe, but even Jobe would have had his fill at this point, so he finally says something. He knew he should have said something before he got this mad, but there's no stopping him now.

"Just a damn minute, Mac barks "I have busted my butt for you two. I haven't been home for my family for weeks because you have taken so much of my time. I've been arguing with my partners all day every day. And I've spent too many sleepless nights worrying about getting this done right and it isn't even my problem. I have argued for weeks that The Company messed up your lives and we had to make it right."

"But now I think that was all bullshit. This problem rests squarely on your shoulders Randy Rodd. The Company didn't make you an immature punk that didn't give a damn if you got girls pregnant. Ricky's mom was the only one dumb enough to have your child, but she wasn't the only one you got pregnant, was she Randy? Three girls had abortions for you, but you still were too selfish to use protection. That was years ago, but you're still a self-centered selfish punk bitchin that the world owes him something."

"The truth is Randy that it wasn't The Company's decision not to use protection, but if you had, you wouldn't have had this problem. (as he points to Ricky) Then **you** cheated on his mom, so she left you. How is that The Company's fault? She did the right thing this time because she knew you weren't going to be there for her and her baby. Now, you were a single parent. You could have taken your parents' help, and I know they offered because I talked with them, but you were too proud." You can't blame that on The Company.

"Then one night you were tired of being a daddy, so you bought a twelve pack of bud, got shitfaced and passed out. The Company didn't pour that alcohol down your throat. You did. That got you locked in Raceland and other people had to take over parenting your son. And I know for sure that you have never reached out to any of those people that you dumped on and apologized. Your dad told me that's all he ever needed from you...a simple apology. An apology would have made your life so much easier. An apology would have gotten you forgiveness from your parents. An apology would have given Ricky a family.

But you have never done anything wrong, so why should you apologize, right?

Wrong. Dead wrong. Your arrogant ego wouldn't let you do something as simple as apologize, when you knew that's all it would have taken to give your son a home, a family, a life and a chance. Your ego cost your son 17 years of his life.

How many more years does Ricky have to pay for your mistakes Randy?

Another man raised your son for you. Major Coynes took Ricky in and raised him as his own. You know this man but have never even said 'thanks. Randy, you run your mouth too often with all your whining and bitching. And now, you're about to lose the deal of a lifetime, but worse, you're about to take the deal of a lifetime away from your son.

"So I don't think The Company owes you anything at all, and I would have told them that except I know Ricky well enough to know that he deserves a dad and a damn good one and if you're still not man enough for the job, I'll give this deal to a man that would be forever grateful and he'd be everything that Ricky deserves. So, if you open your mouth again before I'm through, you are going to find out that I'm as good at getting out of deals as I am at making them."

It's quiet now in the house across the street from Hot Rod High while Ricky and Randy each read their own employment agreement. When they are finished, Mr. Mac says, please turn your contracts to the back page. He hands them each a pen and says "By the way, the only change I made, as I was trying to explain before I was so rudely interrupted, was I changed your paid vacation from four weeks to six. I didn't think you'd mind!" So, if you would, cross out the four and write above it a six. Then, initial the change and return them to me please. I will have these documents recorded for state records and give you each a final executed copy by the end of the week.

Ricky says "Did you hear that. Mac got us MORE vacation time. You jerk. You're an ungrateful total jerk! Dad, you owe Mr. McKay an apology."

Randy says, "What did you call me?"

"I called you, Ricky says loudly, "an ungrateful total jerk!"

"No. Not that part!" Randy yells, then softer "The part where you called me 'dad'." Then the room was quiet.

The tears came slowly at first, down Randy's tired face, but he couldn't stop them, and now there were many and they seemed to be racing. He was a fool that didn't know *how* to say what he knew he *had* to say. What he needed to say. What they needed to hear.

After a while the silence became deafening. It was then that Randy Rodd said something he had never said before. He said, "I'm sorry Mac. I really am. And Ricky, I owe you an apology too. Son, I'm really sorry…. for everything"

That older couple that walked in quietly behind Randy and Ricky Rodd quite a while ago? They heard that apology. And for the first time in years, Randy Rodd Sr and his wife Rickie looked at each other and smiled. They were finally proud of their son.

Mr. McKay then introduced Rickie to his grandparents who were thrilled to meet him. Randy came over and hugged both his parents. shook hands with Mr. Mac and said, thanks for your patience with me. I've never had anything really good happen in my life, and I didn't believe that anyone could do all the things you promised me, so I kept expecting you to fail, and I'd just get back to my screwed-up life. But Mac what you pulled off here is nothing short of a mirac e. I will owe you for ever. I finally figured out that you really worked that hard just to right a wrong and it wasn't even your wrong. I apologize for my horrible behavior in this process, and for ever doubting you. I apologize to you sir, humbly and sincerely. You are one hell of a good man Mr. McKay and possibly the best human being on the planet. Thank you for everything, especially your patience.

Mac said, "Randy, just promise me one thing?" Randy said, "Anything."

Mac said, "Promise me that you'll be the very best dad you can be for your son."

Randy said, "I promise." Mac said, "Then it was all worth it."

Mac smiled for the first time in weeks, gave Randy and Ricky hugs and walked away feeling like he changed their lives forever and it felt really good.

Bully
Shaming

Life Lesson; What's behind you doesn't matter

Enzo Ferrari

Chapter 15
Bully Shaming

Everyone at Hot Rod High was talking about Randy Rodd. There's an adult in Raceland. What? This better not be the start of an invasion. Everyone feels like we don't need adults in Raceland. We've gotten this far without them, so who needs them now. Raceland won't be Raceland if it has adults here too! Those comments dominated social media all day today.

There were two big races planned for Raceland today and Flash has committed to announce them both. That's why he's sitting in Mr. McKays office right now. Mac called Flash this morning and told him that he needed a favor and asked him to meet in his RodKingz office before he reported for work in the booth today.

Flash had only been waiting a couple of minutes when Mr. Mac came out to get him. They were both seated comfortably in Mr. McKay's private office, when the boss started talking. He told Flash about making the deal with the Rodds and how the whole school was not happy with the idea of an adult in Raceland, but they didn't know that Randy had been in there for years. Mac wanted Flash to calm the haters and explain that the track needs at least one mechanic on duty 24 hours a day now due to their growth.

Mac says, "Flash you have to explain it to them in your terms but basically this is where we are: 1. Everyone is racing more often and some of the parts in their cars are beginning to fail. 2. We have to increase maintenance, or we will start having DNFs like NASCAR very soon. 3. Kids don't want to be racing for pinks and win a broken-down car. 4. It's against the child labor laws to hire kids to be mechanics, so we really have no choice.

"The kids seem pretty upset about this, Mac says, "but it's really no big deal. I trust you Flash and I'm sure your fans will follow your lead on this issue. Do I have your support?"

Flash asks Mac, "You're not planning to let any more adults in, are you? And don't forget that our mantra is very popular. You know, it goes like 'no teachers, no parents, no problems.' I think your son Kyle made it up, and everyone loves it."

Mac says, "I promise you Flash. I have no immediate plans to add any more adults in Raceland."

"Can I quote you on that?" Flash asks. Mac says, "of course."

Later that morning, Flash is in his booth doing his thing. After his sound check, Flash G is ready to get started, so he says, "Hello Ladies and Gentlemen and welcome to Raceland, where America's kids come to race! We've got a match race for pinks today. It's a 10-lap event on Track 12, Raceland's Mile oval track."

"This is the 20-minute racers' notice. Will Shelby Hollenbut and Riley Riviera please bring your cars to the starting line." "Shelby is a home-grown talent, and today, she'll be racing her white Ford Mustang GT Gen 3 supercar with a 600+ horsepower V8 from the inside lane."

"Riley races out of New Jersey. She's the Northeast Juniors champ. She'll be racing today in her Black Chevrolet Camaro ZL1, a supercar with a supercharged 650 horsepower V8 from the outside lane."

"Both our racers are approaching the starting line now, and for today's race they'll be using a light tree start. They're ready to go and it's 3 2 1 and they're off. From up here it looked like a clean start, with Shelby using her inside lane advantage all the way around the first turn."

"Riley was content to race wide through that turn and it will cost her sometime today especially if she doesn't change that strategy. Down the backstretch, these two hot racers are still side by side going into the far turn. Again, Riley chooses to run next to Shelby throughout the far turn, even though it's to Shelby's advantage. Riley must think she's faster and can afford to race wide, but I've watched a lot of races, and I haven't seen this strategy pay off very often."

"Riley must be trying to intimidate her opponent. Showing Shelby that she has enough speed to race wide throughout and then beat her down the straightaway to the checkered flags. They are crossing the finish line right now for the 9th time and Riley is sticking with her strategy, running nose to nose down the backstretch, and still side by side around the far turn."

"Now, they are heading for home and these two are still side by side but they're both going faster now. Riley makes a strong move at the ½ mile mark and she "thinks she's got this win, but she doesn't know Raceland's Shelby Hollenbut. Now Shelby has caught back up at the ¼ mile mark, and she's pulling away, Riley starts to get ahead, but Shelby has enough speed to get clear and win by a length and a half in her white Mustang GT. Riley does a cool down lap and pulls into the pits. I can see she's unhappy from up here. "Come on up and talk to me Riley."

Flash says, "Ladies and Gentlemen, a round of applause please for Ms. Riley Riviera." And she gets an ok amount of applause. Flash begins with, "What happened out there? You looked like you got stuck on stupid!" Riley's in shock and says, "Pardon me."

"Well, I don't mean to offend you Riley" Flash says, "but darlin' you ought to know better than to think you're going to beat a racer like Shelby Hollenbut runnin' wide throughout!"

Riley's reply was, "Well maybe I had a different strategy, you freckle faced fruitcake! There's still no excuse for calling me 'stupid'. It just so happened that our cars were very evenly matched, and every time I tried to speed up to take the rail, she sped up and kept me from it. And I've never won a race by braking to get behind someone. What would you suggest I do you little faggot? Like you've ever even raced! I'm betting the only thing you do fast is cowboys."

Flash is so embarrassed and shocked that he can't even respond. He's staring at her and fighting the urge to knock on her butt, when Shelby bursts into Flash's booth. She grabs Riley by her neck and is pulling her out of the chair, and she yells, "Listen you brat, that is not the way we treat people in Sunnyvale, so if you ever plan to return here, you better apologize to Flash right now or I'll kick your dumb butt to the curb, and you'll never race here again."

Riley says, "I apologize Flash. I know I was out of line, but you did start this fight by calling me stupid."

"That's not true Riley." Flash argues, "I watched you run a really bad race and I asked you if you got stuck on stupid. It's just an expression in the South like, 'you drunk or something?" I'm sorry I offended you, but I really wasn't trying to. You've raced here before and I remember I thought you were nice. Listen, the crowd here knows racing so when they watch someone stick with a bad strategy, they are thinking exactly what I said. I honestly wasn't trying to hurt your feelings; I was just giving you a chance to defend your strategy."

Riley responds, "Damn it Flash! Now I feel really bad about the crap I threw at you. I'm sorry and the next time I come down here to see if I'm improving, I assure you I won't be challenging Shelby and I won't be calling you names. You know what? I think your kind of handsome. Can I buy you dinner tonight to make amends?"

"At Houston's?" he asks. "Sure." she says, and Flash says "Then hell yes you can! If I can meet you there later. I've still got to work another race and then I have to close down my show, so is 7:30 ok? Riley says, "perfect Flash. I'll see you at Houston's at 7:30."

"Ladies and Gents, this is the 20-minute Racer's call for Kyle McKay and Steve Speed. Can we get Steve Speed and Kyle McKay to the starting Line on TRACK 12, The Oval Mile please."

"Kyle McKay will be racing his Orange Ferrari named, Terminator from Hollywood, California, and Steve Speed will be racing his Silver Lamborghini called, "Maverick" out of Dallas, Texas in a 5-lap sprint Match Race. These two cars and drivers are pretty evenly matched, and that race should start in 10 minutes."

"While there's a break in our racing action today, it's a good time for a public service announcement. I hate to even think about Raceland Management changing their policy on adults in Raceland, but there's a rumor going around that the Three Kings are considering allowing adults in Raceland.

As most of you know, our mantra in Raceland is 'No parents, No Teachers, No problems!' Now, I want to add, "and no changes!" I was concerned so I went upstairs to talk with the track management."

"I met with Mr. Kevin McKay, one of the 3 Kings earlier today and expressed my concerns. I asked him point blank if he was planning to allow more adults into Raceland. Mr. MacKay is a straight shooter so I believe he would tell me the truth. Mr. McKay said, 'Flash, I promise you, I have no immediate plans to add any adults in Raceland.' You got my guarantee Sunnyvale because you heard it from me, the one and only Flash G!"

"Now, if Shelby is still here, will you start this race for Kyle and Steve. Shelby Hollenbut to the starter's line on Track 12 please." But Shelby has left.

Shelby is making arrangements to put her new car, (Riley's old car, a Black Chevy Camaro ZL1 Supercharged 650) in her Race Space, and almost every person that walked by made a comment to her, and she just realized that they weren't congratulating her for her victory today. Everyone she saw said something about her run-in with Riley. It was crazy. "You're my hero! Way to shut that bully up! Flash isn't even gay! Gay shaming is stupid. Riley's a hater. Everybody in Raceland is now into **bully shaming** and Shelby's their hero!

"Hello out there! This is the 5-minute Racer's call for Kyle McKay and Steve Speed. Can we get Steve Speed and Kyle McKay to the starting Line on TRACK 12, The Oval Mile Immediately, please." Hey guys, It is your responsibility to be on time for all your races. Your fines are being assessed at $100 per minute that you're late.

Now, both Kyle McKay and Steve Speed are officially 5 minutes late so your race is officially cancelled. Sorry guys. I hate to cancel a race because I know it costs you money and it ticks off your fans, but it already cost you guys $500 each and I wanted to stop the bleeding. You know you can just call in if it's 30 minutes before your start time. Anyway, still no sign of you guys so I am saving you money by the minute. Please call and let us know you're both ok.

"Ladies and Gentlemen, this concludes the racing schedule for today. I apologize. Everyone, please come back tomorrow for our… YOU BE THE JUDGE! Game Promptly at noon tomorrow the two racers that stood us up today will stand trial by a jury of their peers (you guys). Each offender will be given a reasonable amount of time (maybe 3 minutes) to explain why they didn't show, we will hear both stories and then the crowd will decide by applause whether 1) they are forgiven their $500 fine, or 2) their fine is doubled to $1000. If they owe money, they will be assigned janitorial duties here at the track, and that work must be completed this weekend.Thank you guys and gals for hangin' out with me today and watching these fools runnin' in circles! See ya tomorrow in Sunnyvale! Flash Out!"

The McKays didn't know that Kyle missed a race today. It got Flash real mad and he tried to get ahold of Mr. McKay, but didn't get an answer. No surprise. Most the cell phones don't work in Raceland because of all the cement they used to build the Sunnyvale Speedway that was on top of this track.

Kyle was supposed to be at the Palace to work with GD on the bots too, but he has disappeared. Tulz and Dub introduced themselves to Gordon, but they couldn't tell him where Kyle went.

Tulz told him that Kyle and Sam had raced earlier, and they were both in good spirits when they showed up at the Palace. They were all working to make space for this bot project.

Then Dub said, "Sam went out back to look for some clean rags. She called for Kyle to come join her. She said, 'Kyle you better come out here right away.' She sounded different, but not mad. Kyle went out the back and a minute later a souped-up old Chevy Vega fishtailed out of here. Tulz and I went back there, but Sam and Kyle were gone. They must have been in a hurry because they didn't even say goodbye."

GD is a a busy guy and he can't wait for Kyle to show up so he goes to work on Sally and Suzi. In no time he has disassembled them and is now analyzing their programs. He brought skin and hair, some modified HGH and some very unique serums and actuators, along with a brand-new mutating material that had similarities to human cartilage. He was amazed that he got all that stuff through airport security, but now he had the stuff necessary to mimic human bodies. He wasn't God and couldn't make these two bots totally human the way Kyle had asked him to. But he could build the next best thing and he was confident that he could engineer these bots well enough for most people. He didn't know Kyle.

Uh Oh!

Life Lesson; Success is getting what you want,
Happiness is wanting what you get.

Chapter 16
Uh Oh

Mac says, "Well Keegan, don't just sit there looking like the Trump Tower just fell over on you! Talk to me, son."

"Pops, Key says "I wish it was that easy. It feels like I've fallen in quicksand and I'm alone. I know what I have to do to catch up, but I can't make me do it. I've got to get out of this funk man, I've just got to." He's silent for a minute or two, then he turns toward Mac and says, "Dad, I need your help." He wondered why that was always so hard to say.

"On the night of the Big Crash, Miles' home got taken from him by his aunt, a bunch of local druggies and a Cartel delivery team. Now, the Cartel is running boatloads of heroin, coke and fetanyl out of there."

Key has lowered his voice like he thought someone may be listening, "The last time Miles was there, it was a nightmare. There was a different kind of party in every room; lots of naked people and lots of needles and smoke. There were people on his bed shootin' up, and he went to his sister Maria's room, but a couple was having loud crazy sex on her bed. He found her under some dirty clothes curled up in the corner. She was crying softly and trying to rock herself to sleep. Miles got her to her dad's house, but that loser has a new coke ho girlfriend that said Maria couldn't stay there anymore because her kids were moving in there now."

"Miles knew that the mens' shelter in Taft was a dangerous place because he'd been staying there the last few nights, but he was all out of choices, so he tried to sneak Maria in there, but he got caught and they got thrown out. They won't let him back in for 30 days. They slept at the Taft City Park in a corner in the men's room. He's been missing school and barely getting any food. We've got our biggest baseball game ever tomorrow night and he's going to try to make it. There's no way he can play if Maria's dad won't take her, but Miles is going to talk to him about it today, so we'll know soon." Key had been looking at the floor the whole time he was talking so he's not sure how long Moms has been there, but she's standing next to his dad now and they're both standing very stiff, like statues, except statues don't cry. "

He had to look back down to continue his story. When his eyes found their spot on the floor, He started again. He said meekly, "There's more."

"Wait a second Keegan, his dad stopped him and said "You said Maria's dad had a new chick suddenly?" Key nods and Mac say, "I've met him somewhere before. Mac's thinking and then says, "I remember. Miles introduced me to him at your football championship game. That man was old and ugly. That sounds like a plant that the Cartel would put in place. Tell Miles not to go near that place again until further notice."

There's a pause while everyone is digesting that thought. Finally, Key picks up his story, "Miles rode his bike over here to pick up his dad's car as he had told M's he would. She had left it exactly where they planned. He popped the trunk to put his bike in there, but it was jampacked with thirteen 2.5 Kilo bags of fentanyl."

"He quickly closed the trunk, put his bike in the back seat, jumped in and almost started driving, but his eye caught some motion in a car down the street. When the guy sat back up, Miles saw this 'banger' that he'd seen the other night, smokin'crack with his aunt. He stayed put until the banger fell asleep, snuck down the street and deflated all 4 of the guy's tires. Then he snuck back to his dad's car, and drove up next to the banger, close enough that the guy didn't have room to even open his door."

"Then, he laid on his horn and cranked the music way up, drawing as much attention as possible. When the guy started climbing out the passenger door, Miles took off and called the cops to report a drugged-out loser was swinging a gun around on their street. He didn't find out until later, but it worked. The guy was arrested and is still being detained because of immigration paperwork issues. One down."

Now, Miles has a whole new set of problems. The fetty in his trunk belonged to the Cartel and so did the banger that was guarding it, so the Cartel now knows that Miles has it. Miles would be happy to just give it back to them, but they don't have a return policy.

His other option is to take it to the cops, but there's two problems with that idea. One is that the Cartel will have the intel on that before Miles gets out of the station, and they will be hunting him like they haven't eaten in a month and he's a big fat turkey on Thanksgiving. After all, they have a reputation to uphold. The other problem with bringing it to the cops is that they will keep Miles' dad's car as evidence for at least a year, so how are Miles and Maria going to live in it?"

Keegan said, "We could probably hide the whole kit and kaboodle in 'The Palace' for a few days but based on the guys I've met from the Cartel so far, they aren't exactly a patient bunch. Realistically, I'd say, that if we haven't delivered every ounce of this to them by sundown…. we're all dead!"

The McKays were just being filled in about Miles Malone's life since the Big Wreck and it's a mess. Keegan says, "This is a huge mess mom and dad and I have tried to keep you guys out of it, but you need to know, because we all need to be aware that our lives are in jeopardy."

"Oops. I left out the part where I tried to help Miles, but probably made the disaster that is his life right now, much worse. And I didn't really get this black eye by tripping into a drinking fountain in school. Sorry for lying about that, but I had to swear to Miles that I would never tell you guys anything about this mess or he would never let me know what was going on with him again. I was worried about my buddy. He had stopped coming to school for the most part, missed one of our baseball games and was late for two others. And don't forget we have our championship tomorrow. I hope he can make it."

"I started watching him a little closer and I noticed he was wearing the same clothes every time I saw him. I didn't say anything at first because they were always clean. The guy's crazy. He's been going into this laundromat in Taft by the shelter and he washes his clothes every other day in there. He brings this dirty towel with him and wears that while his clothes are getting washed. The weirdo is sitting in there wearing just a towel for like an hour, while people are coming in and out."

"He says he avoids most people by going an hour before they close. Plus, he says he doesn't think most people in Taft wear clean clothes, because the place isn't very busy. I didn't stand up for the fine people we know in Taft because my explanation would have to have included the fact that most people have laundromat kind of stuff in their houses, and he just lost his house, so I just dropped it."

"Sorry. I could have skipped that whole part, but I'm probably stalling because the truth about my black eye is going to open a whole 'nother can of worms and I think I may have released enough worms with this conversation already."

"Keegan! Mac raises his voice, "Stop stalling. I know the rest of the story anyway, so I'm just going to catch moms up here. "Keegan had Gordon meet him at Miles' place because he went there and found a ton of drugs and thugs." Gordon dispatched the thugs but not before they had given Miles, Pocket and Key enough reason to never come back...3 black eyes. I had to promise Gordon that I would never let Key know he told me, but he has... Moms interrupted him with, "And you wonder where he gets it? Let's get through this today!"

His dad says, "I suppose you brought Pocket because you needed a ride, right? Pocket has a car, and they needed a ride. But wh...Oh never mind."

Keegan says, "Bottom line is...what can we do with the drugs that doesn't involve Miles losing his car, and stops the Cartel from chasing us?"

Moms asked, "Where is the car now? Where's Miles now? Where's Maria now? And how is Miles driving all over Taft without a license? You won't have these big decisions to make if the cops pull him over."

Key answers, "Ok. "All three are at the Palace."

Moms says, "I don't think that's safe. I mean if the bad guys grew up anywhere around here, they'll know everyone goes there to wrench. Especially your crew."

Mac says, "Key, please call over there and make sure the place is all locked up and stays that way. Have everyone there come straight here. And talk to Miles. Tell him to drive that car straight to the police station. Park it right in front, lock it up tight and make sure the alarm is on. Then he should sit at the top of those steps and wait for Gordon. I'll call Gordon and have him go there now. Miles shouldn't have Maria with him. Have Wendy bring her home with her and tell her we'll pick Maria up asap. Got it?"

Key nods. "Then do it now! Mac barks."

Keegan calls Wendy and reaches her, "Hey Wendy, its Keegan," She replies, "Hey Key what's up? You never call here anymore. Wally and I both miss hangin' with you guys."

"Believe me I miss both of you too, Key says, "and I hate to call you when I need something, but I need something and I have to be rude now, sorry. Please hide Maria in the back seat. Cover her with blankets and come straight to my house. Don't stop for anything. Make sure no one's following you. If you think someone's following, call 911 and go straight to the cop shop, tell them they have to come outside to help you." "Ok? Hurry please!"

He knows Miles doesn't have a phone, so he calls Shelby. He hasn't talked to her much lately and figures she's still mad at him, but he thinks she'll still help. She answers on the first ring.

"Shel, It's Key. Is Miles there?"

Shelby says, "I can tell you're rushed but I would like to talk."

Key says, "Thanks Shel. I miss you and we'll talk soon, but right now can you find Miles for me?"

"Easy, she said. "He's right here. I'll put him on."

"Hey Key, wassup?" Miles asks.

"I need you to get to my house asap. Can you?" Key asks.

"Sure," Miles says. "See ya in a minute."

"Dad, I think they're coming. Key says, "Should we call Gordon?"

Mr. Mac replied, "I already did! Hey, have you seen Kyle?

Keegan and His dad both said, "Uh Oh" at the same time. Shelby and Miles showed up and were in the den talking with Key and his parents.

Mr. Mac said, "Miles I understand your living situation isn't good. You and Maria will be staying here for the rest of the school year anyway. I won't listen to any complaints. You are a good kid and this community is better with you in it, so Sunnyvale is not willing to have your world messed with. You're welcome in our home forever or for as long as you like of course, but I'm going to try to get your house back for you also. First, we're going to make the neighborhood safe enough for Maria to grow up there. The mayor, the sheriff and I are going to be cleaning up your neighborhood and it started tonight. Now let's get started on getting your house titled in your name. Can you tell me if your parents had a will."

Miles said, "I think so, but how can I find out?"

"Can you get me any of their mail?" Mr. Mac asked. "Bank info? Stockbroker? Do you have any of their checkbooks or bank statements. Collect as much of that stuff as you can and come see me at work. Email log ins will help. Do either of them have a tablet, laptop or desktop computer? Bring those with you too. If you can get some of that stuff, I can probably get you your house back. Then we'll just have Gordon and Steve Speed both stay there for a couple weeks. That will send the right message throughout your neighborhood and no bad people will come near your house ever again. But first, let's get your car back."

Keegan says, "Shel, can I talk with you for a second privately.' He nods his head toward the kitchen, and she follows him. Hi. Sorry we haven't talked in quite a while, but I figured you were still mad at me, so I've just been giving you space."

"Anyway, I'm worried about Kyle. I haven't seen him since this morning, and I was hoping you have."

Shelby almost whispers her response, "You're not going to be happy about this Keegan, but I haven't seen Kyle today and I should have. I had a match race today in Raceland and there was a race scheduled after mine that got cancelled for RNS (racer no show). The race was supposed to be Kyle against Steve Speed and neither of them showed up. And Flash was still paging them for quite a while after he canceled their race.

"Uh Oh!" Key almost yelled as he went back into the living room, where he said, "Dad, Kyle had a race scheduled this afternoon in Raceland and he didn't show."

Mr. Mac was on the phone talking with Steven Speed, Sunnyvale's sheriff in seconds. He said, "Evening sheriff. Thanks for taking my call. Hey, I've got a missing kid and I'm afraid there may be foul play. Can you get everyone looking for my son Kyle? I know they call it an 'APB' on cop shows, but I figured we weren't that sophisticated. What? That's awesome. Please keep me posted asap on any news. Yeah. Thanks." And he hung up.

He looked at moms and said, "We're a lot more sophisticated than most towns in turns out. The sheriff took all the photos on record for everyone in Sunnyvale and created what he calls resident cards. They are like trading cards, complete with details like height and weight, address, cell #, email address, etc. along with a kid's latest school picture and adults' license pictures, so he sent out an APB for Kyle before I even asked him. I'm impressed." Shelby interrupts Mr. Mac, "I should have mentioned this earlier, but Kyle's scheduled opponent was the sheriff's son."

Mac redials the sheriff, and when he answered, Mac said,

"Steve, I just found out that Kyle was supposed to be racing your son today and neither of them showed. Have you seen Steve or talked with him this afternoon?"

Steve says, "Hold on Mr. McKay. Give me a second." Then "My son is at home playing a video game with Ben Jr., but we'll find Kyle for you sir."

The doorbell rang and everyone jumped! It was Wendy bringing Maria over.

Miles grabbed his little sister and held her as tight as he could. He told her, "I love you sis and I'm glad you're ok." She looked up at her big brother and said, "I'm glad you're ok too!"

Moms said, "Miles, she looks really tired. Do you want to put her down in the big guest room at the end of the hallway?" Miles was gone without saying a word.

Keegan says, "Shel, you said Kyle was scheduled to race Steve Speed today and they both 'no showed' right? Shelby says, "yeah".

Then Key said, "But Steve's at home, so shouldn't we have asked if Kyle was there? Then he says, "No wait a minute. Are you sure Kyle was supposed to race Steve? I think we better find out where Samantha Speed is."

Mr. Mac, called the sheriff back, Steve answered with, "Samantha and Kyle were last seen at the Pit Stop Two, getting into an old Chevy Vega with two very large black men. We have issued an All-Points Bulletin for both our kids Mac, but I think you better come clean with whatever involvement you may have in this situation."

"Steve, I think you should come over here. We have a few things we need to talk about. After a pause, "Ok, I'll see you then."

Mrs. Mac and been pinging Kyle's phone nonstop for a while, when someone other than Kyle answered it with a deep male voice, "Ola" the voice said.

Mrs. Mac yelled, "You better bring back my son unharmed mister!"

The sheriff was already using the latest tracking program to trace the origin of the call, while Mr. Mac had taken over for his wife. He said, "Where are you and is my son ok?"

Now the person on the other end of mom's phone, sounded smaller somehow, and said, "You know the drill, Mr. McKay so don't get cute. You have something of mine and I intend to get it back at all costs, so why don't you make this easy on both of us. You tell me where to get my fetty and maybe I won't kill your kid."

Mr. Mac says, "I think you misunderstand your negotiating position. I've got all of your drugs, and you only have one of my kids, and that's not even my best kid. And I also know that in two of your last exchange arrangements, you didn't give the kid back anyway, so I'd like to get off this call so I can start taking other calls because I'm pretty sure there are better offers out there. I've got bills bro. I need money. You can't pay your bills in this country with kids. Nobody takes 'em. The Hells Angels already offered us $3.2 million for your drugs though. Have a nice day." And then he hung up! You could hear a pin drop at the McKays' house."

The sheriff said, "Mr. Mac what are you doing? I want my daughter back."

Mac says, "Steve, I want my kid back too but that is true. In two of the last three of these deals, the Cartel killed the hostages. They set a meeting place, and you bring their drugs, and then half of them come from behind you with guns drawn and they just take their drugs and then kill the hostages right in front of you."

Steve says, "I know that's true and if they kill my daughter, I'm likely going to go rogue on their dumb asses and at least get some payback. It felt good to say that, but I'd do anything to get Sam back. Just the thought of those dirtballs handling her makes me sick to my stomach. We have to come up with a plan that gets our kids back."

Mac says, "Do we have any of their guys locked up anywhere that we could hold at gunpoint at the trade site?" Maybe we do a half of the drugs for one kid, so we get at least one back? or we keep the drugs and fill the bags with flour. Come on, let's all think about this. If we don't do something different than just walk into their trap, they have shown that they don't respect that. I'm going to ask my partners for help, and he explains his predicament to Major Coynes and Ben Hollenbut.

Then he realized that he hadn't spoken to Gordon yet about this. He called him now. He explained that Kyle and one of the girls from school had been kidnapped by two large black men who were driving a gold Chevy Vega. They were last seen at the Pit Stop Two. The girl is the sheriff's daughter Samantha Speed. Gordon said, "I'm on it but keep me posted as to what the police are doing, so we don't cross paths."

Gordon had been keeping an eye on Miles' house because he had looked and that metal table was still holding up more than a dozen 2.5 kilo bags of white, with a street value in excess of ten million dollars. He knew that even the biggest drug dealers don't leave a stash like that behind. If the cops that came to pick up the thugs he had apprehended, would have gone up to the house when they were here, they would have confiscated all those drugs. Instead, he sent them away and left the trap to draw their big dog out.

G had a bad experience with this crew before. They had shot

him with a tazer gun from behind that immobilized him and then they tortured him. Fortunately, their fun and games were cut short by their rival gang's arrival. He was able to escape during their battle, but that's where he had seen Gypsy before, and he overheard that she was the leader's half-sister. Her brother was a gangster named Juan Malone. He was the Puerto Rican looking guy at Miles' house that told Keegan his name was Mr. Malone. He wasn't lying and that's why he went to their baseball game. He played for the Puerto Rican national team when he was young and wanted to see his nephew Miles play.

Juan's gang had been trying to take some of the Southeast territory's drug trade, and this was their second failed coup that G knew about. There were likely others too. The good news for the good guys was that Juan's crew has enemies in this territory that are far more powerful than they are, and Gordon was on good terms with one of these top dogs.

He was waiting right now for Juan Malone to come back to his sister's house and collect his stash. He came alone just a few minutes later. G knew that could only mean one thing; Juan Malone intended to steal his own gang's multi-million-dollar stash. There is no other reason to come alone. Juan knew that most of his muscle was locked up in the Sunnyvale jail and the remaining meatheads were kidnapping Kyle. Now G could hear Juan finalizing the plan with his sister, Gypsy downstairs in the laundry room. G slid in quietly and roped and bagged them both in mere seconds and in only about 10 more he loaded them both in his trunk. He pulled closer to the house and loaded all their stash into his car. It filled the whole back seat and the front seat and the floor and there were still two bags left. He threw them on the hood. This way he would know if they started sliding off.

He called Mac and the garage door opened right on time. He

pulled in and told Mac and Sheriff Speed what and who was in his car. He said, "They want to make a trade? It's going to cost 'em." G then took Mac's Porsche and went to the Palace.

He wanted to meet the other Gordon that Kyle calls 'GD'. The two masters of their crafts discussed trade secrets and came up with a very creative plan to get Kyle back. It would require the highest levels of skill in each of their fields but both men loved a challenge. G drew up the plan based on the location he would require the gang to make the trade at. He knew he had all the power because he had all their drugs now and their gang's leader. They were lucky he was talking trade with them. He discussed his plan with Mac and the sheriff, and they loved it!

The next time the kidnappers called, Mac would tell them they would make the trade at midnight tonight in the center of the Sunnyvale Speedway. G asked the sheriff to make sure that Miles' BMW was still in front of the police station and that the 9 hulks that worked for Juan would not be released under any circumstances prior to the planned exchange.

GD was feverishly working on Sally and Suzi to build them exactly as Kyle asked, and to create a third fembot but this one didn't have to be so close to human quality because it was only going to be used for the trade tonight.

Sally and Suzi had to be nearly human, but he had been perfecting that for a few years now and he was sure Kyle would not be able to tell the difference. He had even engineered aging into the bot's skin.

Kyle had a meeting scheduled in 2 days to meet with the 3 Kings to discuss the fembot situation. He had a business plan for them that would include rebuilding Suzi and Sally and making them as human as possible. GD had agreed to do this custom rebuild at no charge, provided The Company didn't return the two new fembots.

Kyle had created a work schedule that would utilize all 4 bots and feature their unique traits at a minimal additional cost to The Company. This deal would make everyone happy. Now, he just had to get away from these stinky kidnappers in time to make his presentation.

G had created an exchange plan that would get our hostages back for sure, get Myles' car and house back and put $10 million in the city of Sunnyvale's bank account.

Now, everyone just had to wait. Well, that was the plan, but something happened on the way to making these deals that no one saw coming. The sheriff demanded a live video of the two kids taken right now. He wanted to make sure they were alive. After all, the dealers had killed the hostages 2 of the 3 last times a trade was agreed upon. At first the drug dealers just refused, but Sheriff Speed stuck by his demand and said there is absolutely no way that his guys would release the drugs and Juan and Gypsy until the gang could get them live footage for proof of life.

No one had required a live video in the last 10 of these trades, so the gang didn't anticipate this problem. Finally, their leader claimed that the kids had gotten away. They were stalling now trying to get the good guys to just make the deal. Their leader said, "Let's just get this trade done. You guys don't want the drugs anyway and you will just have to dispose of them, and that's going to take a lot of man hours. Save yourselves the hassle and the money, the kids got away. They'll come back once we get out of here, but we're not leaving without our drugs."

The sheriff says, "You're not getting a single ounce of your drugs until we get the kids back and that's final." A couple of hours later neither side was bending so the sheriff called off the exchange until the next morning, unless the kids were found prior.

The sheriff and the McKays were sure the gang had killed the kids. They were hoping they were wrong, but it looked very much like the gang had killed Kyle McKay and Samantha Speed. They had gotten away with killing the hostages 2 of the r last 3 exchanges. In those deals both parties agreed to brirg their hostages and the drugs to a trade location. Once they did that the druggies surrounded them, took their drugs back and killed the hostages. That didn't work this time because Kevin McCay didn't bring the drugs here. He's smarter than that. Instead, he took a video of the drugs all being stacked up outside of town. The McKays' team didn't bring the drugs so the dealers couldn't steal them this time. Clearly no trade could be made tonight, but could it happen tomorrow?

Did the dealers kill the kids? That's sure what it looks like.

On the way home, the McKays decided some prayer might speed Kyle home, so they stopped at St. Peter's on the edge of town. This was a beautiful but small church run by Father Tony, and they just happened to catch him closing the church down for the night. He let the McKays in and quickly locked the doors behind them. Kevin McKay starts explaining why they stopped, but the gentle old padre put a finger to his lips, so Kevin stopped talking although he wasn't happy that the priest didn't want to listen to him. The priest pointed at Kevin and then curled his finger in indicating he wanted Kevin to follow him. Father Tony opened the door to a confessional and inside sound asleep were Kyle and Samantha. They walked back to the front of the church, and the kind old priest said they got here about an hour or two ago and asked me to hide them and look after them because some bad people may come looking for them. They were right. A couple of drugged up thugs came in with guns, but I told them no one was here, and I used my old trick and it worked. Mr. Mac asked what old trick that was, and Father Tony said, "I lied. But after I lied, I said I swear to God and that always gets them." Both men laughed and then Father Tony said, "You get the kids Kevin, and I'll go out front and take a good look around. If the coast is clear, I'll whistle, ok?"

Kevin said, "Father you do that, but I'm going to pull my car right up to the church doors and Karen will bring the kids up ok?" He said sure and they all did their parts quickly, and the McKay family was all together and heading home. Kevin called Sam's dad and told him the good news. He asked Steve if he would mind posting an officer at the house overnight, and Steve replied, "No I wouldn't mind at all. I think it's a good idea and if you don't mind, I think it would be smart if we all slept at your house until this ordeal is behind us." Mac liked the idea and contacted both Gordons with the good news and they agreed to stay at the McKay's for the night also.

Moms had been holding onto Kyle since she woke him at the church, and she wasn't about to let go of him now either. Kyle was so tired he couldn't even argue. He and Sam both put a pair of Kyle's pajamas on and those two slept between Mac and Moms all night long. In the morning, Moms and M's cooked breakfast for everyone and it was a big hit with all their guests. Their house was full of pure joy, and then Mac read G's note to everyone

Mac checked the garage and found the Porsche was back and Gordon's car with the drugs, Juan Malone and Gypsy was gone. There was an envelope under the wiper of the Porsche. Mac opened it and went into the kitchen to read G's note to everyone... 'Hey boss, If you're reading this then you know I returned your Porsche and removed my car and all the drugs and hostages from your property. I was able to steal the kids and get them tc St. Peters where Father Tony promised to protect them until the sun comes up. You can find them there and they are in good health. I am going to use the drugs to get all these losers relocated far away. Miles' car is parked in the Bigtime's old driveway. I asked the new homeowners' permission, and they were very nice. I guess this was only their second day in the home. When they get settled, they promise to introduce themselves to your family, and you guys are going to love them. They have 6 kids and a very active family. They haven't chosen a school yet, but I put in a good word for HRH of course.

Anyway, like I said, Miles' car is there and I filled his tank and removed all the drugs so it's good to go. Gypsy and Juan, well, I'm not usually this hateful, but it was these two that were torturing me when I got tazed last year. They won't be back here or anywhere else ever. Also, I put some of the Malones' bank accounts and titles and insurance papers in the glove box. I took the liberty of creating a will granting Miles and Maria the home, the car and all their parents' belongings. Even got it notarized by a friend. Turns out that Miles' dad was a shrewd investor so he left the kids a substantial nest egg that will pay for college for both kids and still leave 'em with a couple million. Those kids are set! (Miles was openly crying)

Been a long couple of weeks but we made some good progress. There is a very good chance that there will never be any drug dealers in Sunnyvale ever again and I think we've got Sunnyvale back on the list of America's safest cities. Good luck to Key, Ky and Miles and all the Speed Demons in that championship baseball game tonight.

And wait until you see what GD and I are doing with the fembots! Your boys will be stoked to the moon. Please tell Kyle I left that pink bracelet on Sally's left wrist.

I think I see the sun coming up. Looks like we're going to have another beautiful day in Sunnyvale. Have a great day boss! G

Mac looked up from Gordon's letter at the faces of so many people that mattered to him, and he saw the stress and the fear get washed away in a tidal wave of relief. It was over. It was a horrible nightmare, but it was over now and everyone was going to be ok.

Finally, he managed to relax a little, and he thanked everyone for their help and support. He looked up at the sky and said, "Thanks God." The emotions were welling up in him as he realized how fortunate he was. He almost lost a son last night. He decided that Gordon was going to get a big hug and a huge raise and he couldn't wait to give his friend both.

The End

Hope you enjoyed the story, but either way,

I'd like you to review it for me. Please email your review

To; ajloft@gmail.com

because you'll either make me proud that I wrote it

or aware of how much better I could have done.

Hopefully, I'll learn from your comments and make Book

Three the best one yet.

Last Life Lesson; Every decision you make along the way will alter your path, so the goal is to start making good decisions now. Trust your judgement. You're a very smart kid, and you're getting smarter all the time because you're reading books. Never stop reading and you'll never stop learning. The world needs you, so never stop being you!!